Disappearing Palestine

Disappearing Palestine

Israel's Experiments in Human Despair

JONATHAN COOK

ZED BOOKS
London & New York

For my daughter Bayan, in the hope that she and the other children of Palestine will one day know a land without walls

Disappearing Palestine: Israel's Experiments in Human Despair was first published in 2008 by Zed Books Ltd, 7 Cynthia Street, London N1 9JF, UK and Room 400, 175 Fifth Avenue, New York, NY 10010, USA

www.zedbooks.co.uk

Designed and typeset in Monotype Van Dijck by illuminati, Grosmont, www.illuminatibooks.co.uk

Cover designed by Andrew Corbett

Printed and bound in Malta by Gutenberg Press Ltd

Distributed in the USA exclusively by Palgrave Macmillan, a division of St Martin's Press, LLC, 175 Fifth Avenue, New York, NY 10010

A catalogue record for this book is available from the British Library Library of Congress Cataloging in Publication Data available

ISBN 978 1 84813 030 2 Hb
ISBN 978 1 84813 031 9 Pb

Contents

Acknowledgements

There are, as ever, too many people to thank individually for their help and support over the years I have been reporting from Israel and Palestine. In particular for this book, I am grateful to: John Hilley for help in locating a source from his excellent archive of run-ins with the media; Peter Lagerquist for bringing the Tel Amal museum to my attention; Gavin O'Toole for his comments on a draft section of the manuscript; Ellen McKinlay at Zed Books for taking on this project and Tamsine O'Riordan for guiding it so skilfully through the later drafts; the staff of *Al-Ahram Weekly* for giving me permission to reproduce three articles, 'Finishing the Job', 'Apartheid Looks Like This', and 'Covering up Gaza'; and the editors of many other publications and websites that have unstintingly promoted my articles, including *Counterpunch*, *Electronic Intifada*, *Dissident Voice*, Anti-war. com, *Znet*, Information Clearing House, *Countercurrents*, AMIN, and the Center for Global Research. Were it not for their support, and the freedom provided by the Internet as an independent, if sometimes chaotic, platform for publication, I might have been forced to abandon journalism some time ago.

My deepest thanks go to: my mother-in-law, Diana Awad Azzam, who has dedicated herself selflessly and with great humour to sustaining me in Nazareth; my UK family – my mother Elena, my father Keith and his wife Clea, my brother Richard, his wife Sue, and their wonderful children Joe and Aliona – on whose long-distance love and support I have come to depend; and my wife, Sally Azzam, and our daughter, Bayan, who make every day special.

Jonathan Cook
Nazareth, April 2008

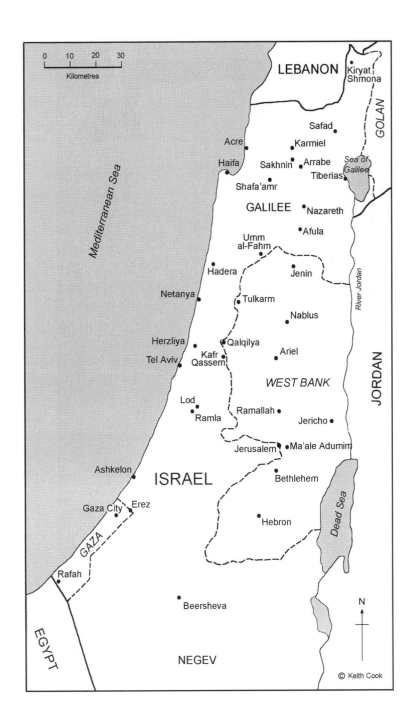

WEST BANK

ISRAEL

JORDAN

Dead Sea

Fragmentation of the West Bank, June 2007
(adapted by Keith Cook from a UN Office for the
Coordination of Humanitarian Affairs map)

Introduction

In spring 2003 I published a commentary in the *International Herald Tribune* about Israel's steel and concrete 'security barrier' that was beginning to wind its way through the West Bank. The path to publication had been arduous. The *Tribune*, published from Paris, is little more than a syndicated version of the *New York Times*, but it does buy in a small number of opinion pieces to broaden its appeal to a non-American audience. I had placed several commentaries in these slots before, but my article about the wall faced stiff resistance from the editorial staff for several months. Then suddenly in May 2003 the *Tribune* put aside its fears and agreed to publish my commentary, possibly because President Bush had just delivered a speech in which he criticized the barrier.[1] In my article I argued, at a time when it did not seem quite the truism it does today, that Israel was using the wall effectively to annex large swathes of Palestinian land in the West Bank, particularly farmland and territory over its aquifers, to destroy any chance of a viable Palestinian state emerging.

I began the piece by quoting from a humorous email circulating among solidarity activists that cited a 'law of diminishing territorial

returns' for Palestinians from the various attempts by outside parties to divide their land over more than half a century. The United
Nations' Partition Plan of 1947 offered the native Palestinians less
than half of their historic homeland, even though they were still
two-thirds of the population after waves of Jewish immigration had
been sanctioned by Britain, the ruling power in Palestine. Unhappy
that their land was being carved up for the benefit of these recent
incomers, the Palestinians rejected the deal. Months later the Jewish
leadership in Palestine declared statehood and in the ensuing war
seized 78 per cent of the Palestinians' homeland. Nearly two decades
later, in 1967, during a lightning strike against its Arab neighbours,
Israel captured the rest of Palestine.

The Palestinians had to wait until 1993 and the Oslo Accords for
another offer. In the proposed final-status negotiations of Oslo, it was
widely assumed that Israel would return to the Palestinians 22 per
cent of their homeland – that is, the territories of the West Bank and
Gaza occupied since 1967. That offer, however, never materialized;
in fact, during the Oslo years the number of Jewish settlers living in
the occupied territories doubled. Instead, in 2000 a new Israeli prime
minister, Ehud Barak, offered the Palestinians yet another deal: about
80 per cent of the two occupied territories, leaving intact the largest
Jewish settlement blocs that had been built in East Jerusalem and the
West Bank in violation of international law. Finally, as Ariel Sharon
began erecting his 'security barrier' across the West Bank from late
2002, the Palestinians found themselves facing a future where they
would be left with only a fraction of Barak's 'generous' offer. 'The
e-mail's payoff line', I wrote, was that Sharon had 'devised an even
more miserly take-it-or-leave-it deal: the Palestinians can have a state
on 42 percent of the 80 percent of the 22 percent of 100 percent of
their original homeland.'[2]

The episode soon taught me why I so rarely read similar commentaries in the American media. A few days later the paper's letters page was dedicated to a single topic: criticism of my article.
From the consistent theme of the letters, it seemed likely that they
were part of an organized campaign. 'What exactly is the historic

Palestinian homeland?' asked Eric Danis from Jerusalem. 'Was there ever a time in history when a country called Palestine was ruled by an Arab-Palestinian who spoke a language called Palestinian?' His conclusion: 'Those who speak about a historic Palestine believe that Israel is illegitimate and that the Jewish people don't have a right to a state of their own.'[3] The implication of all the letters was that the Palestinians were simply 'wandering Arabs', or nomads, passing through at the moment of Israel's birth. On this view they had no historic rights to the land – or, at least, very inferior rights to those of Jews. Such comments echoed an infamous statement made by Israel's prime minister Golda Meir in 1969, in the wake of the Six-Day War, that the Palestinian people 'did not exist'.

We shall examine that claim in detail in Chapter 1, but the important point here is that the controversy aroused by my article suggested that in America the debate about Palestinian rights to statehood had barely moved on from Meir's time. That has been possible because the letter writers represent a constituency whose depiction of the Middle East remains almost unchallenged in the US media.[4] Behind them can be found potent Zionist media lobby groups such as the Anti-Defamation League (ADL), Camera (the Committee for Accuracy in Middle East Reporting in America) and Honest Reporting;[5] and behind them stands the muscular pro-Israel political lobby of the American Israel Public Affairs Committee (AIPAC). These Zionist watchdogs have created what the late Edward Said called 'the last taboo in American public life',[6] moving rapidly to shut down any signs of critical debate about Israeli policies or US support for such policies either in the American media or in Washington's corridors of power. Consequently, my article was leapt on by these groups. The head of the ADL, Abraham Foxman, published a template letter of complaint to the *Tribune* on the front page of his website, while Camera formally submitted a demand for an apology from the paper,[7] backed by 'the largest postbag in our history', as one sympathetic *Tribune* editor confided in exasperation. After I made a lengthy written defence of my article to the editors, they did at least refuse to print an apology.[8] However, my brief relationship with the American media had soured for good.[9]

3

I recount this episode chiefly because it illustrates two of the main themes in this book: that the last remnants of Palestine are being annexed to Israel while its native inhabitants are concentrated into holding pens in preparation for their final ethnic cleansing, to make way for Jewish settlers; and that, faced with the concerted efforts of the Zionist lobby, the Western media – and human rights groups – barely dare mention these obvious developments. As several of the letter writers to the *Tribune* indicated, the erasure of the Palestinian homeland and the concealment of this fact from the wider public are crucial to Israel and its supporters because they are intimately tied to Israel's continuing legitimacy as a Jewish state.

Israel's enduring approach to the Palestinians – and the assumption, in Zionist thinking, of their eventual disappearance – was illuminated to me during a visit to a nature park close by the northern Jewish town of Beit Shean, built on the ruins of the Arab town of Bisan after the 1948 war that established Israel. There I came across a small fortified settlement constructed entirely of wood – a replica of Tel Amal, one of the earliest frontier outposts in Zionism's battle against the Palestinians for territory. The original enclosure and tall watchtower at its centre – known as a tower-and-stockade – was built in 1936 to protect 'Judaized' land in the Beit Shean valley from the Arab Revolt, a Palestinian uprising against Britain's increasingly overt support for Jewish immigration. A militia was stationed at Tel Amal, its members taking turns in the tower to keep watch over their comrades from the neighbouring kibbutz of Beit Alpha working the fields below.[10] Once the land was secure, a new kibbutz, Nir David, was safely established next to the enclosure. The kibbutzniks then extended their reach by building a new outpost further along the valley. Within a few years there were several dozen such tower-and-stockades erected across Palestine.

Tel Amal was the physical embodiment of the Zionist philosophy of 'dunam after dunam, goat after goat': the whole of Palestine could be occupied step by step, and wrested from the natives. Moshe Sharett, one of the Jewish Agency's leaders and a later prime minister, observed that the point of the tower-and-stockades 'was to change the map of Eretz Israel by erecting new settlements, to make it as difficult as possible to solve the problems of this land by means of division or cantonization'.[11] Compromise over territory was not part of the Zionist plan. In 1938, as the tower-and-stockades were marching across Palestine, David Ben-Gurion, the head of the pre-state Jewish government, declared that, once his forces were strong enough, 'we will abolish the partition of the country [between Jews and Palestinians] and will expand to the whole Land of Israel.'[12]

At the end of the war of 1948, when the threat that the Palestinians might reclaim their land had been decisively thwarted, the remaining tower-and-stockades were converted into kibbutzim or moshavim. These rural cooperative communities, which for several decades attracted young people from around the world wanting to show solidarity with the new Jewish state, explicitly ban from membership the fifth of the country's population who are Palestinian (the vestiges of the Palestinian population expelled in 1948). Today such communities control most of Israel's usable land, holding it in trust for world Jewry rather than Israel's citizenry.

Later, after the Six-Day War of 1967, the tower-and-stockade would become the prototype for Israel's land-grabbing settlements in the occupied West Bank and Gaza. In the early stages, armed civilians, usually religious fanatics, were encouraged to move into hostile territory to establish settlements to surround and fragment Palestinian communities. As these settlements were secured, less ideological Israelis were tempted there with offers of financial incentives from the state, such as cheap housing and low-interest loans. Today the job of the tower-and-stockade has passed from these established colonies to what Israelis sometimes call 'illegal outposts', small satellites of the main settlements in the West Bank that the government claims to oppose but that invariably become legal over time. The outposts have proved an ideal way to extend the boundaries of the main colonies and steal yet more land from the Palestinians. Inhabited by the most fanatical and violent of the settlers, the so-called 'hilltop youth', the outposts are sometimes justified as necessary by Israeli politicians because of the 'natural growth' of the main settlements' populations. But in truth their purpose is to consume vast areas of Palestinian land, which disappears as it is 'redeemed', concentrating the rural Palestinian population into ever-narrowing confined spaces or driving them into the main West Bank cities for safety.

Today, the Tel Amal museum is the destination for endless parties of schoolchildren, there as part of their Zionist education to learn about the pioneering spirit of earlier generations. The youngsters are encouraged not only to reimagine conditions in the enclosure's spartan living quarters but also actively to re-create the period, donning the khaki shorts and denim shirts of the kibbutzniks. Scaling the watchtower, the children pretend to survey the horizon, on the lookout for the Arab 'enemy'. At Tel Amal, Israeli schoolchildren have the chance to re-enact the battle of redemption and celebrate the acquisition of territory. In the process, some are doubtless persuaded not only of Israel's glorious past but also of the need to continue the struggle to take land from the Palestinians on Israel's new frontiers in the occupied territories.

Zionism's need to root Jews in the 'Land of Israel' has always required a corollary: the uprooting of the native population. Whether adopting the settlers' messianic language of returning to the Promised Land, the pioneer rhetoric of 'redeeming' the land, or the bureaucratic jargon of 'Judaizing' land, Zionists have been encouraged to regard their national identity as intimately tied to control over territory and the displacement of non-Jews who claim rival ownership. The staking of an indisputable claim to Palestine resonates with Zionists in several interrelated ways, including in the security, imaginary and religious-mythical realms. It promises a personal and collective safety supposedly unattainable for populations that are stateless. It reinvents the supposedly weak Diaspora Jew led to the European gas chamber; he is now liberated, casting off his wandering and compromised nature to toil the land and become a muscular 'Sabra' Jew.[13] And inevitably it feeds on ideas of chosenness and return, the Jewish people's armour against the twin dangers of modernity – secularism and assimilation.

Part One of this book can be read as an introduction, if a very thematic one, to the Israeli–Palestinian conflict. I have tried to encompass in the first four chapters the major developments in Zionism's long history of encroachment on the Palestinian people and their territory. In Chapter 1, the movement's assertion that the Bible provides the historical title deeds to Palestine is examined, as well as the leadership's plan to expel the Palestinians under cover of the 1948 war. I also survey the subsequent battle to wrest land from the remnants of the Palestinian people inside Israel – the so-called 'Israeli Arabs' – in what became a self-proclaimed programme of 'Judaization'. Chapter 2 looks at the period of the Six-Day War, arguing that the traditional account of a 'war of defence' is implausible and that its true goal was the annexation of neighbouring Arab territory, especially the last parts of Palestine. Israel's rapid move to rewrite international law in the occupied territories to facilitate Moshe Dayan's policy of 'creeping annexation' of Palestinian land is described in detail. In Chapter 3, the rise of the settlement enterprise is examined, highlighting how Israel's dispossession of its Palestinian citizens became the template for its large-scale theft of Palestinian land in the West Bank. The chapter ends with a description of the recent expansion of the settlements and growth in the number of 'outposts'.

Chapter 4 seeks to explain the consistent goal of Israeli policy towards the Palestinians over several decades. It is my contention that Israel has turned the increasingly confined spaces left to the Palestinians not only into open-air cages but also into laboratories where experiments to encourage Palestinian despair, and ultimately emigration, are being refined. In fact, these experiments were begun inside Israel, only being 'exported' to the occupied territories after their conquest in the 1967 war. Without the constraints imposed by trying to maintain its image as a Western-style democracy inside its own borders, Israel has been able to develop a more aggressive and transparent form of imprisonment for the Palestinians under occupation. It has 'industrialized' Palestinian suffering through curfews, checkpoints, walls, permits and surveillance systems, creating a lucrative 'homeland security' industry that has grown in importance since the US began a similar occupation of Iraq. The holding pens in which the Palestinians are kept today are ideal places for testing new methods of urban warfare, crowd control and ghettoization, as well as developing techniques for excluding observers such as journalists and aid workers. The gradual ethnic cleansing of the Palestinians from their homeland, on both sides of today's Green Line, is likely to take place with few witnesses to record it.

Despite these developments, the 2005 disengagement from Gaza has encouraged a profoundly mistaken view among many observers that, far from entrenching its occupation, Israel is prepared, and is preparing, to withdraw from Palestinian territory. In fact, not only has Israel continued to maintain strict control of the tiny area of the Gaza Strip since the disengagement, but it has exploited the Western fixation on Gaza to steal yet more Palestinian land in the West Bank and tighten its hold on the Palestinian population there. Even the construction of the 'separation wall', which is in its latter stages and has so far effectively annexed some 12 per cent of the western boundary between Israel and the West Bank, is far from marking the end of Palestinian dispossession. An eastern wall to annex the huge area of the Jordan Valley, though now rarely mentioned, is still on the drawing board. In any case the outlines of this eastern wall have already been delineated on the ground through closures and checkpoints that keep almost all Palestinians out of the Valley. In the restricted spaces that are being carved out by razor wire, concrete walls and checkpoints, Palestinians are being deprived of any economic prospects – even the basic ability to subsist. Their immiseration, far from being the unfortunate by-product of Israel's measures to stop Palestinian terrorism, as Israeli officials would have us believe, is designed with one end in mind: the encouragement of 'transfer', the word Israelis prefer to 'ethnic cleansing'.

Part Two consists of essays I have published over the past six years in newspapers and on websites, embracing a wide range of topics related to Israel's destruction of the Palestinians as a people; the ways a Jewish state dangerously exploits sensitivities about anti-Semitism; and the failure by Western observers, the media, human rights groups and the Israeli left to challenge Israel's attempts at wiping the Palestinians off the map over many decades. The essays have been selected because they elaborate on issues raised in Part One, taking the arguments of that section in diverse new directions, directions that would have made Part One too unwieldy had they been included. The essays closely reflect the original articles: with one bracketed exception in 'Finishing the Job', I have avoided the temptation to update them. That is because, I believe, their chief value and relevance to the rest of the volume lies in the fact that they provide enlightening 'snapshots' of Israeli policy towards the Palestinians. The day-to-day details of Israel's grinding oppression of the Palestinians and the grossly inadequate response of most observers are too often lost in the sweeping narratives of Israeli and Palestinian history, including in the overview provided by Part One. Israel's bad faith – and the unquestioning assumption made by the media and human rights organizations that Israel desperately wants to make peace with the Palestinians – is best revealed in the details of specific moments in the conflict that are usually later forgotten or misleadingly simplified.

Nonetheless, I have made minor edits to these essays to avoid repetition, to flesh out points that subsequently need more context, and, more mundanely, to improve the clarity of the writing in some of the articles written to tight deadlines. But I have not included in the text any information that was not available when an essay was written; where a later development is relevant to an issue in the text, I have added an endnote, a few of them lengthy, to draw the reader's attention to it. I have also made a few corrections, most of them kindly pointed out by readers in the wake of publication. The essays have been sorted into themes and organized in such a way that, I hope, they develop into a clear argument supporting Part One: that the goal of Israeli policy is to make Palestine and the Palestinians disappear for good.

In a year in which the world 'celebrated' Israel's sixtieth birthday, books like this one are needed more urgently than ever. Most of the flag-wavers forgot, or did not care, that this year also marked sixty years since the Palestinians lost most of their homeland. That is because for the past six decades Israel has been working to ensure that the territory of Palestine is erased from historical memory, and that its people remain refugees without a homeland. One of the terrible ironies of this 100-year-old conflict is that, as the Palestinians have finally come to be recognized as a people, their chance of being allowed a real state is at its lowest point ever. The Palestinians may have emerged from the shadows, but Palestine has disappeared. A 'Palestinian state', endlessly talked about as the endpoint of a 'process', has come to seem no more tangible than a dream. The diplomats have even started calling it a 'horizon', forgetting – or, worse, understanding – that horizons, like rainbows, are always out of grasp. Standing in the way of a Palestinian state, of course, is Israel, a self-declared ethnic state that, perversely, much of the international community refers to as a democracy. As should be clear from the arguments contained in this book, I believe there can be no peace or reconciliation between Israeli Jews and Palestinians until Palestine and its people are allowed to reappear.

PART I

I

The Road to Dispossession

For thousands of years, we Jews have been nourished and sustained
by a yearning for our historic land. I, like many others, was raised
with a deep conviction that the day would never come when we
would have to relinquish parts of the land of our forefathers. I
believed, and to this day still believe, in our people's eternal and
historic right to this entire land.

Israeli prime minister Ehud Olmert,
address to US Congress, 24 May 2006

The argument that the Palestinians never existed as a people draws
on the earliest Zionist thinking. In Theodor Herzl's utopian novel
Altneuland (1902), which imagined a future in which Palestine had
become a Jewish state and which became one of the founding Zionist
texts, the natives are undistinguished and indistinguishable 'Arabs',
referred to as 'dirty', living in 'blackened villages' and looking 'like
brigands'. Their anonymity, barbarity and criminality are contrasted
to the nobility of the European Jews who in 'restoring' their connection to the Promised Land bring with them a civilization that
supposedly benefits the natives too. The one Arab character with

a name, Reschid Bey, calls Zionism a 'blessing for all of us'. When asked why he does not regard the Jewish settlers as intruders, he replies: 'Would you call a man a robber who takes nothing from you, but brings you something instead? The Jews have enriched us. Why should we be angry with them?'[1]

Herzl's predictions about the 'Arab' experience of Jewish settlement in Palestine offered a reassuring colonial narrative for the early Zionists, which included several related themes. First, it suggested that the natives had no genuine ties to the land, but were themselves recent intruders or at best 'brigands', descendants of those who had stolen the land from its rightful owners 2,000 years before. This was the argument of a notorious academic hoax, Joan Peters's *From Time Immemorial*, published in the mid-1980s and unmasked a decade later by Norman Finkelstein in his book *Image and Reality of the Israel–Palestine Conflict*. Second, the Jews were presented as a nation waiting for its homecoming, an act of restoration that would return the Promised Land to its former glory as the cradle of civilization. Only a Jewish presence could drag the region out of its primitiveness. Or, as Herzl put it in his earlier book *Der Judenstaat* (1896), a Jewish state was 'the portion of the rampart of Europe against Asia, an outpost of civilization as opposed to barbarism'.[2] And, third, the unavoidable implication of these two other principles was that, should the 'Arabs' reject the civilizing influence of the Jews, it would be proof not only of their incorrigible barbarity and unfitness for the land they had usurped but also of their anti-Semitism.

For most later Zionists, these themes had solidified into a political philosophy by the time of Israel's birth. The problem of two nations claiming the same land could be safely ignored as long as one of the nations had no right to consider itself a nation and consequently no right to ownership of the land. According to these Zionists, the Palestinians did not exist as a people because they were simply 'Arabs', part of a much larger nation that had been given many other states across the Middle East. As the Palestinian scholar Nur Masalha has noted of this argument, 'if the Palestinians did not constitute a distinct separate nation [separate from the Arab nation] and were not an integral part of the country and were without historical ties to it, then they could be transferred to other Arab countries without undue prejudice.'[3] The Jews, on the other hand, had a unique historical connection to the territory now known as Palestine, where they had lived long ago as a nation before their forced exile. Were further proof needed, the Zionists argued, it should be remembered that the Palestinians had never enjoyed statehood in this territory – unlike the Jews.

Zionism's Denial of History

In order to bolster their claim to the Promised Land, the Zionists, even secular ones, sought historical justifications in the Bible. Benjamin Beit-Hallahmi, a professor of psychology at Haifa University, points out:

> The historization of the Bible is a national enterprise in Israel, carried out by hundreds of scholars at all universities. ... The Israel Defence Ministry has even published a complete chronology of Biblical events, giving exact dates for the creation of the world, the killing of Abel and the exodus from Egypt.[4]

Or, as peace activist and former Knesset member Uri Avnery observes, the Bible was soon being treated 'as if it were a history book. ... That is the history that all of us [Israelis] learned in school, the foundation upon which Zionism was built.'[5] It is no surprise, then, that many leaders of Labor Zionism, despite its professed socialist and progressive outlook, zealously pursued biblical archeology. Israel's first president, Yitzhak Ben Tzvi, and feted generals like Moshe Dayan and Yigael Yadin took a passionate interest in uncovering ancient artefacts they believed were the Jewish people's title deeds to Israel. When asked what he was looking for in his many digs, Dayan answered: 'The ancient land of Israel. Everything that ancient Israel was. Those who lived there then. ... I sometimes feel I can literally enter their presence.'[6]

Even were it possible to treat the Bible as documented 'history', why would the fact that the Jews were a nation 2,000 years ago in an ancient Israel confer on their descendants a right to dispossess the Palestinians now? Or as the Israeli sociologist and peace activist Jeff Halper concludes about the Zionist narrative: 'Although the ancient Israelites and Judeans had sovereignty over the country for only 1,300 of its 10,000 years of recorded history (and a third of which was under Babylonian, Greek or Roman suzerainty), in Zionist thought our claims trump any others, including the 1,300 years of Muslim rule.'[7] But, in fact, the concerted efforts of Israeli historians and archeologists to find the physical evidence necessary to prove that the Bible is a genuine record of the Jewish people's history have failed dismally, as a growing number of Israeli academics have conceded. Ze'ev Herzog, a professor of archeology at Tel Aviv University, caused a storm in 1999 when he admitted that archeology had failed to find evidence that an ancient Jewish nation ever existed:

> This is what archaeologists have learned from their excavations in the Land of Israel: the Israelites were never in Egypt, did not wander in the desert, did not conquer the land in a military campaign and did not pass it on to the 12 tribes of Israel. Perhaps even harder to swallow is the fact that the united monarchy of David and Solomon, which is described by the Bible as a regional power, was at most a small tribal kingdom.

In fact, Herzog's research, and that of other archeologists, suggests that, when a historical entity called Israel briefly did emerge, it was pagan and Jerusalem was not its spiritual centre. Herzog says of the response in Israel to his findings: 'Any attempt to question the reliability of the biblical descriptions is perceived as an attempt to undermine "our historic right to the land" and as shattering the myth of the nation that is renewing the ancient Kingdom of Israel.'[8] On cue, Tommy Lapid, at the time a member of the Israeli parliament and later a justice minister and leader of the avowedly secular Shinui Party, responded to Herzog's conclusions: 'The attempt to prove that the Bible is wrong is really an attempt to prove that Zionism is wrong and Israel is wrong.'[9]

So who were the ancient Israelites, if not, as the Bible tells us, one of three rival ethnic nations, along with the Canaanites and the

Philistines, living in Palestine? Another professor of archeology at Tel Aviv University, Israel Finkelstein, argues that the Israelites were not in reality a people apart but themselves Canaanites, possibly pastoral hill shepherds who eventually broke away over religious differences. According to Niels Peter Lemche, a biblical scholar at the University of Copenhagen, 'the real difference between the Canaanites and the Israelites would be a religious one and not the difference between two distinct nationals.'[10]

Another controversy flared in early 2008 when Shlomo Sand, a history professor at Tel Aviv University, published a book in Hebrew called *When and How Was the Jewish People Invented?* According to a sympathetic review by the Israeli journalist Tom Segev, Sand debunks Israel's official history that today's Jews are descendants of the Jewish community in Palestine 2,000 years ago, a community that was supposedly exiled by the Romans in 70 AD. He argues instead that most of the Jews and Christians in the region converted to Islam several hundred years later, when the Arabs conquered Palestine.[11] Interestingly, this view was shared by at least two of Israel's founding fathers, Yitzhak Ben Tzvi and David Ben-Gurion. They believed that many modern Palestinians were descended from the region's Jews. In the 1920s the pair even dabbled with a plan to convert the native Palestinians back to Judaism, only abandoning the idea when confronted a decade later with an intensification of Palestinian resistance to Zionism during the Arab Revolt of 1936–39.[12]

How, then, does Sand explain today's widely dispersed Jewish Diaspora if there was no exile? These Jews, he argues, are in fact the descendants of non-Jews who converted to Judaism, thereby explaining the great ethnic diversity to be found among the modern Jewish population. In Sand's view, Judaism was a proselytizing religion that competed for converts with the new upstart faiths of Christianity and Islam. It had most success among pagan populations, particularly the Berber tribes located in north Africa, the Arabs of southern Arabia, and Turks in south Russia, who converted from the fourth century AD onwards. 'The people did not spread, but the Jewish religion spread', Sand observed in an interview.

Judaism started to permeate other regions – pagan regions, for example, such as Yemen and North Africa. Had Judaism not continued to advance at that stage and had it not continued to convert people in the pagan world, we would have remained a completely marginal religion, if we survived at all.

Only later, it seems, did the Jews become a closed ethnic and religious group.

Most damagingly to the Zionist idea of a Jewish 'return', Sand argues that Ashkenazi Jews, the first immigrants to Palestine following the pogroms in eastern Europe and today's ruling class in Israel, have no historic connection to Palestine. Sand and other scholars believe they were originally Khazars, a Turkic people who created a kingdom 1,000 years ago in what is now southern Russia. The Khazar king, says Sand, converted himself and his subjects to Judaism. In partial support of this theory, Paul Wexler of Tel Aviv University argues that Yiddish – generally assumed to be a Germanic tongue – is, in fact, a Slavic language.[13] Sand admits his research is likely to damage his academic career in Israel, adding: 'The revelation that the Jews are not from Judea [ancient Israel] would ostensibly knock the legitimacy for our being here out from under us. ... There is a very deep fear that doubt will be cast on our right to exist.'[14]

The Clash of Nationalisms

In 1969, Israel's prime minister, Golda Meir, made an infamous observation during a newspaper interview:

> There were no such thing as Palestinians. When was there an independent Palestinian people with a Palestinian state? It was either southern Syria before the First World War, and then it was a Palestine including Jordan. It was not as though there was a Palestinian people in Palestine considering itself as a Palestinian people and we came and threw them out and took their country away from them. They did not exist.[15]

Meir's analysis intentionally ignored the recent history and colonial experience of the Middle East, as well as distorting commonly understood political realities. The idea of the nation-state, which ties the sovereignty of a group to a particular piece of territory, is a relatively modern political development even in Europe, where it has been the basis for relations between peoples for little more than two centuries. Nationalists claim that some groups have an inherent or primordial right to live as a 'nation' in a state of their own because they share a common ancestry, ethnicity or destiny. Most modern scholars, however, view nationalism in a different light, seeing it as an attempt to create an 'imagined community' based on myths, language and culture – and exploiting the means of mass communication made possible by industrialization – to construct a national identity and consciousness.[16] For this reason, the claim by peoples to nationhood is often contested; ideas of nationality, rather than being immutable, change and adapt over time. Even well-established nations face internal challenges from groups claiming a right to separate nationhood, from the Scots in Britain to the Basques in Spain.

In the Middle East, long part of the Ottoman Empire, a different system of governance existed: the region was ruled from Turkey as a series of separate provinces, defined by geographical features and the culture and language of the inhabitants. Peoples within the empire regarded themselves as primarily tied to a religious or ethnic community, as had Europeans before the arrival of nationalism, and further defined their identity in relation to a particular area, language or culture rather than a state. Only when the Ottoman Empire collapsed at the beginning of the twentieth century did the European imperial powers, particularly Britain and France, step in to impose the nation-state model on the region. However, they did so in ways that suited their interests: they largely ignored the informal territorial boundaries established by the region's ethnic or religious communities and instead created weak and fractious nation-states by including these potentially hostile communities within the same borders. Iraq, an amalgam of Sunni, Shia and Kurdish groups, was a typical example. This ensured that the newly 'independent' regimes would still need the support of their colonial patron to survive.[17]

Britain, committed as we shall see to creating a Jewish homeland in Palestine, had every reason to suppress any sign of an awakening Arab or Palestinian nationalism following the demise of Ottoman rule. Nonetheless, in the face of an aggressive Jewish nationalism being advanced by the Zionists in Palestine, a fledgling Palestinian nationalism was evident from the early 1930s. The very first Palestinian *intifada* (uprising), usually referred to as the Arab Revolt, against Britain's rule and its support for the Zionists, was launched in 1936 and lasted three years. The revolt began as a sixth-month general strike and boycott of the British- and Zionist-controlled parts of the economy, in what the historian Rashid Khalidi observes 'was the longest anticolonial strike of its kind until that point in history, and perhaps the longest ever'.[18] According to Khalidi, the strength of Palestinian opposition required savage force from the British to quell, with more than 10 per cent of the Palestinian population killed, wounded, imprisoned or exiled as a result. Britain, facing the aggressive ambitions of Germany and Italy for control of the Mediterranean, was forced reluctantly to divert a huge number of soldiers into Palestine during this period.

> The repression of the revolt had an impact not only on the populace, but also on the Palestinians' ability to fight thereafter, and on the already fractured capabilities of their national leadership. A high proportion of the Arab casualties included the most experienced military cadres and enterprising fighters.[19]

In contrast to its treatment of the Jewish community in Palestine, Britain also prevented the emergence of any national institutions for the Palestinians. As Khalidi notes,

> successive British governments simply were not prepared to countenance any progress toward Palestinian self-determination, or toward the linked principle of representative government, that would enable the country's overwhelming Arab majority to place meaningful obstacles in the way of the Zionist project. They were committed to holding fast to such a position at least until Jewish immigration brought about a Jewish majority, at which stage it would become a moot point and perhaps democracy could be admitted.[20]

20

In other words, unlike the situation in the other Mandates of the Middle East, where power was slowly being transferred to Arab leaders, Palestinians were denied any experience of self-rule or any hope of eventual statehood. In contrast, the Jews were given communal autonomy within British rule and the chance to build national institutions, one of the reasons they were in a position to declare statehood the moment Britain departed Palestine.

Meir's argument that there had been no Palestinian nation, moreover, ignores the obvious parallels between Jewish and Palestinian nationalisms. Until the advent of Zionism at the tail end of the nineteenth century, those who called themselves Jews identified either as a religious community or as an ethnic group. Zionism's self-declared goal was to transform these traditional identities into a common national identity. To achieve this end, Zionism, like other nationalisms, had to set about creating national myths, drawing heavily, as we have seen, on the Bible; to revive a non-living language, Hebrew; and, hardest of all, to establish a common culture. The first Zionist Congress was held in 1897, but its agenda of Jewish nation-building in Palestine was espoused only by a tiny minority of Jews until the rise of Hitler in the 1930s. Of the 4 million Jews who left Europe between 1880 and 1920, only 100,000 went to Palestine.[21] Or, as the Israeli novelist A.B. Yehoshua has observed: 'If the Zionist party had run in an election in the early 20th century, it would have received only 6 or 7 percent of the Jewish people's vote.'[22] The idea of a cohesive and unified Jewish nation made little sense when most Jews identified as Poles, French, Moroccans or Iraqis, sharing no language or culture. Karl Kraus, an Austrian-Jewish writer and early critic of Zionism, derided the idea that any 'common bond ought to hold together the interests of the German, English, French, Slavonic and Turkish Jews'.[23]

In short, neither Palestinians nor Jews could claim a convincing and generally accepted national identity until well into the twentieth century. And if Palestinians could not, as Meir observed, point to the existence of a Palestinian state, neither could Jews until Israel's creation in 1948. Fully aware of the fact that their argument would fail to resonate with the great majority of Jews, the early secular leaders of Zionism emphasized biblical ideas of chosenness and divine promise. Ben-Gurion observed: 'The message of the Chosen People makes sense in secular, nationalist and historical terms.... The Jews can be considered a self-chosen people.'[24] And, although Herzl considered both Palestine and Argentina to have merits as the site of a Jewish homeland, he admitted: 'Palestine is our unforgettable historical homeland. Its name alone would be a powerfully stirring rallying cry for our people.'[25]

'A land without a people'

Refusal to recognize the Palestinians as a nation was the inevitable development of an ideology that denied the existence of any significant non-Jewish presence in Palestine. At the turn of the last century, Zionists began popularizing the notion that Palestine was an 'empty land' waiting to be colonized by Jews. The Anglo-Jewish writer Israel Zangwill coined the slogan of 'a land without a people for a people without a land' – referring to the Palestinians as an 'Arab encampment' on another occasion.[26] These myths buttressed the Zionist claim that it was incumbent on all Jews to 'return' to the Promised Land[27] – or make an 'ascent', as the Hebrew word *aliyah* denotes – and 'redeem' the territory by settling it. Consideration of the Palestinian inhabitants and their rights inside their homeland was swept aside as Zionism's hunger for land and statehood grew.

Unfortunately, this wilful blindness to the physical realities of the region was shared by the colonial rulers of Palestine. In 1917, as the Ottoman Empire was breaking up and shortly before Britain took control of Palestine, the London government issued a letter, known as the Balfour Declaration, under strong pressure from its local Zionist lobby. Britain promised to help establish in Palestine 'a national home for the Jewish people', even though at the time Jews comprised only 10 per cent of the population, including a significant group, the Orthodox, who were not Zionists. The declaration referred to the majority indigenous population as 'existing non-Jewish communities', which, it was further noted, had civil and religious rights but, unlike the small community of Jews in Palestine, no political or national rights. The League of Nations subsequently gave Britain a Mandate to help the Jews create their national institutions in Palestine. As Khalidi points out, the Mandate's 28 articles included nine on local antiquities but not one on the Palestinian people, who were variously and vaguely referred to as 'a section of the population', 'natives' or 'peoples and communities'.[28]

Whatever the popular Zionist slogans of the time, the Jewish political and military leadership in Palestine was only too aware of the threat to its plans for statehood posed by the existing, large native Palestinian population. A campaign to buy farmland in Palestine, mostly from absentee landlords,[29] was spearheaded by an international Zionist organization, the Jewish National Fund (JNF), but failed to bear significant fruit: by 1948 only about 6 per cent of Palestine was Jewish-owned, half of it by the Fund.[30] Instead the Zionist government-in-waiting began plotting the removal of the Palestinians from their homes and homeland, as the Israeli historian Ilan Pappe has documented in his book *The Ethnic Cleansing of Palestine*. In the first decades of Zionist colonization, Jewish officials began building up a detailed picture of the Palestinian population. In addition to buying land, the JNF was given the task of amassing an archive of files on the hundreds of Palestinian villages. Soon the 'village files' were recording precise details of 'the topographic location of each village, its access roads, quality of land, water springs, main sources of income, its socio-political composition, religious affiliations, names of its mukhtars, its relationships with other villages, the age of individual men' and so on.[31] These files prepared the ground for a series of military plans to destroy the Palestinian villages under cover of war and evict the native population.

As Britain prepared to abandon its Mandate in Palestine, the burden increasingly fell to the recently formed United Nations. A committee established to decide on Palestine's future issued a plan for partition in November 1947. Contrary to the impression given by Israel's supporters today, the Partition Plan offered little succour to the Zionists of the day – even though it largely ignored, in line with the Balfour Declaration, the rights of the native Palestinian population.[32] Rather than granting the native population independence, Palestine was to be divided: more than 800,000 Palestinians were to share their state with 10,000 Jews, while 500,000 Jews were to share their state with nearly 440,000 Palestinians.[33] The city of Jerusalem was to become an internationally administered zone populated by equal numbers of Palestinians and Jews. Under the Partition Plan, the Jewish state, on a little over 55 per cent of Palestine, was given control of much of the best land, in particular the fertile coastal plain and the hilly eastern Galilee around Lake Tiberias.

The Jewish leadership accepted the plan reluctantly, however, aware that, with far higher Palestinian birth rates, the Jewish state would be doomed within a decade or two to become a second Palestinian state. As the Israeli historian Benny Morris points out: 'Large sections of Israeli society ... were opposed to or extremely unhappy with partition and from early on viewed the [coming 1948] war as an ideal opportunity to expand the new state's borders beyond the UN-earmarked partition boundaries.'[34] Tom Segev points out: 'The Zionist movement invested great efforts into attaining a majority in favor of partition, but the borders proposed by the UN were far from being an answer to its yearnings. Had the Arabs agreed to those lines, the Zionists might have rejected them.'[35] Fortunately for the Jewish leadership, the Palestinians did not. A war for Palestine drew nearer.

In August 1948, in the midst of the fighting, David Ben-Gurion, Israel's first prime minister, would note the problems of the Partition Plan. He told *Time* magazine: 'There are eleven million Jews in the world. I don't say that all of them will come here, but I expect several million, and with natural increase I can quite imagine a Jewish state of ten million.' Would the partition boundaries cope with so many Jews, he was asked. 'I doubt it,' he replied, adding: 'We would not have taken on this war merely for the purpose of enjoying this tiny state.'[36]

Meeting in Tel Aviv on 10 March 1948, more than two months before Britain's exit from Palestine, the Zionist leadership agreed a final version of their ethnic cleansing programme, Plan Dalet, which was immediately sent out to military commanders in the field. According to Pappe, the army was to forcibly evict Palestinians from their homes and land using various prescribed strategies: 'large-scale intimidation; laying siege to and bombarding population centres; setting fire to homes, properties and goods; expulsion; demolition; and finally planting mines among the rubble to prevent any of the expelled inhabitants from returning.'[37] Plan Dalet was in keeping with the earlier thinking of the Zionist movement's leadership. Ben-Gurion had warned the Zionist Congress of 1937 that the issue of 'transfer', or ethnic cleansing, should be dealt with 'carefully'. But he continued:

> Transfer of inhabitants [Palestinians] happened in the past, in the [Galilee's Jezreel] Valley, in the Sharon [coastal plain] and in other places. We know of the Jewish National Fund's actions in this regard. Now the transfer will have to be carried out on a different scale altogether. In many parts of the country new Jewish settlement will not be possible unless there is a transfer of the Arab peasantry. ... The transfer of the population is what makes possible a comprehensive [Jewish] settlement plan.[38]

In a similar vein, three years later Yosef Weitz, one of the heads of the Jewish National Fund, wrote in his diary:

> It should be clear to us that there is no room in Palestine for these two peoples. No 'development' will bring us to our goal of independent nationhood in this small country. Without the Arabs, the land will become wide and spacious for us; with the Arabs, the land will remain sparse and cramped.[39]

Jewish military commanders were well aware of the nature of the task they had been set: their operations against the Palestinians were described as *tihur* ('purifying'), *biur* ('rooting out') and *nikkuy* ('cleaning').[40] They did not wait for Britain's departure before advancing the ethnic cleansing programme. By the time of the British exit on 15 May 1948, Jewish forces had expelled or forced into flight a quarter of a million Palestinians and occupied 200 of their villages.[41] A series of well-publicized massacres of Palestinians, again under Britain's watch, and most notoriously at the village of Deir Yassin on the outskirts of Jerusalem, only added to the mass exodus.[42] As the campaign of expulsion intensified, Ben-Gurion saw the advantages of widening the war to the main area of the Galilee, where some 100,000 Palestinians, as well as tens of thousands of refugees from the fighting, were living on land that had been assigned to the Palestinian state under the Partition Plan. 'Then we will be able to cleanse the entire area of Central Galilee, including all its refugees, in one stroke,' he announced.[43]

Rise of the Jewish State

Despite the mythical narrative promoted today, Israel's victory on the battlefield was rarely in doubt. During the first stage of the offensive, before Britain's departure, Jewish forces were in effect fighting a civil war against disorganized Palestinian militias, which had not recovered from their crushing by the British army during the three-year Arab Revolt a decade earlier. In the next stage, after Israel's Declaration of Independence, the Arab armies entered the war but were unprepared and lacked coordination, as the Israeli historian Shlomo Ben-Ami notes. The Arab leaders were less concerned about defending the Palestinians' national rights than 'establishing their own territorial claims or thwarting those of their rivals in the Arab coalition'.[44] Neither the Palestinian militias nor the Arab armies were a match for the Israeli forces: in fact, they were outnumbered throughout the fighting. As Benny Morris points out: 'It was superior Jewish firepower, manpower, organization, and command and control that determined the outcome of battle.'[45] The 'ruthless, successful offensive' by the new Jewish state set a pattern for its behaviour in the future, adds Ben-Ami, by unleashing 'a momentum of territorial expansion that [its] leaders ... would not allow to be interrupted by premature diplomatic overtures'.[46]

The ruthless offensive of 1948 included dozens of massacres and rapes, the destruction of more than 400 villages, including communities that had signed non-aggression pacts with their Jewish neighbours, and the purging of the Palestinian inhabitants of a dozen ethnically mixed cities.[47] This outcome is celebrated by Israelis as their War of Independence, but mourned by Palestinians as the *Nakba* (Catastrophe). As the historian Walid Khalidi observes, Israel's rapid and comprehensive dispossession of the Palestinian people in 1948 was 'one of the most remarkable colonizing ventures of all time'. Strikingly, Palestine was colonized 'in the wake of the (at least verbal) espousal by the Western democracies of the principle of national self-determination' and 'in the modern age of communication'.[48]

Tales of atrocities are legion on both sides of the fighting, but perhaps one incident more than any other gives a flavour of the Israeli leadership's intentions during the war. In July 1948, the neighbouring Palestinian towns of Ramla and Lydd, halfway between Jerusalem and Tel Aviv, were almost entirely emptied of their inhabitants on Ben-Gurion's orders, despite the fact that they had been designated part of the Arab state under the UN plan. As Lydd was attacked, a large number of men sought refuge in the local Dahamish mosque. When they eventually surrendered, they were massacred by Jewish forces led by Yigal Allon and his deputy, Yitzhak Rabin, a later prime minister. Some 176 bodies were reportedly recovered from the mosque. Allon then rounded up the 50,000 inhabitants of Lydd (today the Israeli city of Lod), who were forced at gunpoint to march many miles to the Jordanian border; some died en route of exhaustion.[49] Years later Rabin recalled how Ben-Gurion indicated what he wanted done with the inhabitants: 'Yigal Alon asked: what is to be done with the population [of Lydd and Ramla]? Ben-Gurion waved his hand in a gesture that said: "Drive them out!"'[50]

As Israel signed the armistice agreements with its Arab neighbours in 1949, at the close of the war, the Jewish state found itself in possession of 78 per cent of Palestine, far more territory than the 55 per cent allotted it by the UN Plan.[51] Under the same agreements, the tiny coastal strip of Gaza was occupied by Egypt, and Jordan acquired control of the West Bank and the eastern half of Jerusalem, the consequence of an earlier secret pact with Israel that prevented the two armies from engaging in serious fighting.[52]

The UN classified some 750,000 Palestinians as refugees, the great majority of them by then living in makeshift camps across the Middle East.[53] Ben-Gurion was determined that they should not be allowed to return. 'Land with Arabs on it and land without Arabs on it are two very different types of land', he told his party's central committee in March 1949.[54] Fearful that the UN might insist on the return not only of the refugees but also of the areas of Palestine like the Central Galilee not assigned to the Jewish state under the Partition Plan, he cautiously referred to these regions as 'administered' rather than as part of Israel. His worries were unfounded, however. In May 1949, as Israel was admitted to the UN, Pappe notes, 'all distinctions disappeared, along with the villages, the fields and the houses – all "dissolved" into the Jewish State of Israel.'[55]

For a considerable time, government officials, private citizens and especially soldiers enjoyed free rein looting Palestinian homes of their valuables. One government minister reported seeing the army take 1,800 truckloads of property from the single, largely deserted city of Lydd, while another admitted that 'the army does what it wants'.[56] The government sought to reassert control with new emergency regulations.[57] One, passed in late 1948, ended the legal definition of land as 'abandoned' and instead declared the Palestinian owners 'absentees'; their seized property was then reclassified as 'state land'.[58] In an attempt to make this land grab appear legal, the same regulation invested authority in an official, the Custodian of Absentee Property, whose job was supposedly to safeguard the property of the Palestinian refugees. According to a statement in 1980 from the Custodian, about 70 per cent of Israel's total territory was 'absentee' land – that is, rightfully the property of Palestinian refugees.[59]

Although officially a trustee, the Custodian – and in turn the State of Israel – was soon reaping the profits from rental income from buildings, farmland and religious endowment land; from his newfound ownership of large Palestinian businesses; and from the sale of produce from the refugees' olive and citrus groves, their tobacco, fig, apple, grape and almond crops, and their quarries.[60] Of items from the large store of confiscated merchandise – from clothes to furniture

– the army was given first refusal. Remaining goods were put up for sale, with priority going to disabled war veterans, soldiers' families and government employees.[61] Palestinian bank accounts were seized too. When Ben-Gurion was told that refugees' deposits totalling 1.5 billion Palestinian pounds had been discovered in the banks of Haifa, he noted simply in his diary: 'The banks are willing to hand this property over.'[62]

The historian Michael R. Fischbach reports that a UN committee set up to evaluate Palestinian losses produced a very conservative estimate in the mid-1960s that Israel had confiscated at least 1.75 million acres of land (or seven million dunams, in the traditional unit of measurement used by the Ottomans)[63] – about a third of Israel's total territory.[64] This land was valued at close to $1 billion in the prices of the day and would be worth many hundreds of billions more today.[65] If confiscated Palestinian moveable property such as bank accounts, jewellery, artworks, safe deposit boxes, bonds, as well vehicles, furniture, agricultural equipment and herds of animals was included, the total was pushed far higher. To the Palestinians, of course, their homeland was priceless. None of the successive Custodians, however, regarded their role as the protection of the refugees' property. Mordechai Schattner, the incumbent in 1953, observed: 'All money accruing from these sales should go the development authorities. This means, in fact, that it would be used for the settlement of new [Jewish] immigrants.'[66]

Decades later, in 1990, Israel's state comptroller demanded a list of the refugees' moveable property as part of an audit of the Custodian's office. Seven years on, the Custodian had still not complied, claiming that the task was 'impossible' because some of the records were lost and others incomplete and because he had no computer. He added that 'it would require 500 workers to sit for two years' to prepare a complete list. On another occasion, in 1998, when an Arab legal group, Adalah, requested information about the property under the country's Freedom of Information Act, the Custodian replied that he could not divulge details because he needed to protect the refugees' privacy. When pressed further, the government responded in 2002 on the Custodian's behalf that such information would 'damage relations with foreign governments'.[67] And when Israel and the Palestinians came to the negotiating table at Camp David in 2000 to reach a final-status agreement, Israel's attorney general, Elyakim Rubinstein, disclosed that the Custodian's records were no longer available and that the income from Palestinian assets had been spent. 'We have used them [the monies] up. It is up to the international community to create funds for this [a final settlement with the Palestinians].'[68]

Unwelcome Citizens

The new Jewish state faced an uncomfortable twofold legacy from the war.

First, the remains of several hundred Palestinian villages dotted the countryside, not only an embarrassing reminder of the native population that had recently been expelled but also a testament to the war crimes that had been committed during the ethnic cleansing campaign. Furthermore, there was a general fear among the leadership that, should the villages remain standing, Palestinian refugees might successfully lobby the international community for their right to return.[69] Israel therefore invested much energy after the war in the mammoth task of erasing the villages. A significant number of the more impressive homes in cities like Jerusalem, Haifa, Lydd and Ramla were used to house Jewish officials or new immigrants,[70] but most rural communities were destroyed by the army, which either dynamited them or bombed them from the air.[71] Maps were changed too: over the course of several years a Jewish National Fund committee replaced Arab place names with Hebrew ones, often claiming as justification to have 'rediscovered' biblical sites. The committee hoped to invent an ancient, largely mythical landscape all the better to root Israeli Jews in their new homeland. The real landscape of hundreds of destroyed Palestinian villages was entirely missing from the new maps.[72] Cleared of Palestinian traces, the 'empty' lands were handed over to Jewish agricultural communities, the kibbutzim and moshavim, for their exclusive use.

By the 1960s, however, dozens of remoter Palestinian villages could still be found intact across Israel. During a search of the official archives, a history professor at Tel Aviv University, Aharon Shai, discovered that in 1965 the Israeli government had recruited the JNF and prominent archeologists to a project to 'clean' the land of these last Palestinian blemishes. Several arguments for renewing the destruction programme were offered, according to Tom Segev:

> The deserted villages spoiled the beauty of the landscape and consti-
> tuted a neglected nuisance. There were pits filled with water which
> endangered the well-being of visitors, particularly children, as well
> as many snakes and scorpions. The Ministry of Foreign Affairs was
> concerned about the 'unnecessary questions' which tourists would
> present regarding the deserted villages.

The Association for Archeological Survey issued the permits needed by the government to make the destruction 'lawful', while a body called the Society for Landscape Improvement lobbied to preserve any architecturally important buildings.[73] Historic or scenic mosques were sometimes left intact: one in Caesarea became a restaurant and bar, for example, while another in al-Zeib was incorporated into the site's seaside complex.

The second problem was that Israel had acquired, along with most of Palestine, a small rump population of Palestinians, about 150,000,[74] who had managed to remain within the new borders in more than 100 Palestinian communities that were spared.[75] They constituted then, and continue to constitute today despite subsequent waves of Jewish immigration, nearly a fifth of the total population.[76] Israel worked quickly to 'de-Palestinianize' the minority, who were officially re-ferred to either as 'the minorities' or as 'Israeli Arabs'.[77] State policy was to encourage group identification at the sectarian and ethnic levels – in a classic strategy of divide and rule – by accentuating communal differences. In 1949, for example, the Education Ministry was advised to 'emphasize and develop the contradictions' between the Druze, Christian and Muslim populations to diminish their Arab and Palestinian identities.[78]

There was no official interest in integrating the Palestinian population. As a commentator observed in the *Ha'aretz* newspaper in 1954, 'the authorities did not even try to think, after the establishment of the State, about the possibility of "Israelizing" the Arab minority.'[79] Eleven years later, the *Ma'ariv* newspaper reported an election speech by Moshe Dayan in which he dismissed the idea of integration: 'This is going too far. It shall not be.'[80] Having expelled Palestinian intellectuals and eradicated Palestine's urban centres, the minority could be kept in an almost permanent state of social, economic and political underdevelopment. Meron Benvenisti, a former deputy mayor of Jerusalem, notes that decades later 'no urban society worthy of the name has been created [for Palestinian citizens] in Israel. There are, indeed, Arab towns in Israel, but they are merely dormitory communities.'[81]

No single reason can explain why the Palestinians who remained inside Israel were not expelled too. Some belonged to the small Druze community – 10 per cent of the new Palestinian minority – whose leaders had backed the Jewish forces during the fighting. A few Christian communities in the Galilee, most notably Nazareth, were left in peace for fear of the international reaction,[82] and other Christians, such as those in the village of Eilaboun, were allowed to return under pressure from the Vatican. Some villages, such as Jisr al-Zarqa and Fureidis, were untouched after local Jewish communities, which relied on their Palestinian neighbours for manual labour, lobbied on their behalf. Other villages were spared by individual Jewish commanders who refused to carry out expulsion orders. A number of Palestinians, including some Bedouin in the Negev, managed to sneak back over the porous borders after they were driven out. And, finally, 30,000 Palestinians living under Jordanian rule in an area of the West Bank known as the Little Triangle were belatedly handed over to the Jewish state as part of the 1949 armistice agreement with Jordan.[83]

Most of these Palestinians eventually received citizenship, though that was not the original intention. As the fighting subsided, the authorities issued Palestinians inside the borders of Israel with a variety of residency permits. The primary purpose was to distinguish the permit holders from the refugees outside Israel, and so ensure the continuing exclusion of the overwhelming majority of Palestinians and prevent them from returning undetected to their properties.[84] Only later did the permits entitle their holders to citizenship. The first Nationality Law, drafted in 1950, for example, proposed that the Palestinian minority inside Israel be denied citizenship and left stateless. The law was not ratified, notes Meron Benvenisti, because it became clear 'it would irrevocably deface the state's image in the eyes of the international community'.[85] Citizenship was finally conferred on most of the Palestinian minority two years later in a different draft of the law.[86]

Nonetheless, the Jewish leadership still hoped the numbers of Palestinians could be significantly reduced. Sabri Jiryis, a Palestinian lawyer who lived through those early years, observes: 'Apparently there were many [in the leadership] who hoped to be rid of the Arabs, if not by "sending" them after their brothers beyond the borders, then at least by "exchanging" them for Jews from the Arab nations. International events stifled such hopes.'[87] Researching Israel's archives, the Palestinian scholar Nur Masalha has found evidence of almost continual plotting by governments in the first decade to expel these new Palestinian citizens. Some schemes, such as offering incentives for whole communities to relocate to Brazil, Argentina or Libya, remained on the drawing board.[88] But other plans were carried out: 2,000 inhabitants of Beersheva were expelled to the West Bank in late 1949,[89] while 2,700 inhabitants of al-Majdal (now Ashkelon) were driven into Gaza a year later;[90] as many as 17,000 Bedouin were forced out of the Negev between 1949 and 1953;[91] several thousand inhabitants of the Triangle were expelled between 1949 and 1951;[92] and more than 2,000 residents of two northern villages were driven into Syria as late as 1956.[93]

In the most ambitious plan, Operation Hafarferet, Israel hoped to find a pretext to expel to Jordan what had become 40,000 inhabitants of the Little Triangle on the eve of the Suez War of 1956. The plan was shelved, however, when a brigade of soldiers implementing the early stages of the plan by enforcing a curfew massacred 49 Palestinian citizens, including women and children, returning to their village of Kafr Qassem.[94] Later, in 1964, according to Uzi Benziman, political editor of *Ha'aretz* newspaper, Ariel Sharon, then head of the army's Northern Command, asked his staff to work out the number of buses and trucks needed to expel the country's 300,000 Palestinian citizens in time of war.[95]

Judaizing the Land

Visiting the north in the 1950s, Ben-Gurion expressed his shock at the number of Palestinian villages still to be found there. 'Whoever tours the Galilee gets the feeling that it is not part of Israel,' he declared.[96] His concern was widely shared. The Galilee had been assigned to the Arab state under the UN Partition Plan, and Israeli officials feared that the neighbouring Arab countries might make a case for the region's secession unless Jews were quickly settled there. The government therefore set its primary goals as containing the Palestinian population within the tightly delimited boundaries of their remaining villages and confiscating their wider lands for the benefit of Jewish immigrants, in what the state was soon referring to as a 'Judaization' programme. Joseph Nahmani, the long-time head of the Jewish National Fund, set out the rationale for Judaization in a memo to Ben-Gurion in 1953:

> The Arab minority centred here [in the Galilee] presents a continual threat to the security of the nation. … The very existence of a unified Arab group in this part of the country is an invitation to the Arab states to press their claims to the area. … At the very least, it can become the nucleus of Arab nationalism, influenced by the nationalist movements of the neighboring states, and undermining the stability of our state.

It was, therefore, 'essential to break up this concentration of Arabs through Jewish settlements', and create '*faits accomplis* which will make it impossible for the government, for all its good intentions, to give up any of the uncultivated land for the Arabs to live on'.

Nahmani added that the safest way to achieve this would be to 'hand over all abandoned or government-owned land to the JNF'.[97]

Much of the Palestinian minority's land was easily taken. In the Absentee Property Law of 1950, the state defined one in four Palestinian citizens as a 'present absentee': an Orwellian classification that registered those internally displaced by the war, however briefly, as officially 'present' in Israel but 'absent' from their property.[98] The UN, which numbered these internal refugees at 46,000, provided them with aid until 1952 when they officially became citizens under the Nationality Law.[99] Like the refugees outside the country, however, they were denied all rights to their homes, land and bank accounts, as were their descendants.[100] Their properties and those of the other refugees were taken by the Custodian, who then passed them on to a government body known as the Development Agency, which classified them as 'state land'.[101] The agency, in turn, used the land for national projects, handed it on to Jewish agricultural communities, or sold it on the cheap to the Jewish National Fund.[102] 'The looting of Arab property was given the guise of a huge land transaction that the state had conducted with itself', observes the historian Gabriel Piterberg.[103] By 1953, an additional 2 million dunams (675,000 acres) had been passed on to the JNF as part of these transactions.[104]

Other tactics were needed to wrest land from the rest of the Palestinian population inside Israel. In the latter stages of the war the government imposed a military government on the minority that would last until 1966.[105] Although formally citizens, with the right to vote in Knesset elections, the minority was dealt with entirely separately from the Jewish population. The point of military rule, noted Shimon Peres in 1962, when he was deputy defence minister, was to 'directly continue the struggle for Jewish settlement and Jewish immigration'.[106] The military government's legal authority derived from some 150 emergency regulations promulgated by the British in 1945, supplemented by a raft of new Israeli ones.[107] The arbitrary and often brutal rule of the military governors prevented Palestinian citizens from leaving their communities without a permit and banned them from organizing demonstrations, forming political parties and publishing independent newspapers. Leaders who opposed these measures were placed under 'administrative detention' – or jailed without charge – by special military tribunals. There was no possibility of appeal.[108] Despite the strong arm used against the Palestinian minority, Tom Segev notes of the minority in this period, 'They were a frightened, leaderless people; they caused no danger to state security.'[109]

Severe restrictions on the minority's freedom of movement did offer many benefits, however, even if most were unrelated to security. Any danger of relations developing between the Palestinian and Jewish populations could be averted by isolating the minority;[110] expulsions of Palestinians from areas intended for Jewish settlement were made easier;[111] Palestinian workers could be prevented from competing for jobs with Jewish workers; and the minority's votes could be bought by the governing party through its powers of patronage.[112] But the two most important benefits to the state related to land. First, by exploiting the need of the population for travel permits to work and see family, the military government was able to recruit an extensive network of informers and collaborators who helped in alerting the authorities to attempts by the external refugees to 'infiltrate' and return to their villages.[113] And second, having confined most Palestinian citizens to their communities, the military government was able to carry out unopposed the confiscation of large tracts of outlying farmland.

Palestinian citizens soon found themselves facing a series of legal and bureaucratic ruses to strip them of their land no less arbitrary than those faced by the present absentees. During the 1950s, for example, the Bedouin tribes of the Negev were evicted from their ancestral lands, covering some 2 million dunams,[114] and 'concentrated' in what was called the *siyag*, or 'fenced-in' area, close by Beersheva.[115] The authorities then engaged in a war of attrition to force the tribes to abandon their way of life as farmers, as well as their claims to the pastoral lands on which they grazed their herds of sheep and goats, and instead settle in a handful of bleak townships – a battle that has only intensified with time. So far the government has succeeded in corralling half of the Negev's 160,000 Bedouin into these townships. The other half live in communities 'unrecognized' by the state, which deprives them of all public services, from electricity to water, demolishes their homes and sprays their crops with herbicides.[116] Governments regularly refer to the Negev's Bedouin as 'criminals', 'squatters' and 'trespassers'.[117]

Similarly in the country's north, the other area heavily populated with Palestinians, a succession of land confiscations was approved. These came in various guises: land was sealed off as 'closed military zones', before being developed on behalf of Jewish communities;[118] tracts of farmland were taken after officials claimed they were uncultivated, often because they fell within the closed military zones, again only to fall into the hands of Jewish developers soon afterwards;[119] an Ottoman law entitling Palestinians to common land they had been cultivating for at least ten years was amended to require possession of twenty years;[120] Palestinian land was taken in the 'public interest', for major infrastructure projects, including highways, reservoirs and the National Water Carrier;[121] and forestation programmes invariably required wholesale confiscation of the outlying lands of Palestinian villages.[122] In this way, some 70 per cent of land belonging to the Palestinian minority was seized by the state.[123] Compensation, when it was offered, was a fraction of what the land was worth.[124]

Those Palestinian citizens who tried to continue farming faced further obstacles, including limited access to national markets, reduced prices for their produce and tough restrictions on water allocations for irrigation.[125] With farming unprofitable, some were persuaded to sell their land to the state or the Jewish National Fund. As a result of all these measures, Palestinians in Israel were quickly transformed from independent farmers and landholders into landless casual labourers, commuting to Jewish areas to service the construction, quarrying and agricultural industries of a Jewish economy. Anger over the sweeping confiscation of their lands reached a peak in 1976 with a one-day general strike that the government crushed by sending in the army. As a result, six unarmed Palestinians were shot dead in the Galilee – an event commemorated annually by Palestinians as Land Day.

Within a few decades the state had nationalized 80 per cent of Israel's territory, officially holding it in trust for the Jewish people around the world. Transfers of land to the Jewish National Fund meant that the Zionist organization was in possession of a further 13 per cent. The purpose of this massive nationalization programme was explained by Ariel Sharon during a Knesset debate in 2002. Israeli Arabs, observed Sharon, had 'rights *in* the land', whereas 'all rights *over* the Land of Israel are Jewish rights'.[126] In other words, Palestinian citizens were merely tenants, temporary or otherwise, while the Jewish people were the landlords of Israel (though typically, it should be noted, Sharon left unclear the extent of the territory to which the Jews held the title deeds).

Today, only 3 per cent of Israeli territory remains in the hands of either Palestinian communities or private Palestinian landowners. Even then they have little say over what is done with much of this land. Jewish planning bodies typically refuse to issue local master plans, making it all but impossible to build legally or expand the municipal limits of towns and villages. Palestinian communities are almost always excluded from national priority areas and development zones, making it difficult to attract businesses and industry. And, in addition, the state has refused to establish a single new Palestinian community since Israel's founding six decades ago. As a result, Palestinian citizens find themselves living in spaces that increasingly look like overcrowded ghettoes. According to official figures, 82 per cent of land use in Palestinian communities is residential, 1 per cent light industrial, and 8 per cent set aside for public parks. In Jewish communities, by contrast, less than half the land is residential, eight times as much is in industrial use (meaning Jewish communities have a much larger tax base) and there is three times as much park land.[127] Even Palestinian-owned fields and olive groves yet to be confiscated by the state are invariably placed under the juris-diction of Jewish-controlled regional councils, which enforce national master-plans designed to keep Palestinian communities boxed in.[128] In the Galilee, where most of the minority live, only 16 per cent of the land comes under Palestinian municipal control, even though Palestinian citizens are 72 per cent of the region's population.[129]

The JNF Shell Game

The Palestinian refugees have had no hope of accessing their former lands as long as Israel, backed by the international community, has been able to ignore their right to return under international law. But more pressing for the Jewish state has been the fear that Palestinian citizens might one day find a way to demand a right under Israel's domestic law to reclaim their confiscated lands. To avert this danger, Israel has created a further deception to add to its existing and elaborate hall of legal mirrors.

The role of the Jewish National Fund, an international Zionist organization founded in 1901 to buy land in Palestine on behalf of the Jewish people, should have come to an end with the creation of Israel in 1948. Sole responsibility for regulating land transactions and administering state-owned land would then have devolved to state agencies governed by Israeli law. Instead, the opposite has happened: the JNF has grown ever stronger in relation to the state. As already mentioned, soon after Israel's creation the Israeli government transferred ownership of large areas of the country to the JNF, to the point where estimates are that a majority of the Jewish population are living on its land.[130] In 1953 the Knesset passed the JNF Law, granting the organization independent status as a landowner on behalf of the state. And the JNF has been given a key role in directing the policy of the Israel Lands Authority, the government body that manages both the 80 per cent of lands belonging to the state and the 13 per cent belonging to the JNF.

The significance of this legal sleight of hand is that by virtue of its charter the JNF is bound to lease land only to Jews.[131] By giving the organization ownership of 13 per cent of Israeli territory – including most of the country's inhabited land – and allowing its officials to set policy in relation to a further 80 per cent, Israel has successfully veiled the exclusion of Palestinian citizens from most 'state land'. The authorities have thereby managed to deflect attention from the fact that they are violating the country's anti-discrimination laws.[132] Other legislation requires that the JNF not sublease to non-Jews and that heavily subsidized water quotas set aside for the JNF not be transferred to owners of non-JNF lands, a way to ensure Palestinian smallholders cannot compete with Jewish-run agribusinesses. The JNF has also launched campaigns of intimidation against Palestinian communities in an attempt to persuade them to sell their lands. In the early 1960s, for example, special military outposts were set up by the JNF at the entrance to recalcitrant Palestinian villages as a way to increase psychological pressure.[133] Today, the JNF is party to regular reconnaissance flights over Palestinian communities to photograph their land in the hope of demonstrating that it is not being cultivated and can therefore be confiscated.[134] Nonetheless, despite the JNF's enforcement of blatantly racist policies, it is still registered as a charity in the United States and most of Europe.[135]

The Fund's most visible activity is managing forests across Israel, often planted over Palestinian villages that Israel destroyed after the 1948 war. In fact, according to the research of one Israeli remembrance group, Zochrot, JNF parks have been established on the lands of eighty-six destroyed villages.[136] These forestation programmes have been held up as an inspiring example of sound environmental management, with the JNF boasting on its website that it has planted 240 million trees in Israel and cares for 100,000 acres of 'natural woodlands'.[137] What is not mentioned is that the tree of choice has been the fast-growing European pine, useful for rapidly concealing the rubble of Palestinian homes underneath the forest's evergreen canopy, and that in the process the JNF has decimated indigenous species to make way for the pine.[138] The resulting nature parks are open to Israelis without distinction, but still enforce a separation between the Jewish and Palestinian population at a deeper level. The very accessibility of the forests, popular for walks and barbecues, both validates the crimes committed in establishing the parks and conceals their true purpose: yet further 'Judaization' of the land and the continuing exclusion of Palestinian refugees. As the Israeli scholar Uri Davis notes of the forestation activity: 'It is not charitable, as the JNF would have you believe, it is a war crime. The forests of the Jewish National Fund are there to veil this criminality.'[139]

The process of 'Judaizing' Israel, and the JNF's role in it, is far from over.[140] In an age when racist laws and policies are judged harshly, Israel is struggling to maintain the fiction that it is an enlightened liberal democracy rather than an ethnic state that enforces a territorial segregation guaranteeing ever larger privileges for the Jewish 'landlords' compared with the Palestinian 'tenants'. Sensitive to Israel's image abroad, the country's High Court issued a ruling in 2000 against the state's practice of excluding Palestinian citizens from the hundreds of rural cooperative communities such as the kibbutzim and moshavim controlling most of the country's land.[141] This exclusion had been achieved by allowing Zionist organizations like the JNF and the Jewish Agency to oversee building programmes on state land and to control the admissions committees that vet applicants. The court ruling sparked a heated debate among Israeli and Diaspora Jews about the continuing need for Zionist organizations to carry on with the mission of 'Judaizing' Israel. 'We are still fighting for our future existence as a Jewish state', declared Yehiel Leket, head of the JNF. 'In order to strengthen the Jewish state it's justified to have a Jewish organization strengthening our presence here.'[142] Most of Israel's legislators apparently agreed. In 2007 they passed by an overwhelming majority the first reading of a bill to reverse the court decision and ensure that all JNF lands be allocated to Jews only.[143] Shortly afterwards a poll revealed that 81 per cent of Israeli Jews wanted JNF land reserved for Jews.[144]

The High Court decision in 2000 concerned one Palestinian family, the Qaadans, who were seeking the right to lease a plot of land in a rural Jewish community.[145] Both the JNF and the Israeli government quickly recognized the potential threat posed by the verdict, even though it applied to a single family. Under an agreement between the JNF and the state reached in 1962, all JNF land is managed by a government body, the Israel Lands Authority – though, as noted earlier, the JNF largely directs the Authority's policy through its dominance of the ILA's board of directors. The court ruling now made that convenient alliance look like a liability: the ILA might be forced to end the exclusion policies it enforces against Palestinian citizens on behalf of the JNF. The legality of the relationship was under threat of being tested again in 2004 when other Palestinian families petitioned the court over their exclusion from JNF-owned land managed by the Israel Lands Authority in the northern Jewish development town of Karmiel.[146] The attorney general, Menachem Mazuz, declared his opposition to JNF policy in 2005, fearing that a decision in favour of the Palestinian families might set a legal precedent against discrimination in land allocation. In response, the JNF threatened to withdraw from its arrangement with the Lands Authority.[147]

The petition was held at bay while the court gave the government time to review its position. The Gadish Committee on land reform, set up the year before the Karmiel case was initiated, had already proposed a solution: a land exchange in which the JNF would give up part of its lands in the developed centre of the country in return for undeveloped state land in the rural areas of the Galilee and Negev. As the Adalah legal centre pointed out, such an exchange, while ending some of the discrimination in principle, would actually increase it in practice. Not only would the JNF continue to own 13 per cent of land in Israel, but it would also own more land in the peripheral regions where most Palestinian citizens live.[148] An agreement between the government and the JNF looked near at hand by early 2008. Reports in the Israeli media suggested that the JNF would give up 60,000 dunams (15,000 acres) of land it had developed in the Jewish-dominated centre of the country in exchange for open space in the rural north and south. The deal was held up as the two sides haggled over the amount of compensation the JNF should receive from the state.[149]

These frantic legal manoeuvres were not needed to prevent Palestinian citizens from buying state land: all the land in question – 93 per cent of Israel – is held in trust for the Jewish people and cannot be bought, either by individual Jews or by Palestinians. What the Israeli government and the JNF were seeking to ensure was that the area of land Palestinian citizens could access even as 'tenants' – through leases rather than sales – was as negligible as possible.

A Demographic Timebomb

If the question of how to ensure Israel's Palestinian citizens were confined to ghettoes – leaving the rest of the territory for Jews – had been largely solved by the time of the second intifada, another important issue had not. From Israel's establishment, the state has been seeking ways to limit the growth of its Palestinian population, while increasing that of the Jewish population. Monetary prizes, child allowances, even the preferential provision of family-planning clinics have been devoted to this end.[150] But during the second intifada, concern about the country's demographic trends reached a new fever pitch. The Herzliya Conference, an annual security convention, was launched in late 2000, its theme the threat posed by the growth of the Palestinian minority and its connections to its ethnic kin in the occupied territories. From this conference new kinds of legislative assault on the citizenship of Palestinians emerged. In 2003 the government amended the 1952 Nationality Law, one of its fundamental pieces of legislation, to bar any Palestinian citizen from bringing to Israel a spouse from the West Bank or Gaza. Officials feared such marriages might allow a Right of Return for Palestinian refugees 'through the backdoor'.[151]

It was not surprising that opinion polls soon found similar worries among the Jewish public. A survey in 2003 showed that 57 per cent thought Palestinian citizens should be encouraged to emigrate, through inducements or force.[152] In a follow-up poll in 2006 the figure had risen to 62 per cent.[153] In another survey that year 68 per cent of Israeli Jews said they did not want to live next to a Palestinian citizen.[154] These racist views have been encouraged by leading journalists, academics and politicians of all persuasions, who regularly refer to the Palestinian minority as a 'demographic timebomb' that, if not urgently defused, will destroy the state's Jewishness one day. Many advocate drastic action. One favoured measure is a policy of 'transfer' – or ethnic cleansing – of the Palestinian minority. Such talk has been heard regularly, from the revisionist historian Benny Morris and rabbis to former prime ministers Binyamin Netanyahu, Ariel Sharon and Ehud Barak.[155]

Leading the charge in promoting 'transfer' is Israel's far right, particularly Avigdor Lieberman, a Moldovan immigrant and leader of the increasingly popular Yisrael Beitenu party. Lieberman, once director general of the Likud Party, has been promoting a 'Separation of Nations' Plan whereby mutual transfers of territory ensure Jewish settlers in the occupied territories are included inside an expanded Israeli state, but as many Palestinians as possible are relocated to what he calls a future Palestinian state – though, like most Israelis, he appears to mean by statehood no more than a patchwork of ghettoes in the West Bank and a besieged prison in Gaza. He has powerful allies in Washington, including former US secretary of state Henry Kissinger.[156] In putting forward his proposal, Lieberman has exhumed the idea of transfer from the dark recesses of Zionism, freeing Israeli politicians to speak about it openly, especially as part of what may be presented as a potential 'peace agreement' with the Palestinians of the occupied territories. In particular, he has made respectable the idea of transferring the Little Triangle, a small area of Israeli territory close to the West Bank and densely populated with 250,000 Palestinian citizens, to a future Palestinian state. He also proposes a loyalty oath for Palestinian citizens who remain inside Israel, not to their country but to Israel as a Jewish state. Those refusing would presumably be expelled.

In October 2006 Prime Minister Ehud Olmert appointed Lieberman to his cabinet as deputy prime minister. Shortly afterwards, on a trip to the US, Lieberman explained his vision of conditional Israeli citizenship to American Jewish leaders at the Saban Center for Middle East Policy in Washington: 'He who is not ready to recognise Israel as a Jewish and Zionist state cannot be a citizen of the country.'[157] In January 2007, for the first time, the government backed loyalty legislation proposed by a right-wing legislator, under which Israeli citizenship could be revoked for participating in 'an act that constitutes a breach of loyalty to the state' – that is, loyalty to Israel as a 'Jewish and democratic' state.[158] A consensus appears to be forming behind the Lieberman approach. Shortly before the Annapolis peace conference in November 2007, called by President George W. Bush

44

to revive the peace process stalled since Camp David in 2000, Israel's foreign minister, Tzipi Livni, observed that a Palestinian state would be the 'answer' to Israel's Palestinian citizens: 'They cannot ask for the declaration of a Palestinian state while working against the nature of the State of Israel as home unto the Jewish people.'[159] Earlier, in August 2007, President Shimon Peres, in a post intended to embody the nation's unity, proposed exchanging Jewish settlement blocs in the occupied territories for Palestinian areas inside Israel.[160] All these ideas are in line with the political instincts of prime minister Ehud Olmert. He has repeatedly stated that he supports the goal of two states for two peoples, Jews and Palestinians. But, as we shall see, all indications are that by 'Palestinian state' he and Israel's other leaders mean life inside a set of 'holding pens' managed by the Israeli army.

2

Greater Israel's Lure

To a large extent, the creation of the state [of Israel] was an act of self-defense. ... But now the issue at hand is conquest, not self-defense. As for setting the borders – it's an open-ended matter. In the Bible, as well as in our history there are all kinds of definitions of the country's borders, so there's no real limit. No border is absolute.

> *David Ben-Gurion, Israel's first prime minister, in discussion*
> *with political aides before a meeting with Egyptian negotiators*
> *over the terms of the armistice agreement, 13 January 1949*[1]

By the mid-1960s Israel finally felt confident that it had secured physical and legal control over the land inside its own borders from the threats posed by the Palestinian refugees and its own Palestinian citizens. It is either historical irony or a convenient coincidence that in June 1967, within months of Israel ending military rule over its Palestinian minority, the Israeli army was conquering the remnants of Palestine – the West Bank and Gaza – in another war and re-creating in these newly captured territories the recently defunct military regime.[2] The rapid acquisition of Palestinian territory would, however, resurrect the 'demographic' demon that had supposedly been buried by the 1948 war: Israel found itself ruling over a substantially enlarged population of Palestinians inside its newly expanded borders.

The 1967 war is usually presented in the West in simplistic terms, as a war of self-defence by an Israel faced with imminent destruction by its hostile Arab neighbours. The main evidence cited is that Egypt's leader had menacingly massed his troops in the Sinai, leaving Israel with no choice but to attack pre-emptively. Just as with the 1948 war, it has taken many years for a different picture to emerge, largely thanks to the work of revisionist historians. True, most of the neighbouring Arab states, led by Egypt under Gamal Abdel Nasser, were keen to restore their lost honour after the comprehensive defeat of 1948, and to remove the presence of an aggressive Western-backed colonial state in their midst. The dispossession of the Palestinians in 1948, and the refugee crisis that had ensued, were seen as a destabilizing influence on the region, undermining Nasser's plans for pan-Arab unity. But equally, it seems, Nasser was more than aware that he and other Arab leaders did not have the forces to take on and defeat the Israeli army.

Israel, meanwhile, had its own interests, unrelated to self-defence, in confronting and crushing the Arab states, especially the most powerful, Egypt – that was, after all, why a decade earlier it had so enthusiastically joined Britain and France in their venture to humiliate Nasser in the Suez War. Not least Israel wanted to cement its relations with Washington by proving that it was an invaluable military ally in controlling the Middle East. In addition, it hoped to land a decisive blow against the Arab states in order to hammer home their powerlessness against the might of the Jewish state – Israel's famous 'deterrence' principle. And finally, there were many in the leadership who hoped to free Israel's hand to take the last remnants of Palestine from Jordan and Egypt, partly from a sense of historical entitlement and partly based on the idea that expanded borders would be easier to defend. As General Ezer Weizmann, the army's chief of operations, explained on the eve of the Six-Day War: 'We are on the brink of a second War of Independence'.[3] It was therefore hardly surprising that, in a dangerous game of Cold War brinkmanship, Israel chose to strike first, defeating the combined forces of Egypt, Jordan and Syria in a few days.

Despite the David and Goliath mythology surrounding the war, subsequent statements from the architects of Israel's military strategy reveal that they knew Nasser did not pose a threat to Israel, that he did not want war and that Israel's victory would be a foregone conclusion. According to Matityahu Peled, a senior member of the General Staff in 1967, for example, the claim that the Egyptian army threatened Israel's existence 'is an insult to Zahal [the Israeli army]'. Yitzhak Rabin, the Chief of Staff at the time, took a similar view: 'The two divisions he [Nasser] sent into the Sinai on May 14 would not have been enough to unleash an offensive against Israel. He knew it and we knew it.'[4] Elsewhere, Rabin called the build-up of Egyptian forces 'a demonstrative move'.[5] The political echelon understood the balance of forces in the region too. Abba Eban, Israel's ambassador to the UN, later wrote: 'Nasser did not want war. He wanted victory without war.' And Menachem Begin, leader of the opposition, admitted there was little evidence from the movements of the Egyptian army in Sinai that Nasser ever planned to attack. Begin told Israel's National Defence College: 'We must be honest with ourselves. We decided to attack him.'[6]

Shlomo Ben-Ami, a historian and one of Israel's chief negotiators at Camp David in 2000, concludes that the Israeli attack was preemptive. The fear among the leadership was that the West would force Israel into 'a diplomatic compromise' that would undermine the army's reputation in the region, consolidating 'an image of Israel as a nation at the mercy of the goodwill of the West'.[7] It seems that many in the senior command also hoped to prove their military prowess to the Americans. Ben-Ami points out that the prime minister of the time, Levi Eshkol, 'valiantly resisted the army's call for war against almost all odds', but growing public hysteria, fuelled by the army's strenuous lobbying, pushed inevitably towards war. According to the notes of his aide, Eshkol told his impatient generals a few days before the war:

> I never imagined that if an Egyptian army is deployed near our border this inevitably means that we must wake up in the middle of the night and destroy it.... You wanted a hundred more aircraft. You got it. You also received the tanks you asked for. You received everything that is needed to win a war if a war becomes necessary. You did not receive all these weapons in order for you to say that now that we are ready and well equipped to destroy the Egyptian army, we must do it.[8]

Politically weakened, however, by his public disagreements with the army, Eshkol had little choice but to restore confidence by conceding the post of defence minister to a belligerent general, Moshe Dayan. A few days later the army got its way and the attack on Egypt was launched.

A 'Miraculous' Victory

Traditional accounts argue that, in the immediate wake of capturing the West Bank and Gaza, as well as the Golan from Syria and the Sinai from Egypt, Israel had no intention of remaining in the occupied Palestinian areas. Instead, on this reading, it hoped to exchange the captured land for peace with its neighbours. Or, as Moshe Dayan famously suggested a few days after the war in an interview with the BBC: 'We are awaiting the Arabs' phone call. ... If anything bothers the Arabs they know where to find us.' Slowly, or so the argument runs, Israel gave up waiting and instead caved in to the wave of religious sentiment and secular hubris unleashed by its 'miraculous' victory. Thus was born the settlement enterprise, an entanglement that supposedly the Israeli leadership came to regret.[9] And yet, as we shall see, all the evidence suggests that large sections of the Israeli government and the army had decided before the war, or immediately after it, that such a trade of land for peace with the Arab states was of no or limited interest. Dayan said of peace talks in the same BBC interview: 'We ourselves won't make a move. We are quite happy with the current situation.'[10]

The Arab states, as the revisionist historians have also shown, did try to initiate negotiations, almost at once and repeatedly, and yet their overtures were always rebuffed. Even Ben-Ami, a reluctant revisionist, is forced to concede that the readiness of the Arab states to make peace after 1967 'was either misread or overlooked by Israel's leaders'.[11] And when the Israeli leadership did briefly consider withdrawing from the territories occupied in 1967, it was only the Sinai and the Golan, and talks with Egypt and Syria, that were under discussion. The debate inside the cabinet about the West Bank and Gaza was restricted to how best to incorporate them into Israel without annexing the population. Israeli politicians hoped, notes Henry Siegman, a former senior fellow at the US Council on Foreign Relations, that some form of local autonomy would 'in time allow them to establish the Jordan river as not only Israel's security border but as its internationally recognised political border as well'.[12] This is hardly surprising once we factor in Zionism's long-term territorial ambitions, its philosophy of 'dunam after dunam', and the idea, traceable back to at least Herzl, of a Jewish historical entitlement to all of Palestine, based on title deeds to be found in the Bible. Equally revealing if Israel's priority was truly peace is the fact that its first acts were to change the geography and demography of the most cherished part of the newly captured territories, the West Bank.[13]

The evidence suggests that, just as in 1948, Israel hoped to cleanse the West Bank, as well as Gaza, of as many Palestinians as it could under cover of war. But the speed of victory and the war's greater 'visibility' in a media age meant that a wholesale ethnic cleansing campaign like the earlier one was not feasible. Nonetheless, determined efforts were made to expel Palestinians on a large scale. At least 250,000 Palestinians in the occupied territories, or about one in four of the total population, fled in terror or were expelled.[14] A quarter of a century later, the president of Israel, Chaim Herzog, admitted that he had secretly organized the expulsion of 200,000 Palestinians as the first military governor of the West Bank. Men aged between

20 and 70 were rounded up and put on buses to take them to the border with Jordan. In a separate interview, Uzi Narkiss, who was in charge of the Central Command in 1967, alluded to the same, or related, expulsions: 'The number began with 600 and 700 persons a day, and then it began to decline until it reached a few scores, and after two or three months the operation stopped.'[15]

When in early July Israel offered the refugees the chance to return, 120,000 applied but only 14,000 were allowed back.[16] Meanwhile those men, women and children who tried to cross back unofficially over the River Jordan to the West Bank risked being shot dead, as the army adopted a free-fire policy along the border.[17] Today, after the combined mass expulsions of the 1948 and 1967 wars, at least 70 per cent of Palestinians are refugees, with 4 million to be found in the Middle East alone.

With the failure to implement more general expulsions, Israel faced a different outcome from 1948: this time the Jewish state had acquired not only the territory it wanted but much of the native population too. Also unlike 1948, the United Nations was adamant that the conquered lands would not be considered part of Israel, but rather as occupied. Nonetheless, Israel was soon resorting to the same methods of control and dispossession it had mastered in dealing with its own Palestinian citizens during nearly two decades of military government. Israel's ghettoization of its Palestinian minority under military rule would be the template for handling the Palestinians in the occupied territories, whether in East Jerusalem, the West Bank or Gaza. Or, as two Israeli analysts noted, Israel exploited 'the experience and know-how that had been accumulated during the eighteen years of military rule inside Israel', as well as drawing on 'the culture and mentality of military occupation of a civilian population'.[18]

Facts on the Ground

Israel's first moves following the 1967 war should have been a warning of its longer-term goals. Within three days of the Palestinian half of Jerusalem falling to the Israeli army, bulldozers moved in to create the first facts on the ground. The government chose the most sensitive site imaginable: the walled Old City of Jerusalem. Even before the 1948 War, Israeli leaders desired sovereignty over this area, which includes the Western Wall, the main Jewish holy site in Palestine. Not least they believed that it would provide their Jewish state with a symbolic heart, one that could be presented as the birthright of all Israelis and thereby unite religious and secular Jews in the pursuit of a Greater Israel. In the wake of the 1967 war, they grabbed their second chance.

During the night of 19 June, a demolition crew arrived to raze part of the Muslim quarter close by the Noble Sanctuary (Haram al-Sharif), where the ancient al-Aqsa and Dome of the Rock mosques are located. The plan was to destroy the homes to clear space for a wide plaza in front of the Western Wall, the embryo of what would soon be a Jewish quarter. But in staking their claim to the prayer wall, it seems, the leadership was also laying further claim to ownership of the raised terrace behind it, on which stood the two mosques. The elevated site, known as Temple Mount to Jews, is believed to contain the ruins of the First and Second Temples, the latter destroyed in 70 AD. As the first Israeli troops entered the Old City, the army's chief rabbi, Shlomo Goren, rushed towards the Temple Mount clutching a Torah scroll and blowing a ram's horn – in a foretaste of the new religious nationalism about to be unleashed.[19] Soon the bulldozers would wreck the Mughrabi Quarter, demolishing the first home with the family still inside and terrorizing a further 1,000 Muslim residents into flight.[20] The other Christian and Muslim inhabitants of the Old City might have been evicted from their homes too, had senior cabinet ministers got their way. However, the official put in charge of East Jerusalem, Yehuda Tamir, opposed such a move, arguing it would cause problems with the international community. Instead he chose another path, making it a priority to expropriate Palestinian land close by the Green Line in East Jerusalem and begin implanting Jewish settlements like Givat Hamivtar, Ramot Eshkol and French Hill.[21]

At the same time the cabinet was holding a heated discussion about how to annex East Jerusalem. It agreed to do so without legislation, simply by declaring an enlargement of the western city's municipal limits to encompass the Palestinian half, in a 'municipal fusion' as it was misleadingly referred to.[22] Official annexation would have to wait until 1980, but in the meantime Israel behaved as the new sovereign ruler. The authorities relentlessly confiscated land, 'Judaizing' it by building settlements around and between the Palestinian neighbourhoods of the city's eastern half. Jerusalem's municipal boundaries were massively enlarged, almost tenfold, annexing by stealth a huge area of extra land, including twenty-eight outlying villages in the West Bank, and moving Israel's new border deeper into Palestinian territory to point where it virtually reached the Jordan Valley. The municipal boundaries were redrawn from 38 sq km to 108.[23]

The main goal, it soon became clear, was to destroy any chance of Palestinian statehood, both by isolating Jerusalem, the economic hub of any future Palestinian state, from the rest of the West Bank, and by cutting the West Bank in half at its waist. Meanwhile, Palestinian natural growth in East Jerusalem was curbed using every legal and administrative trick that could be devised, including many that had been refined under the military government inside Israel. In particular, East Jerusalemites – with a status of 'permanent residents' rather than citizens of Israel – were denied building permits in the hope they would abandon Jerusalem and move to the West Bank, after which they could be stripped of their residency rights. As overcrowding grew, and rental prices soared, it is estimated that more than 60,000 Palestinians were forced out of Jerusalem.[24] By the outbreak of the second intifada, East Jerusalem had been physically and demographically transformed, and now has as many Jewish settlers as Palestinians. The latter have been forced into ghettoes, which, as the long-time mayor of Jerusalem Teddy Kollek explained, were deprived of most services. Asked in 1990 what he had done for the city's Palestinian residents, he responded:

> Nothing! Sidewalks? Nothing! Cultural institutions? Not one! Yes, we installed a sewerage system for them and improved the water supply. Do you know why? Do you think it was for their good, for their

welfare? Forget it! There were some cases of cholera there and the Jews were afraid they would catch it.[25]

At the time of the Mughrabi Quarter's levelling, Eshkol was pondering the dilemmas Israel would face if it stayed in the West Bank and Gaza: 'We'll have to devote some thought to the question of how we'll live in this land without giving up what we've conquered and how we'll live with that number of non-Jews.'[26] The direction in which the new winds were blowing was suggested by the actions of Israeli army commanders, who initiated several wrecking sprees close to the Green Line in an attempt to cleanse the areas of Palestinians. Former Knesset member Uri Avnery notes that the army tried to destroy two cities on the armistice line, Qalqilya and Tulkarm, though both projects had to be abandoned as they came to light.[27] More successful was the razing of four Palestinian villages in a strategic area known as the Latrun Salient, a strip of land jutting out from the West Bank that overlooks the main road between Jerusalem and Tel Aviv. The failure to capture the area in 1948 had been an enduring regret of many army commanders, and they were in a hurry to rectify matters during the 1967 war. Narkiss observed in his memoirs: 'I was determined that the Latrun enclave, that thorn in our side, would never be returned.' The 10,000 inhabitants of the West Bank villages – Imwas, Yala, Beit Nuba and Deir Ayub – paid the price: an Israeli journalist who witnessed the forced evacuation described the refugees as wandering 'without food, without water, some dying on the road' as they were expelled towards Ramallah.[28] Foreign journalists showed no interest in the story; one who did, Michael Adams of the *Guardian*, lost his job.[29] A few years later, the Jewish National Fund – again drawing on its experience of erasing evidence inside Israel of the hundreds of destroyed villages – used charitable donations from Canadians to plant a forest over the villages' lands, which were renamed Canada Park.[30]

In creating faits accomplis in Jerusalem and at the Latrun Salient, the Israeli leadership had shown it would move quickly to shape the landscape in ways it believed were most pressing. But soon Israeli minds would be preoccupied with longer-term goals, no different from those pursued after the war nearly two decades earlier. The first goal was to find a pretext for expelling more of the native population of the occupied territories. The second was to assert sovereignty over vacant and vacated land wherever possible, using the twin weapons of the law and settlements to transform its status in a manner begun with the tower-and-stockades of the pre-state period and continued after 1948 with a 'Judaization' programme. 'Dunam after dunam' would be the Zionist motto yet again.

Redrawing the Map

If Golda Meir's observation that the Palestinians 'did not exist' was widely noted, Israel's practical implementation of the policy was not. After 1948 Israel had begun the systematic removal of Palestinian place names from maps to make the former Palestinian presence invisible. Now the government initiated the same process by erasing from official maps the Green Line, the boundary with the West Bank created by the armistice agreement with Jordan and internationally recognized as Israel's eastern border.[31] The Green Line was removed from schoolbooks too, making Greater Israel not only the dream of Israeli officialdom but also a reality in Israeli classrooms.[32]

It was the West Bank, supposedly rich in connections to the Jewish faith, rather than Gaza that most fired the imagination of Israeli Jews. They were now encouraged to refer to the territory as the Biblical regions of 'Judea and Samaria',[33] integrating it into an imagined Greater Israel even before the necessary physical changes could be effected. The shift in thinking was easily achieved. After all, Israel's 'miraculous' victory over the Arab armies appeared to echo stories from the Bible, whether it was David defeating Goliath, or the Israelites under Joshua bringing down the walls of Jericho. Moreover, the conquest of the West Bank had supposedly 'returned' to the Jews their ancient heritage, including the city of Jericho itself. In 1948 Ben-Gurion had called the failure to capture the West Bank a cause to 'lament for generations';[34] now the grieving was over. As the Israeli journalist Amos Elon observed shortly after the war:

The territory of Israel prior to the Six-Day War, though rich in Roman, Byzantine, Nabatean and Crusader ruins, actually had very few historical monuments testifying to the Jewish past here. The old territory never embraced the ancient territory of the Hebrews – who were people of the Hills – but rather that of their plainland enemies, the Philistines, as well as the Edomites' Negev and 'Galilee of the Gentiles'.[35]

Elon also pointed to a rash of archeological 'discoveries' being made – 300 within a few months of the war – to bolster Israel's claims to the occupied territories. Prophetically, he noted that the Jewish religion was rapidly being reinvented:

> While reminiscent in many ways of Catholic practice – the cherishing of bits of the cross, or the handkerchief or footprint of Jesus – a new element was here being introduced into the traditionally abstract character of Jewish religious worship. To judge by sounds and sights alone, the Wailing Wall was paralleling the mass gatherings in southern Italy following a 'miracle'.[36]

The JNF Naming Committee was also revived, having completed its job inside the 1948 borders, to assign Hebrew names to the captured territories. Again, biblical place names were preferred for the West Bank, thereby adding more fuel to the fledgling territorial ambitions of the religious-nationalist fanatics determined, as the inheritors of a covenant with God, to settle Palestinian land in the occupied territories promised to the Jewish people.[37] Just as in 1948, it was easy for Israelis to deceive themselves that these renamed lands belonged to no one, that the territory was 'empty', not necessarily, as the Palestinian scholar Nur Masalha explains, in the sense of an 'actual absence of its inhabitants, but rather in the sense of civilizational barrenness – justifying Zionist colonization at the expense of the native population and their eventual removal'.[38]

Although the West Bank no longer existed on Israeli maps, its future preyed heavily on the minds of Israel's military strategists. The main problem, everyone agreed, was that formal annexation would entitle the Palestinians there to Israeli citizenship. Commenting on that possibility, cabinet minister Yisrael Galili observed: 'I know how serious that is, not only from a moral, abstract democratic perspective but also because of the concrete risks.'[39] Others were concerned with damage to Israel's image. A month after the war, a Foreign Ministry memo warned that 'internationally, the impression could be created ... that Israel is maintaining a colonial regime'.[40]

Blueprints for the Future

The two most important strategists were Moshe Dayan and Yigal Allon, rivals who were considered potential successors to prime minister Eshkol and worked separately on plans to integrate large parts of the West Bank into Israel. Both appeared to vacillate between, on the one hand, support for the creation of a small autonomous Palestinian 'entity' surrounded on all sides by annexed land colonized with Jews and, on the other, returning fragments of the territory to Jordan, when the conditions were right.[41] But as the weeks passed, the amount of land the pair considered surrendering diminished. According to journalist Amos Elon, the pair were soon 'engaged in a race to declare more and more patches of occupied territory to be "inseparable parts of Israel's ancient heritage"'.[42]

Allon, a venerated leader of elite Jewish forces in 1948 and the country's deputy prime minister in 1967, produced by late July what would become the blueprint for later visions of the West Bank's future. He believed the region's accepted geography must be altered without delay, with Israel pushing its eastern border to the Jordan river and annexing the long fertile Jordan Valley as well as the West Bank south of Jerusalem, including Bethlehem and Hebron. Agricultural settlements 'camouflaged as military strongpoints' would be erected on the annexed land, while the Palestinians inside their enclaves would live autonomously under what Allon called 'home rule'.[43] He argued that 'the integration of civilian settlement in the defense plan, especially for outlying locales and the vulnerable regions, will provide the state with permanent advance lookouts.' The settlers could stop a surprise attack or at least 'delay the enemy's progress until the army takes control of the situation'.[44] The result would be 'the Whole Land of Israel strategically and a Jewish state demographically'.[45]

Moshe Dayan, the defence minister, proposed an alternative strategy: Israel would take control of the mountain ridge above the Jordan Valley, the spine of the West Bank and the location of its water aquifers and major cities, creating five large army bases next to which would be built civilian settlements connected to Israel by roads. The two nationalities – Israelis and Palestinians – would live side by side, connected to different countries, with the Palestinians remaining Jordanian citizens.[46] The goal of Dayan's plan, unlike Allon's, was to break up the continuity of Palestinian areas so that the inhabitants would never be in a position to unite and demand independence. Then, he hoped, Israel would be able to win over the Palestinians by offering them employment servicing the economy of the settlements, or, as he expressed it, 'bind[ing] the two economies so that it will be difficult to separate them again'.[47] Over the next decades the settlement project would draw on both plans for inspiration.

The army and its allies in the government took an early lead in defining the problems posed by the occupation and the necessary solutions. Among the first concerns were the Palestinian territories' large refugee camps. The refugees who had been expelled from their villages during the 1948 war and ended up in either the West Bank or Gaza were seen by the senior command as teeming masses who might soon demand the right to return to their original homes inside Israel now that the Green Line had been erased. They apparently constituted the bulk of the Palestinians forced on to Herzog's expulsion buses: Uri Avnery recounts that soon after the war the large refugee camps next to Jericho had been entirely emptied of their 100,000 Palestinian inhabitants.[48] Meanwhile, Israeli officials hastily arranged for the demolition of any abandoned Palestinian villages inside Israel still standing.[49]

In fact, it seems that the problem of the refugees exercised Israeli military minds even before the 1967 war was launched. According to Tom Segev, the leadership held discussions about what to do with the Gaza Strip's refugees days before the war, with Allon apparently favouring their expulsion to Egypt, and the prime minister, Levi Eshkol, toying with expulsion to Jordan and Iraq.[50] 'I want them all to go, even if they go to the moon', Eshkol reportedly told his officials.[51] Israel's inability to remove most of the refugees from the occupied territories would haunt the leadership for years to come. After the war Dayan worked hard to negotiate a mass transfer of the refugees in the West Bank and Gaza to neighbouring Arab countries, in what he hoped would be considered a formal exchange of populations for Jewish communities that had either left or been forced out of the Arab states following Israel's creation. Dayan later admitted that every Arab leader rejected his scheme.[52] In 1971 Ariel Sharon proposed destroying the camps and driving their inhabitants out, although the government was not persuaded his idea was viable. Instead, at a cabinet meeting ministers agreed to 'widen the camps' streets' – to ease Israeli military access – and surround and contain them with settlements, as had occurred to Palestinian communities inside Israel.[53] This was referred to as a 'pacification' campaign.

But the military and political leaderships saw eye to eye on the main prize within their grasp: inclusion of the two newly conquered territories in an expanded Jewish state, the realization of the long-standing Zionist ambition for a Greater Israel. They also understood the main problem associated with such a manoeuvre. Annexation would provoke international opposition and threaten the Jewishness of the state by dramatically increasing the number of Palestinians entitled to Israeli citizenship. The solution, in Defence Minister Dayan's view, was 'creeping annexation'. If it was carried out with enough stealth, the illegality of Israel's actions under international law would go unnoticed and the army would also have the time and room to 'thin out' the Palestinian population. As Dayan observed in the early 1970s, creeping annexation would give the Palestinians a blunt message:

> You shall continue to live like dogs, and whoever wants to can leave – and we will see where this process leads ... In five years we may have 200,000 less people – and that is a matter of enormous importance.[54]

Small-scale expulsions of Palestinians from the occupied territories continued to be carried out, just as they had been after the 1948 war. A secret government unit was established to 'encourage' the departure of Palestinians, particularly Gazan refugees, by offering them paid-for, one-way tickets to South America. In Eshkol's words: 'It's possible to move people there that no one would even know about their existence in the world.'[55] Government records show that in May 1968 an intelligence agent told Eshkol that up to 1,200 refugees a week had been successfully enticed to leave the Gaza Strip, but that the number was rapidly dwindling. As a result, the idea of emptying Gaza of its refugees had to be shelved, according to Colonel Shlomo Gazit, Dayan's right-hand man in the territories.[56]

Strictly coercive measures were also resorted to. From its creation in 1948, Israel has been exploiting emergency regulations inherited from the British Mandate – in fact the Knesset has renewed the state of emergency annually ever since. After 1967 Israel used these same regulations, as well as a raft of new military orders, to put into effect a 'deportation' policy. 'Unwanted' Palestinians included not only those who were suspected of resisting the occupation but also those who offered intellectual or moral support. Expulsions were used against: members of 'illegal' organizations; anyone classified as an 'infiltrator'; prisoners who agreed to leave the territories, either under duress or in exchange for a reduction in sentence; and anyone falling foul of Israel's web of personal registration requirements. Up to 2,000 Palestinian men are believed to have been directly expelled this way in the first decade of occupation, with spouses and children often following soon afterwards.[57]

Occupation's Legal Infrastructure

If most Palestinians could not be expelled from the West Bank and Gaza, a different strategy would be required. Israel would need both to encourage Palestinian emigration by making life intolerable, and concurrently to enable Jews to colonize the land in the occupied territories that had been vacated. One of Israel's national war heroes,

Meir Har-Tzion, summed up the philosophy in 1979: 'I do not say that we should put them on trucks and kill them. ... We must create a situation in which for them it would not be worth living here, but [better to leave] to Jordan or Saudi Arabia or any other Arab state.'[58] In fact, as Israel's leaders rapidly came to appreciate, the colonization process itself contributed significantly to the deterioration in Palestinian living conditions.

The most pressing obstacle to the policy of 'creeping annexation' was international law. In cases of military occupation, the rights of the civilian population in the occupied territory are safeguarded by the Hague Regulations and the Fourth Geneva Convention. Two important provisions in these conventions require of the occupying power that: it prohibit the transfer of its own civilians into the occupied territory; and it respect the prevailing laws in force there. Both provisions are designed to prevent the occupying power from trying to change political, demographic and physical realities in the occupied territory in its favour. But this was precisely what Israel needed to achieve if it was to empty the West Bank and Gaza of their Palestinian populations and annex the territories to a Greater Israel.

A nation rich in lawyers, Israel lost no time in erecting a legal facade to justify the abuses of international law it was determined to carry out. One of the Israeli army's first proclamations in the wake of the 1967 war was that the provisions of the Fourth Geneva Convention relating to occupied territory would be observed by its newly established military courts. (The first military orders had been drafted well before the Six-Day War, presumably in expectation of Israel's military conquest of land belonging to a neighbouring state, and were put into immediate effect.) However, two months later, as a political consensus quickly formed behind the idea of keeping the territories, the provision was repealed. Subsequently, Israel argued that West Bank and Gaza were not occupied but 'administered' territories whose status was yet to be determined. The legal pretext was that the two territories had not been under the sovereign rule of any state when Israel seized them in war. Both Jordan and Egypt had themselves been occupying the territories since 1948, and before that they were ruled by the British under a Mandate. Needless to say, Israel's self-serving reading of the Fourth Geneva Convention has been rejected by the International Committee of the Red Cross, the International Court of Justice, the United Nations, experts on international law and even most Israeli academics.[59]

By refusing to accept the West Bank and Gaza as occupied, and by engaging in legal sleights of hand, Israel freed itself to slowly erode the protections that should have been enjoyed by the Palestinian population. Most notably Israel issued hundreds of military orders designed to change radically the laws that were already in force in the occupied territories. According to international law, Israel's military administration could only alter local laws if the changes satisfied one or both of two considerations: military needs and the welfare of the occupied population. But Israel's primary goals – of encouraging the emigration of the Palestinian population, and of usurping the vacated land for colonization by Jews – fitted neither criterion. In fact, by moving large numbers of Jewish colonizers, including some who were armed, into the occupied territories, Israel created a conflict zone that placed both the colonizers and Palestinian civilians in danger.

A Palestinian lawyer, Raja Shehadeh, based in Ramallah, is perhaps the most knowledgeable critic of Israel's labyrinth of legislation in the occupied territories, having founded a Palestinian non-governmental organization, al-Haq, in the late 1970s.[60] He notes that more than 1,000 military orders have been passed since 1967, one set for the West Bank and another for Gaza before the disengagement, controlling almost every aspect of Palestinian life. The military regime in the occupied territories – misleadingly renamed a 'Civil Administration' in 1981[61] – is little different from the military government that existed inside Israel for nearly two decades. The raft of military orders was designed to adapt existing laws – a mixture of Ottoman laws, British defence regulations, and Jordanian and Egyptian laws that had applied in the West Bank and Gaza until 1967 – in ways beneficial to Israeli aims. The orders were secret until their publication in 1982, by which time the contours of the occupation had been firmly shaped. Few of these orders are compatible with Israel's obligations to the Palestinian population of the occupied territories.

According to Shehadeh, Israel's military government used the orders to accrete to itself almost unlimited powers in the occupied territories by:

- confiscating vast swathes of private land and resources on security grounds;
- controlling the issuing of all personal documents, as well as licences and official permits;
- replacing the local civilian and criminal courts for Palestinians with unaccountable military courts;
- creating and enforcing a separation of authority, both governmental and judicial, between the Palestinian natives and the new Jewish colonizers (just as Israel had earlier applied a military government to Palestinian citizens but not to Jewish citizens).

In this way, the Civil Administration was able to control and manage the details of Palestinian life, such as seizing most of the West Bank's substantial water resources; restricting the import and export of agricultural produce to favour Israeli producers by creating a captive Palestinian market; banning political meetings and the publication of newspapers to prevent dissent; holding Palestinians without trial in 'administrative detention'; levying special taxes, the proceeds of which are unaccounted for but impoverish Palestinian society; and withholding money from organizations Israel defines as hostile, also exploited as a way to retard the emergence of civil society.[62] Much like the earlier military rule inside Israel, the immediate benefit to Israel of these controls was to recruit a large class of Palestinian collaborators who depended on favours from the military administration to survive the deprivations of occupation.

One noted analyst of Israel's military court system, Lisa Hajjar, points out that the Military Advocate General of the time, Meir Shamgar, later admitted that he had been preparing for the establishment of a military administration from the early 1960s, long before the Six-Day War.[63] Shamgar, who would become president of the Supreme Court, also made several legal innovations in Israel's rule over the occupied territories. The most notable was his decision in 1968, as attorney general, to allow Palestinians to petition the Supreme Court against the decisions of the military administration. Judicial oversight of the occupation was crucial in persuading many observers that Israel's rule over the West Bank and Gaza was 'benign' or even 'enlightened'. But at the same time Shamgar ensured that the court's ability to safeguard Palestinian rights was severely curtailed.

First, Shamgar ruled that, although the provisions of the Fourth Geneva Convention did not apply to the occupied territories, Israel would voluntarily abide by the 'humanitarian' provisions of the Convention. Shamgar and his successors have never specified which provisions are humanitarian, though the Red Cross, the guardian of the Geneva Conventions, regards the whole body of these codes as humanitarian and considers them to be indivisible. Israel's official evasiveness, however, has allowed the court to claim in its judgments it is respecting international law, while ignoring it in practice or selectively referring to it in ways helpful to the occupation regime.

Second, Shamgar argued that, as the Palestinians had never enjoyed statehood, they could not be considered the rightful sovereigns of the West Bank and Gaza. This meant that in the court's view, while the Palestinians were considered to enjoy rights as individuals, protected by the so-called humanitarian provisions of the Geneva Conventions, they did not have any national rights. Hajjar points out: 'Shamgar's focus on the status of land ... rather than the population (with national rights to self-determination) was a strategic legal maneuver to separate the land from the people residing there.'[64] In this way the Palestinians in the occupied territories were stripped of their collective and national rights, including to their land as a national resource and asset, just as Israel's Palestinian citizens had been before them. The Palestinians would now arrive in court as separate individuals, whereas the settlers and the state would be able to claim national rights, particularly in relation to what would soon be called 'state land' that they desired for settlement.

Shamgar's innovation of allowing Palestinian petitions to the Supreme Court became the legal equivalent of Golda Meir's erasure of the Green Line, annexing the territories to Israel de facto and forcing the Palestinians to legitimize the annexation. Or as two Israeli analysts noted: 'It coerced the [Palestinian] inhabitants, who had no other legal recourse, to appeal to these courts in their quest for justice, and thus recognize, whether they wanted to or not ... the authority of the Israeli judicial system over them'.[65] Similarly, it persuaded most Israeli Jews that the Palestinians' rights were being safeguarded and that the occupation was 'legal'.

In reality, however, the military courts routinely approve the abuse of the Palestinian population's civil and political rights, and ignore international law, with little or no effective oversight from the Supreme Court. The myriad military orders sanction various collective punishments: house demolitions, curfews, closures of schools and colleges, restrictions on family unification, confiscations of private land, restrictions on movement enforced through permit systems and checkpoints, and prohibitions on organized activities. In early 2008 the Israeli Committee against House Demolitions launched a campaign to highlight the fact that 18,000 Palestinian homes had been destroyed by the army over four decades, making tens of thousands of individuals in the occupied territories homeless.[66] The Civil Administration also inflicts sweeping reprisals on the male population in the hope of crushing any resistance to the occupation, including general round-ups, detention without charge, torture and deportations. Figures from the Palestinian Bureau of Statistics show that over the course of the occupation hundreds of thousands of Palestinians have been arrested.[67] Children have not been immune from harsh treatment at the hands of the army either. The Swedish branch of Save the Children estimated that nearly 30,000 Palestinian children needed medical treatment after being beaten by soldiers in the first two years of the first intifada, in the late 1980s. Some 10,000 had broken bones as a result, and a fifth of the injured were under the age of 5.[68]

A report on the military courts system by the Israeli human rights group Yesh Din in late 2007 found systematic and comprehensive abuses of Palestinian detainees' rights. According to the report, 150,000 Palestinians have been prosecuted by the courts over the past seventeen years without due process. Pre-trial detentions are almost always approved and renewed in hearings lasting only minutes, and sometimes seconds. Public scrutiny of hearings is severely compromised, with little chance of access for family or friends. Detainees and their lawyers are notified of the charges against them only in court, when it is too late for them to mount a defence. Charges are in Hebrew, a language many do not understand, and translation of documents, when it does occur, is 'partial or sloppy'. Severe restrictions are placed on lawyers to prevent them from providing an effective defence for their clients, or even having access to them, and typically there are lengthy delays until the trial begins. In only a tiny number of cases do Palestinians receive a proper trial where witnesses are called and evidence provided; instead, in 95 per cent of cases the hearing concludes in a plea bargain. And minors are regularly treated as adults. The report concludes that in the more than 9,000 cases heard in 2006, only about a quarter of 1 per cent of detainees were found innocent of the charges they faced.[69]

Confronted with the overwhelming evidence that Israel's occupation has not been conducted with the welfare of the occupied population in mind, Israel's Supreme Court has shown little interest in upholding the principles of international law. Thousands of petitions have been brought by Palestinians over four decades, but, as one of Israel's leading jurists, David Kretzmer, has noted:

> the Court has interfered infrequently in decisions of the military. . . .
> [I]n almost all of its judgments relating to the Occupied Territories,
> especially those dealing with questions of principle, the Court has
> decided in favour of the authorities, often on the basis of dubious legal
> arguments.[70]

Two Systems of Rule

Of course, the growth and expansion of the Jewish colonies in the occupied territories would not have been possible had the settlers been subject to the same laws and administrative practices enforced against the Palestinian population. Israel avoided this problem by creating an entirely separate system of rule for the Jewish population in the territories. Whereas 'creeping annexation' required that the Palestinians be kept fragmented, unrepresented and oppressed, it also needed to offer protection and privileges to Jews to entice them to live in potentially hostile terrain. Moshe Gorali explains what this meant in practice: 'To describe a situation where two populations, in this case one Jewish and the other Arab, share the same territory but are governed by two separate legal systems, the international community customarily uses the term "apartheid".' Not, however, in the case of Israel's rule in the occupied territories. The best legal minds in Israel, Gorali adds, have also refused to name this system of separation as apartheid. Even Amnon Rubinstein, the country's foremost constitutional expert, 'coined an alternative phrase, "enclave-based justice".'[71]

From 1979 Israel established a network of local and regional councils for the settlements, modelled on local government in Israel rather than the Jordanian system that applied to Palestinian communities.[72] It also began building an extensive network of roads for the settlements, integrating them into Israel proper, that were off-limits to Palestinians. By the time of the second intifada, access to most main roads in the West Bank was physically impossible for Palestinians as the exits from their villages had been sealed off with giant concrete blocks. If they had reason to try to travel on these roads, they needed a special permit from the Civil Administration to get past the growing number of checkpoints. In one notorious case, a major road – Route 443, connecting Jerusalem to Tel Aviv via a section of the West Bank – was closed to Palestinians, despite the fact that its construction on private Palestinian land had been approved by the Israeli courts in 1982 only because it was promised that the local Palestinian population would benefit from its construction.[73] The decision to reserve this road for Israelis exposed 'judicial hypocrisy', in the words of jurist David Kretzmer.[74] In 2004 Israel went cap in hand to the international community for more than $100 million to pay for the completion of an 'apartheid road' system, upgrading circuitous cross-country tracks linked by tunnels, to keep Palestinians away from the West Bank's main roads.[75] A year later the *Ma'ariv* newspaper reported on plans for strict segregation on the West Bank's roads: 'The purpose is to reach, in a gradual manner, within a year or two, total separation between the two populations ... roads for Israelis only and roads for Palestinians only.' The human rights group B'Tselem reported that Palestinians were barred from or had restricted access to more than 700 km of West Bank roads.[76]

In fact, a separation of rights between Palestinians and Jewish settlers was institutionalized from the outset of the occupation. In July 1967 the Knesset passed a law giving Israel's domestic courts a parallel jurisdiction with the military courts in the territories as a way to ensure that the settlers were not subject to military and emergency laws.[77] In the words of Amnon Rubinstein, there are two sets of laws that have created two kinds of people in the occupied territories. 'There are Israeli citizens with full rights, and there non-Israeli non-citizens with non-rights.'[78] Even more than this, as analysts Akiva Eldar and Idith Zertal document at length, Israeli law has been attenuated in the occupied territories, not only allowing the settlers great latitude in harassing and physically attacking ordinary Palestinians but also treating them extremely leniently when they do so.[79] One typical case occurred in 1988, in the early stages of the first intifada. A settler, Pinchas Wallerstein, chased after a group of Palestinian youths firing several rounds of his automatic weapon at them after he came across them burning a tyre on the road. He killed one youngster and injured another, and was sentenced to four months' community service. In reaching his decision, the judge overturned the principles of jurisprudence by arguing that 'one should not judge one's fellow until one is in his place'.[80] Later Wallerstein explained that his actions were not in self-defence but a show of force. He went on to become a leader of the settlers' supreme body, the Yesha council, and a much-respected public figure in Israel.

By military order, the settlements have also been given special powers to defend their colonies with patrols and guards, and the inhabitants have been permitted to carry arms and make arrests. The combination of creating armed militias in the occupied territories and weakening the law controlling them to the point where they are rarely held to account has opened the door to regular abuse of the Palestinian population. During the second intifada, there was a spate of reports from the West Bank of armed settlers stealing the olive harvest from neighbouring Palestinian farmers and assaulting Palestinians trying to access their land. This menace was briefly noted by the mainstream media in October 2002 when the 150 inhabitants of Yanun, a small Palestinian village near Nablus, where forced out in their entirety by marauding settlers from the nearby colony of Itimar, who attacked the villagers' homes, killed their livestock, poisoned their wells, and burnt their generator, all as the army stood by.[81]

In ignoring rights violations committed against the Palestinians, the courts have conspired with Dayan's ambition to encourage Palestinians to leave by making them 'live like dogs'. Or as Raja Shehadeh commented back in 1985, the policies approved by the Supreme Court 'seem to indicate that the Israeli goal is gradually to drive out the local Palestinian population and to annex the territory'.[82] Israel's right-wing parties openly express such sentiments on a daily basis, rarely making a distinction between Palestinian citizens of Israel and those in the occupied territories. Benny Elon, a rabbi, a settler, leader of the Moledet party and the tourism minister in one of Ariel Sharon's governments, put it this way: 'I will close the universities to you, I will make your lives difficult, until you want to leave.'[83]

In addition to abusing the Palestinians' political and civil rights, Israel has prevented the development of an independent Palestinian economy and plundered key resources. Military Order No. 92, for example, transferred all powers over water in the occupied territories into the hands of military officials, allowing Israel to control the mountain aquifers that have subsequently become one of the country's main sources of potable water. Furthermore, the order allowed Israel to integrate the West Bank into the Israeli water grid, effectively denying the two areas' separateness. After 1979, responsibility for the West Bank's water was transferred from the military government to the Israeli water company, Mekorot.[84]

With the Palestinian economy stunted by the decisions of Israeli officials, tens of thousands of the occupied territories' workers once poured into Israel each day seeking employment, doing the most menial jobs for wages no Israeli would accept.[85] Harvard scholar Sara Roy argues that Israel's decades-long policy has been actively to achieve what she calls the 'de-development' of the West Bank and Gaza. From the native population, she observes, have been taken

> its most critical resources, namely land, water and labor, and the capacity and potential for developing those resources. Not only are Palestinians exploited economically, they are deprived of their livelihood and developmental potential, national identity and sovereignty. The result is ... the deliberate, systematic and progressive dismemberment of the indigenous economy by the dominant one.[86]

The occupation's goal has been described by the late Israeli sociologist Baruch Kimmerling in more graphic terms as 'politicide': 'the dissolution of the Palestinian people's existence as a legitimate social, political and economic entity.'[87] In other words, behind a mask of false legitimacy, Israel has carried out the destruction of Palestinian identity and living space and the theft of resources. It has argued that its actions in the occupied territories are needed to prevent terrorist activity and protect its existence from the pathological hatred of the Palestinian population. And as the Jewish colonies have spread and become entrenched in the occupied territories, a further justification has been available: the army must ensure the colonizers' physical safety.

3

Dunam after Dunam

We have forgotten that we have not come to an empty land to inherit it, but we have come to conquer a country from a people inhabiting it, that governs it by virtue of its language and savage culture. ... [I]f we cease to look upon our land, the Land of Israel, as ours alone and we allow a partner into our estate – all content and meaning will be lost to our enterprise.

Moshe Sharett, who was to become Israel's first foreign minister and second prime minister, in a letter to friends, 12 February 1914[1]

Just as inside the Green Line, the key Palestinian resource in the occupied territories desired by the Israeli leadership was land. Confiscations from Palestinians realized Israel's twin goals of de-developing the Palestinian living environment to encourage emigration while enabling Jewish colonization. In fact, the military and legal strategy behind the land grab in the territories was lifted almost straight from Israel's successful record of stealing land from the Palestinian refugees and its own Palestinian citizens after 1948. Raja Shehadeh, whose al-Haq legal organization has been at the forefront of Palestinian challenges to this aggressive programme of land expropriation, explains

71

the Israeli rationale for the confiscations in the occupied territories, though his analysis could apply equally to events inside Israel. In accordance with Zionist philosophy,

> A Palestinian only has the right to the property he resides in. Once he leaves it for whatever reason, it ceases to be his, it 'reverts back' to those whom the Israeli system considers the original, rightful owners of 'Judea and Samaria', the Jewish people, wherever they might be.[2]

In other words, the principle laid out by Ariel Sharon regarding Palestinian citizens' rights to land in Chapter 1 is considered to apply with equal force in the occupied territories: Palestinians should never expect to be more than tenants, whereas the Jewish people are the landlords of the entire Promised Land.

For similar reasons, thousands of Palestinians have lost their residency rights in the occupied territories since 1967. One high-profile victim of this policy is Afif Safieh, today the Palestinian ambassador to Washington, who was studying abroad in 1967. After the Oslo Accords were signed in 1993, he submitted several requests to be reunited with his family in Jerusalem but his applications were rejected.[3] The court's view of such claims from Palestinians is recounted by an Israeli lawyer, Avigdor Feldman. One of his clients who had moved to Norway after marrying a Norwegian woman tried to return to his West Bank village several years later when the couple divorced. 'The army barred his entry, claiming he had lost his residence status. I recall Supreme Court Justice Miriam Ben-Porat cynically remarking that my client was really a "Norwegian".[4] In order to prevent condemnation from the international community, Israel has allowed many Palestinians denied their right to residency to live in the occupied territories on tourist visas instead, having to leave the country and renew them every few months. Some Palestinians have been living like this for a decade or more. But in early 2006 the Israeli government ended this practice, effectively evicting thousands of Palestinians with foreign passports from their homes, and separating them from their families, spouses and children in the occupied territories.[5]

Theft by Stealth

This gradual erosion of Palestinian residency rights, designed to pass unnoticed by the international community, has been mirrored by a similar territorial policy of theft by stealth. In the early days of the occupation, the Civil Administration could simply have taken possession by force of land in the West Bank and Gaza it wanted for colonization. However, as Shehadeh notes, it preferred to devise 'legal' manoeuvres to justify its actions and avoid bad publicity.

> The Zionists have been concerned with projecting an image of a community ruled by the principles of justice and the rule of law. In order to preserve that image, it was necessary to employ a dynamic and creative approach to law and legal systems and to manipulate existing systems so that Zionist aims could be achieved under a semblance of adherence to the rule of law.[6]

It is worth examining in some detail this careful manipulation of the legal framework relating to land ownership in the West Bank to understand how the large-scale theft of Palestinian land was hidden behind a facade of legality.

One of Israel's first moves, with obvious echoes of what had occurred after 1948, was to confiscate as absentee property any land belonging to a Palestinian who was not residing in his or her home at the time of the capture of the West Bank and Gaza in 1967. The absentee's property was seized by the army as abandoned and passed to an official whom we have already noted: the Custodian of Absentee Property. The land was then allocated on a long-term lease to the settlement division of the World Zionist Organization or a subsidiary company of the Jewish National Fund called Himanuta for colonization by Jews.[7] (The JNF avoided getting publicly involved in settlement of the occupied territories for fear that its direct participation would threaten the charitable status of its work inside Israel.)

Land did not always need to be abandoned, or the owner absent, for it to be classified thus. According to an Israeli court ruling in 1982, the Custodian could still expropriate a Palestinian's private land and transfer it to the Israeli authorities as long as he did so in 'good faith', believing the land to be absentee property. Shehadeh reports on a case in which he represented a Palestinian, Francois Albina, who had 70 dunams confiscated this way for the benefit of a nearby Jewish settlement.[8]

Belatedly, in 2004, Israel tried to resurrect the 1950 Absentee Property Law for use against West Bank Palestinians who owned land in East Jerusalem, taking advantage of an 800 km 'separation wall' being built by Israel through the West Bank since 2003. Justified on the grounds that it would prevent suicide attacks, the steel and concrete wall divided sections of East Jerusalem and sealed the enlarged area of the city off from the West Bank.[9] Land owners in the West Bank cut off from their lands by the wall were informed that they had now been classed as absentees, and their land was being confiscated. When the policy came to light shortly after a ruling against the routeing of the wall on Palestinian land by the International Court of Justice in the Hague, it provoked international condemnation. Israel's attorney general, Menachem Mazuz, hastily ordered the practice stopped, arguing that it could 'have grave diplomatic repercussions on the separation fence ... This is an issue where clearly Israel's interest would be to avoid opening new fronts in the world and in international law.'[10] Mazuz's comments, however, suggested this would only be a temporary reprieve until the land could be taken without being noticed. And, true enough, the Housing Ministry announced in early 2008 plans to build 1,000 apartments for Jewish settlers on 'absentee land' – on the other side of the wall – owned by 600 Palestinian families from Beit Sahour, near Bethlehem.[11]

Appeals against arbitrary decisions in the case of absentee property are heard by a committee of military officers, headed by a senior legal adviser to the Israel Lands Authority, a government body dedicated to the 'Judaization' of land.[12] As Shehadeh observed a quarter of a century ago, the Israeli government and the Custodian had never had the intention of holding the absentees' property in trust until a solution to the conflict was found: 'The Custodian is transferring property of absentees to [Israeli and Jewish] third parties for use in a long-term, permanent manner.'[13]

Other methods for taking private land from Palestinians, or restricting their ability to control what land they possessed, were also sought in the early years of the occupation. Leading the way was Himanuta, an 'independent company' almost entirely owned by the Jewish National Fund that pursued the same tactic of purchasing land carried out in Palestine by the Fund before 1948. Himanuta has concentrated on buying land inside the occupied territories but near the Green Line in an attempt to erode the armistice line's significance. A former official in the JNF, Avraham Halleli, noted the logic behind this approach in 2005: 'The Green Line is not a border line; the "border" can take on a different shape, changes can be made.'[14] Although little is known about Himanuta's activities, the Israeli media report that it has bought thousands of dunams of land, much of it paid for by Israel or the World Zionist Organization. However, the purchases have been a very minor element in Israel's land grab. Outside East Jerusalem, where settler tactics have been much more intimidating and underhand, few Palestinians have been willing to sell to Jewish colonizers, even when their land has been stripped of its value by Israel's changes to local planning and zoning laws. When the land is bought, it is often though middlemen, usually Palestinian collaborators posing as independent land buyers.

More successful have been confiscations on administrative grounds.[15] Under the Fourth Geneva Convention, an occupying power is entitled to make changes only if they are necessary for its security or if they benefit the local occupied population. This provision should have forestalled any plans on Israel's part to confiscate land for settlement. But shortly after the 1967 war Israel's chief adviser on international law, Theodor Meron, advised that confiscations could occur on one condition: 'it is vital that [the expropriation of land] be done by military bodies and not civilian ones ... in the framework of [establishing] bases'. The bases should be temporary in nature too, he warned.[16] In the first years of the occupation, therefore, Israel was careful to cite security as the reason for taking Palestinian land and to establish what it claimed were military camps known as Nahal outposts. The first colony approved by Eshkol in the West

Bank, Kfar Etzion, between Jerusalem and Hebron, was settled in September 1967, officially as a military outpost. However, in what quickly became a pattern, not one of the settlers was a soldier and none carried out any military duties at the outpost. Nonetheless, the Israeli media dutifully reported that it was a military base, as did US officials.[17] Three months later, Yigal Allon helped a group of religious fanatics led by Rabbi Moshe Levinger settle in the midst of Hebron, one of the largest Palestinian cities in the West Bank.[18] These two settlements were soon joined by three in the Jordan Valley and the first neighbourhoods in East Jerusalem.

During the early 1970s the number of Nahal bases grew dramatically, with additional land confiscated to provide them with services such as roads, electricity and water. Other land was requisitioned for firing ranges and training grounds as the occupation entrenched. But these bases were soon divested of their military purpose and matured into civilian colonies, often home to religious-nationalist groups belonging to a new extremist settlement movement called Gush Emunim (Block of the Faithful) that had sprung up in the wake of the 'miraculous' victory of the Six-Day War.[19] This became an endlessly reinforcing process, with more military bases needed to secure and protect from possible attack the newly civilianized settlements and their access roads. Around the military camps and civilian settlements large tracts of land were declared security zones, supposedly to offer yet more protection.[20] During this period, the settlers and the army began to forge close, often intimate relations, as described at length in a book, *Lords of the Land*, written by two Israeli analysts, Idith Zertal and Akiva Eldar.[21] Those commanders who dared take on the settlers invariably found their careers soon suffering. Today, religious-nationalist settlers dominate the higher ranks of the army, as well as the bureaucracy of the Civil Administration.[22]

A Civilian Army

At the end of the first decade of occupation, nearly a third of the West Bank was under Israeli military control. According to figures released in 1979, of the land requisitioned by the military since 1967 about two-thirds had been transferred to civilian settlers.[23] Expropriation was carried out in line with Dayan's programme of 'creeping annexation', maintaining the pretence that security needs alone were driving the settlement project. Labor's favoured sites for colonization followed the Allon Plan by concentrating chiefly on the Jordan Valley in the West Bank and the area around and inside East Jerusalem.

That all changed, however, in 1977 with the rise to power of the right-wing Likud Party. With its open espousal of a Greater Israel philosophy, it pursued a far more aggressive and unabashed settlement policy, which not only continued to placate the religious-nationalist settlers but also created what one observer has called a 'free market' in colonization: economic incentives were offered to tempt Israeli Jews to relocate to the occupied territories.[24] Under Likud, the settlements would start spreading across the West Bank, uninhibited by either the need to claim a security justification or whether they were close to Palestinian cities and villages.

This new approach to settlement was mirrored by a change in land confiscation policy following a court case in 1979 over the founding of a religious settlement, Elon Moreh, near the city of Nablus, deep in the West Bank. In June that year the army requisitioned 700 dunams of land from seventeen Palestinian landowners for 'military needs'. Two days later religious settlers began moving on to the land to establish Elon Moreh, demonstrating a new confidence in the wake of a court ruling months earlier that had approved the founding of a civilian colony, Beit El, next to the Palestinian city of Ramallah.[25] Religious settlers belonging to the Gush Emunim movement interpreted the ruling as carte blanche for them to settle the West Bank's biblical sites, whether or not they were located on private Palestinian land and however close they were to existing Palestinian communities.

In the Elon Moreh case, however, the Palestinian landowners not only appealed to the Supreme Court but also presented written testimonies from two senior Israeli military officers arguing that the new settlement would 'not contribute to Israel's security'. The justices, aware of the dangerous precedent they had just unleashed with their Beit El decision, were looking for a way to withdraw their approval from the new overtly civilian settlement drive on private Palestinian land. They issued an interim order freezing construction at the Elon Moreh site while they investigated the case. In the meantime, a settler leader, Menachem Felix, submitted a sworn statement in which he agreed that 'security' had not been the motivation for establishing Elon Moreh. Instead he argued that the settlers were fulfilling a holy mission: 'this is the place where the land was promised for the first time to our first forefather.'[26] Seizing on this admission, the justices ruled that Elon Moreh was not needed for security and ordered the settlers to leave – the first setback in the colonization process.[27]

The Likud government, promising it would no longer colonize Palestinian private land, faced the ruin of its Greater Israel project unless new grounds for confiscating Palestinian land could be found. A senior legal official in the Justice Ministry, Plia Albek, came to the rescue. She was entrusted with surveying the West Bank to find out how much of it could be classified as 'state land', and could therefore be claimed as Israeli territory ripe for settlement. A helicopter was regularly put at Albek's disposal as she flew over areas desired for colonization to check whether the lands were sufficiently cultivated by their Palestinian owners to avoid confiscation. Obligingly, she was soon approving large-scale expropriations of Palestinian land. Or as Moshe Gorali, *Ha'aretz*'s legal analyst, explained: 'She transformed the High Court's prohibition concerning the expropriation of private land into massive authorization for seizure of public land in the territories.'[28] When Palestinians petitioned the Israeli courts to stop Jewish settlement building on 'state land' in the occupied territories, the judges refused to intervene, arguing that it was a matter that should be 'settled in political negotiations' at some future stage.[29]

Albek's work and that of other officials dramatically increased the number of settlements and expanded the amount of land under Israeli control in a few years. In 1978 there were 39 colonies home to 7,400 settlers, while by 1983 there were 67 colonies home to nearly 23,000 inhabitants.[30] To understand how this land grab was achieved, we must examine the land laws applying in the occupied territories before 1967. According to international law, Israel had to abide by the laws already in force when the territories were occupied – meaning, in the case of the West Bank, Ottoman laws along with minor modifications made by the British and Jordanians. Israel, however, hijacked the existing laws, mischievously reinterpreting them so as to define much of the occupied territories as 'state land' – a category all but unheard of in Palestine.[31] As the new sovereign ruler, Israel could then argue that it had legal ownership of this 'state land', which was being officially held in trust for the Jewish people and from which Palestinians could legitimately be excluded – just as had occurred on the other side of the Green Line after 1948.

The Great 'State Lands' Swindle

Israel, however, was grossly mischaracterizing Ottoman law. The Ottoman ruler, the Sultan, had been the owner of all of his empire's territories, including Palestine, only in the same theoretical legal sense as the British monarch is the ultimate owner of all land in England. But, just as with Crown land, the Sultan's supreme ownership had little bearing on what actually occurred on the ground: the use of land was granted to private individuals through a system of tenures and leases. Palestine's land had in effect come to be divided into different legal categories of usage and hence ownership:

- *waqf* land had been placed in an Islamic trust by families who retained its private use even though ownership was invested in God – usually as a way to ensure that state officials did not try to seize it on behalf of the Sultan;
- *mulk* land was private land in the modern sense that the owners could produce documents registering their ownership;
- *miri* land, the bulk of Palestinian land, had not been formally registered. Some was land in communal or public use (*matrouk*), such as lakes, rivers, wadis, forests, pastures, roads, and the cultivable areas close by villages; and the rest was considered dead or

79

unused (*mawat*), such as rocky hills, and unclaimed land far from villages.

For centuries Ottoman law had made it possible for an individual to convert *miri* land into *mulk* land, or land in private use, simply by building on it or starting to cultivate it. In fact, ownership of much of the agricultural and pasture land in Palestine had been determined by custom and usage only, with the same family or clan cultivating parcels of land for generations. In the late 1850s the Ottomans introduced a Land Code, modelled on the French legal system, to regulate the private use of agricultural land by demanding that landholders pay a sum in return for the title deeds (*tabu*) to a plot of land. Anyone failing to cultivate farmland for three consecutive years lost the *tabu*, and ownership reverted to the Sultan, whose officials would then reassign the land to another private landholder. In this sense, *miri* land under the Ottomans was not the same as state land, any more than Crown land in England is state land. Rather the Sultan's officials were arbitrators and overseers in the transfer of *miri* land between potential claimants. Both Britain and Jordan sought to formalize this system by registering more land in the name of private owners, but the process was slow and far from complete by the time of the 1948 and 1967 wars.

Israel, as the occupying power, reinterpreted the Ottoman Land Code and exploited the lack of a proper registration process – despite the clear prohibition in international law on changing the status of occupied land. In May 1979 Israel declared that all *miri* land was henceforth to be considered 'state land', belonging to the Jewish people.[32] Such land could then be passed on to the army or to Jews for colonization. To maximize the amount of land that was classified as state land, Israel issued military orders freezing the registration process for Palestinians who had been cultivating land or even for those who had received the *tabu*. It also suspended all arbitration services to settle land disputes, meaning that Palestinian owners could often not prove their title to the land. In appeals against the declaration of areas as 'state land', the burden of proof always rested with the Palestinian claiming ownership of the land. In more difficult cases, where private Palestinian land was wanted despite its registration, Israeli officials simply forged sales contracts or deeds.[33] In short, rather than continuing the role of the Sultan's officials in arbitrating between private land owners, Israel seized the land for itself and the Jewish people.

In addition, Israel classed as state land all *mawat* land, or unused land, determined in the old-fashioned way: by the Sultan's representative, in this case an Israeli army officer, standing next to the outer houses of the village and shouting. At the point at which his voice could no longer be heard, the land was considered 'dead' and therefore could be reclassified, in Israel's view, as state land. Before this innovation, such dead land had been a reserve for Palestinian villages as they grew. Now the villages were tightly boxed in, confined to their homes and the land next to the village that they had been cultivating at the time of the land survey.

Even in the tightly defined municipal areas left to them, Palestinians found that they had no control over planning matters, which were handed over to committees of Israeli military officers. The committees refused permission to change the use of agricultural land so that villages could expand their built-up area. In consequence, Palestinian villages were turned into overcrowded ghettoes, much as had happened earlier to Palestinian citizens of Israel.[34] In another move, Israel dismissed local mayors of Palestinian towns and installed Israeli mayors, who were willing to cooperate with the army and the local settlement drive. Master plans were also not approved for Palestinian communities, making it difficult, if not impossible, for their inhabitants to build legally.[35] As a result, thousands of demolition orders against Palestinian homeowners have been issued and, as we noted earlier, some 18,000 homes actually destroyed.

In the late 1980s, by the time the land survey had been completed, Israel recognized about a third of the land in the West Bank as registered to Palestinian owners. The rest was treated as belonging to Israel. A report by the Israeli human rights group B'Tselem in 2002 revealed that 42 per cent of the West Bank had been directly seized by the settlements: nearly 7 per cent fell within the boundaries of their municipalities and a further 35 per cent had been allocated to their regional councils.[36] A further 20 per cent of the West Bank was 'state land' controlled by the army or Civil Administration, including areas designated as national parks. These vast areas under the jurisdiction of the settlements are defined as 'closed military zones', from which Palestinians are banned. However, a report published by Peace Now in 2007, citing Civil Administration figures, revealed that the settlements were officially only using about 12 per cent of the area under their jurisdiction.[37]

Nonetheless, the land area under the settlements' control is constantly encroaching on parts of the West Bank belonging to the Palestinians. The Peace Now report also showed that, despite the wealth of land available to the settlers, a third of the land they were using fell outside their jurisdiction. One method by which the councils have grabbed private Palestinian land was revealed in a court case in March 2008. According to the testimony of a leading settler, the councils had been 'laundering' territory since the mid-1990s. Under the scam, the councils leased private Palestinian land just outside their municipal boundaries to individual settlers. Once a settler had been assigned the plot, the army were required to prevent the Palestinian owner from accessing it to safeguard the settler. After three years, the council could apply to the Civil Administration for the land to be confiscated from the Palestinian owner and declared state property on the grounds that he had failed to cultivate his land for that period and thereby lost his right to ownership.[38] Dayan's creeping annexation was triumphing.

Shehadeh points out that even apparently beneficial acts by the Civil Administration, such as declaring parts of the West Bank nature reserves, as occurred from 1974, were really devious measures to strip more land from the Palestinian population. A military order passed much later, in 1996, forbade Palestinians from entering extensive parts of the West Bank known as 'Area C' that were designated by the Olso accords as under Israel's absolute control and included all the nature reserves.[39] In fact, the 'Area C' of Oslo comprised 60 per cent of the

West Bank – exactly those parts that already fell under the control of the settlements and the Civil Administration and were regarded as belonging to the Jewish people.

With Israel's master plan for the West Bank unfolding before his eyes, Shehadeh recounts in one of his memoirs how he came to realize that he and other Palestinians in the occupied territories might have realized earlier what was happening to them had they listened to the warnings from Israel's Palestinian citizens, who had already suffered the same treatment at the hands of a Jewish state:

> They would tell us: 'You don't know a thing about Israel. We can
> tell you what is coming: land expropriations, biased zoning that will
> strangle your towns, and unfair taxation that will impoverish you.' And
> we would look with condescension at them and think they had lived for
> so long under Israel that they had become colonized, unable to think
> beyond their narrow claustrophobic reality.[40]

Goals of Colonization

Ariel Sharon's 'disengagement' in 2005 removed 8,000 settlers from twenty-one colonies in Gaza and a handful more Israelis from four isolated and unviable settlements in the northern tip of the West Bank. Despite the fanfare of publicity that greeted the withdrawal, the evacuees were survived by the overwhelming majority of the settlement population: 270,000 living in 120 official colonies in the West Bank; a few thousand settlers in more than 100 tiny outposts, usually land-grabbing extensions of the settlements that lacked official recognition but were secretly supported by both the army and government; and nearly 230,000 settlers living in the Jewish neighbourhoods of East Jerusalem, the Palestinian half of the city annexed to Israel since 1980.[41] Today, these half a million settlers and the army that protects them control 60 per cent of the West Bank. The remaining ghettoes – islands of Palestinian land surrounded by a sea of Israeli-controlled territory – are nominally ruled by the Palestinian Authority, a kind of Palestinian government-in-waiting created by the Oslo agreements of the mid-1990s.

Shortly after the Gaza evacuation, Sharon advised his Likud Party of the urgent need to expand the surviving colonies in the West Bank without attracting attention: 'There's no need to talk. We need to build, and we're building without talking.' Indeed. In the year of the disengagement, the settler population actually grew, with an estimated 14,500 new settlers in the West Bank more than making up for the loss of the 8,000 from Gaza. Dror Etkes, an expert on the settlement enterprise, warned in the wake of the disengagement that Israeli officials were seeking to pre-empt any final peace agreement being considered by the US: 'They don't know how long they've got. That's why they're building like maniacs.'[42] In 2006, 27 per cent of all the apartments purchased by Israelis were situated in the West Bank.[43] And in the first half of 2007, the settler population grew by 5.5 per cent, several times the rate of increase inside Israel proper.[44] In places like Ma'ale Adumim and Ariel, the settlements have evolved into proper towns, numbering tens of thousands of inhabitants and strategically located to destroy any chance of a territorially coherent Palestinian state emerging. The half a million settlers, nearly a tenth of Israel's Jewish population, with ties to friends and families on the other side of the Green Line, are a powerful constituency that few Israeli politicians choose, or want, to confront.

As we have seen, the colonization of the occupied territories was far from accidental: for four decades it followed the general outlines proposed by Allon and Dayan in 1967. However, over time officials grew more confident that more specific and brazen goals of settlement could be achieved. An idea of their thinking was offered by the World Zionist Organization, an unaccountable quasi-governmental body overseeing settlement policy in the occupied territories on behalf of the state in a role mirroring the activities of the Jewish National Fund inside Israel's borders. In 1978, in the immediate wake of Israel's agreement, under US pressure, to return the Sinai to Egypt, the WZO drafted a report on the settlements, the Drobless Plan, named after its principal author, Mattiyahu Drobless. Hoping to avert any danger that a similar agreement would be repeated with the occupied Palestinian territories, Drobless asserted bluntly that 'settlement

throughout the entire land of Israel' – that is, including the West
Bank and Gaza – was 'our right'. An amended version of the plan
was issued two years later that was even clearer about the aims of
settlement. Israel was in 'a race against time' and must concentrate on
'establishing facts on the ground. ... There mustn't be even a shadow
of a doubt about our intention to keep the territories of Judea and
Samaria [the West Bank] for good'.[45] Drobless envisioned a million
settlers in the occupied territories by 2013, an ambition that may
have looked deluded at the time but today looks less unrealistic.[46]

The report offered a strategy for how to settle the land – one, as
the Middle East expert David Hirst notes, that

> was expressly modelled on techniques which, since 1948, had been
> applied to the organized remnants of the Palestinian community in the
> original Israel, despoiling yet more of their land and villages, fragment-
> ing them geographically, paralysing them politically and reducing them
> to a condition of abject dependence on the Jewish economy.

Settlement, Drobless suggested, should be not only *around* Palestinian
communities, to contain them, but also *between* them, 'in accordance
with the settlement policy adopted in Galilee', to fragment them.[47]
The settlements, and the infrastructure needed to integrate them
into Israel proper, would break up the continuity of the Palestinian
living space, preventing the emergence of any future Palestinian
state. Or, as Sara Roy observes, settlement was designed 'to normal-
ize and institutionalize land expropriations by eroding the 1967
borders making territorial retreat difficult if not impossible.'[48] Sharon
gave voice to precisely this ambition on a helicopter flight over the
Gaza Strip in 1980 when he was agriculture minister. Accompanied
by the Israeli military governor of Gaza, who wanted to know how
he was supposed to contain the Palestinian refugee camps below,
Sharon replied: 'I want the Arabs to see Jewish lights every night
500 meters from them.'[49] The Palestinians had to be made to accept
that Jewish dominion in the occupied territories was an irreversible
fact of life. In the different context of the second intifada, but
expressing much the same sentiment, Chief of Staff Moshe Ya'alon

called for Israel's invincibility to be 'burned into the Palestinian and Arab consciousness'.[50]

For the settlement drive to succeed in fragmenting the Palestinians and disabuse them of any hope of ever attaining statehood, Israel required a large number of Israelis to move from the safety of their homes inside Israel to a more uncertain life in the occupied territories. Despite Israel's long-term intentions, its formal position was that the settlements were only temporary and might one day be dismantled as part of a peace agreement. Apart from in the case of East Jerusalem, which had been annexed to Israel, the undecided status of the West Bank and Gaza explained the reluctance of the wider Israeli population to settle in the territories in the first decades of occupation. Israel therefore invested huge sums of money on the settlements, making them attractive to families who needed cheap housing or a better quality of life away from the overcrowded centre of the country.

Subsidizing the Settlers

A report by the B'Tselem human rights group during the second intifada noted that Israel had 'carried out a vigorous and systematic policy aimed at encouraging Israeli citizens to move to the settlements. One of the main tools serving this policy is the granting of benefits and significant financial incentives to settlers.' Much of the money had been funnelled either through the settlers' local councils or by classifying the settlements as 'national priority areas'. In these areas, settlers received a reduction on their income tax, special loans at discounted rates, greater expenditure on their local schools and subsidized housing and transport, while businesses were eligible for large grants.

The total amount spent by Israel on the settlements will probably never be known, as the figures have been buried deep in the general budgets of government ministries. This was done to avoid both international censure and the likely outcry from ordinary Israelis appalled at the waste of public money. However, in 2003 the *Ha'aretz* newspaper did try to estimate the additional cost of the settlements to the Israeli taxpayer after excluding all military expenditure. It admitted that its calculations were intentionally 'very conservative', that it had not factored in the whole period of the occupation and that it had excluded the half of the settler population that lives in East Jerusalem. Nonetheless, it found that at least 50 billion shekels ($12 billion) had been spent on benefits for the settlers over and above what would have been spent on them if they had remained inside Israel.[51] Given that for much of the occupation there were no more than a few tens of thousands of settlers in the occupied territories, it was a truly astounding sum.

The other factor encouraging Israelis to move into the occupied territories, paradoxically, was the signing of the Oslo peace agreements in the mid-1990s that established the Palestinian Authority under the leadership of Yasser Arafat. During the short, seven-year period of Oslo, the number of settlers doubled to some 200,000. Raja Shehadeh sheds some light on this strange phenomenon. The Declaration of Principles, approved by the Palestinian leadership in Tunis, was

> achieved at the price of keeping the settlements out of the jurisdiction of the Palestinian Authority. ... With one blow, political expediency led to the acceptance [by the Palestinian leadership] of all the illegal changes we in the Occupied Territories had been struggling to nullify for two decades.[52]

Or as the Foreign Ministry's legal adviser, Alan Baker, himself a settler, told an Israeli newspaper in 2003:

> It was resolved – and the Palestinians agreed – that the settlements' fate would be determined in a future peace agreement. After we signed those [Oslo] accords, which are still legally in force, we are no longer an occupying power, but we are instead present in the territories with their [Palestinian] consent and subject to the outcome of negotiations.[53]

Israelis came to believe, and were encouraged to think by their leaders, that, with the signing of the Oslo Accords, the settlement blocs had received Palestinian acceptance and international legitimacy.

A sign of the extent to which Israeli society and the wider international community had allowed themselves to be deceived by the legal facade of the settlement enterprise recently came to light. *Ha'aretz* revealed in October 2006 that a secret report on the settlements had been compiled by General Baruch Spiegel, special adviser to the defence minister. Military sources described its contents as 'explosive'.[54] Following the newspaper's investigation, an Israeli group, Peace Now, petitioned the courts under the country's Freedom of Information Act to force the government to publish the details. Officials countered by arguing that publication would 'damage the state's security and foreign relations', a presumed reference to the fact that the report's findings would embarrass the United States, whose billions of dollars in aid had been secretly siphoned off to prop up the settlement drive. Only later, in early 2008, was information from the report leaked to Peace Now. It showed that more than a third of the 120 colonies in the West Bank had been built on private Palestinian land, officially seized temporarily and out of military necessity. It further revealed that 19 of these 44 settlements had been built after 1979 when the cabinet took a decision, in the wake of the Elon Moreh case, to build on 'state land' only. The list of the settlements included many of the largest and most famous, including Ariel, Efrat, Kiryat Arba, Ofra, Beit El, Psagot, Kedumim and Shiloh. Peace Now pointed out that the data showed many of the settlements were illegal even according to the perverse rules laid down by Israel. A legal source warned improbably that the courts might demand that the state hand back the land on which these settlements were built to their Palestinian owners.[55]

The brief bout of soul-searching in Israel prompted by these revelations allowed Israelis to avoid pondering the deeper purpose of the settlements. It was left to an Israeli journalist, Amira Hass, to offer a dissenting view:

> The exaggerated concentration on private ownership feeds into the Israeli denial of the fact that the Palestinians' right is to all of the territory that has been occupied. Not as private individuals, but rather because they constitute an indigenous national group in this land.[56]

Hollow Pledges

The expansion of the settlements, as Raja Shehadeh points out, 'was a state project' that was 'not going to be hampered by questions of law'.[57] But what Israel craved from the outset of the occupation was that at some point all or most of the 'facts on the ground' it had created inside Palestinian territory would be officially sanctioned by its principal sponsor, the US. That moment came in April 2004 with an exchange of letters between Ariel Sharon and the US President, George W. Bush. Following Sharon's announcement of his plan to disengage from Gaza, Bush wrote:

> In light of the new realities on the ground, including already existing major Israeli population centers [ie Jewish colonies in the West Bank], it is unrealistic to expect that the outcome of final status negotiations will be a full and complete return to the armistice lines of 1949.[58]

That was diplomatic longhand for saying that the US was now prepared to allow the larger and better-established settlements to be annexed to Israel in a final peace agreement. A year later, at a meeting at his ranch in Texas, Bush confirmed his commitment to Sharon.

Bush's backing for the 'settlement blocs' has only intensified Israel's clandestine building programme in the West Bank, in the hope that the US will also concede these new facts on the ground. The work has had to be done quietly because Israel is still officially obliged by the terms of a US-sponsored diplomatic peace plan, unveiled in late 2002, known as the Road Map. That requires Israel to halt all expansion of the settlements as part of a first phase of confidence-building measures. Prime Minister Ehud Olmert confirmed Israel's commitment to freezing all settlement construction again in November 2007 shortly before the Annapolis conference, called by Bush to revive the moribund peace process. However, the same month, a British newspaper reported that Israeli companies were unashamedly offering newly built homes in West Bank colonies at UK property exhibitions.[59]

In truth, Israel has barely bothered to conceal its determination to flout these public commitments. In particular, settlement expansion has continued openly in East Jerusalem, which Israel publicly considers to have a different status from the West Bank. In a comment that defies international law, a government spokesman explained in late 2007: 'Jerusalem is our capital. It is Israeli sovereign territory.'[60] By early 2008 Israel had announced a building bonanza in East Jerusalem, with hundreds of new apartments at the Har Homa settlement and a reported minimum of 10,000 apartments in a new neighbourhood of Atarot, 'the biggest settlement project since 1967'.[61]

Less noticed, settler associations backed by the government, state officials and wealthy donors such as the American billionaire Irving Moskowitz continue to exploit the planning and zoning laws that favour Jewish expansion in East Jerusalem. One preferred tactic is for armed settlers to take over buildings in Palestinian areas of East Jerusalem desired for 'Judaization', including in the Old City, and then seek to terrorize their Palestinian neighbours into leaving. Another is declaring areas of East Jerusalem archeological sites, as a pretext for taking the land.

Both tactics have been used successfully in the neighbourhood of Silwan. There Israeli officials have long turned a blind eye to settler families forming military-style encampments in buildings erected illegally in the heart of the neighbourhood.[62] Today there are a dozen armed settlements dotted around Silwan. Meanwhile, since 1998 a settler organization, Elad, has been given permission by the municipality and the Israel Nature and National Parks Protection Authority to run the 'City of David' National Park in Silwan, supposedly the original location of Jerusalem. The settlers have fenced off most of the neighbourhood's green areas, declaring them archeological sites and posting armed guards to protect them. Several settler homes have already been built inside these parks, and dozens more are planned.[63] Elad has also lobbied for the homes of nearly a hundred Palestinian families to be demolished to make way for yet another archeological park. So far international pressure has kept the demolitions on hold.[64] However, in a sign of the close coordination between state bodies and the settlers, Elad has subcontracted the Israel Antiquities Authority to conduct a disruptive dig under the homes of Silwan's Palestinian residents in the hope that their lives can be made so miserable that they will leave.

In another example of collusion, the Israel Lands Authority has been encouraging settlers belonging to a particularly active settler group, Ateret Cohanim, to wrestle control of a large olive grove in East Jerusalem's Sheikh Jarrah neighbourhood from its Palestinian landowners.[65] Like Silwan, Sheikh Jarrah, which lies close to the armistice line that once separated East and West Jerusalem, is regarded as a key area for Judaization. Jewish control of these strategic areas would seal off the Old City from Palestinian access.

Settlement expansion and building is widespread outside Jerusalem too. Peace Now published a report just as Olmert was preparing to fly off to Annapolis showing that construction was being carried out in 88 of the 120 West Bank colonies.[66] In March 2008 even the pretence of a freeze on settlement expansion was dropped when it was announced that 750 homes were being built in the West Bank, in the Givat Ze'ev settlement north of Jerusalem.[67] Most of the new construction work is taking place in areas Israel expects eventually to annex, once they have been cut off from the rest of the West Bank by the separation wall, as part of a future peace agreement. In spring 2008, in what appeared to be a rebuke to the White House for focusing on the issue of settlement growth, Sharon's former senior adviser Dov Weisglass claimed that US Secretary of State Condoleezza Rice had confirmed in a secret agreement just before the Gaza disengagement that Bush's letter of 2004 gave Israel permission to expand the colonies it intended to keep. Taking advantage of Weisglass's comments, Olmert gave an interview to the *Yediot Aharonot* newspaper in which he thumbed a diplomatic nose at Washington:

> It was clear from day one to Abbas, Rice and Bush that construction would continue in population concentrations – the areas mentioned in Bush's 2004 letter. I say this again today: Beitar Illit will be built; Gush Etzion will be built; there will be construction in Pisgat Ze'ev and in the Jewish neighborhoods in Jerusalem. It's clear that these will remain under Israeli control in any future settlement.[68]

Another colony, Modi'in Illit, established in 1996, already has a population of 40,000, making it both the largest settlement in the West Bank and the fastest growing. By 2020 it is expected to be home to 150,000 settlers. As Israeli historian Gadi Algazi observes, Modi'in Illit is evidence of a new trend in settlement building, the result of an alliance between state officials wishing to take more Palestinian land and private real estate developers looking for a quick and easy return on their money. Built specifically for Israel's poorest Jewish community, the ultra-Orthodox, investors have benefited from non-enforcement of building regulations and reduced taxes, and the creation of a captive labour force of conservative religious women prepared to work for minimum wages.[69] The settlement project has benefited greatly too. For reasons related to their reading of the Bible, the ultra-Orthodox identify little with Zionism and generally do not support the occupation. However, Israeli officials have cynically recruited them to the settlement drive by building cheap housing and providing the ready-made infrastructure of a religious community in several locations in the West Bank.[70] With the highest birth rate of all the country's Jewish communities, the ultra-Orthodox are contributing significantly to the total settler population. In what has been a rapid demographic transformation of the settlement movement, it was reported in late 2007 that a third of the West Bank's settler population live in four large ultra-Orthodox colonies.[71]

In late 2005 it was revealed that officials had expanded Modi'in Illit by building a new 'neighbourhood', Matityahu East, on the private land of the nearby Palestinian village of Bil'in – land that had been made inaccessible to the villagers because it was on the 'wrong' side of the separation wall that cuts Bil'in off from its fields. However, the construction of Matityahu had taken place in violation of Israeli planning rules, and no master plan was ever approved for it. When this 'irregularity' was discovered, the construction work was simply approved retrospectively.[72] Over the past three years, while the Israeli courts have deliberated on the case, Matityahu has continued to grow. This kind of settlement expansion is far from exceptional.

Israeli journalist Akiva Eldar explains how such privatized 'territory laundering' works:

> Building companies owned and managed by settler leaders and land dealers acquire lands from Palestinian crooks and transfer them to the Custodian of Government Property in the Israel Lands Administration. The custodian 'converts' the lands to 'state lands', leases them back to settler associations that then sell them to building companies. In this way it has been ensured that the Palestinians ... will never [be able to] demand their lands back.[73]

The Final Pieces in Place

In recent years, the main focus of territorial expansion has not been established settlements like Modi'in Illit or Ma'ale Adumim. The real work has fallen to small groups of religious-nationalist extremists prepared to rough it in caravans on West Bank hilltops. The tiny colonies they inhabit – known in Israel as 'illegal outposts' because they are still waiting for official authorization from the government – have been a feature of the settlement enterprise since the 1980s. Many of today's settlements started as 'illegal outposts', winning official approval much later. However, the recent concentration on building outposts represents a strategic shift by the settlers, according to a *Ha'aretz* editorial:

> The term 'outposts' embodied a change in the settlers' perception of their struggle for the greater land of Israel. Whereas in the past, they sought to move as many people as possible into the West Bank and Gaza Strip, in order to defeat the Palestinians demographically, at some point, they decided that it was easier to gain control of the territory physically, one hill after the other.[74]

The outposts are usually satellites of the larger settlements, built some distance from the mother colony, sometimes with several outposts radiating from this centre. Once the outposts have become established, they are reclassified as neighbourhoods of the original settlement, eventually becoming part of a 'settlement bloc' of the kind Bush sanctioned as irreversible in his 2004 letter to Sharon.

This process of slowly turning the outposts into 'legal' settlements has offered two obvious advantages to Israeli governments: first, it has largely shielded from public view the incremental expansion of the colonies in the West Bank; and, second, it has helped to manipulate public perceptions such that the very illegality of the outposts can be used to confer an unwarranted legality on the settlements. In other words, if Israeli officials can concentrate public attention on the battle against the criminality of a handful of settlers, it can divert it from the criminality of hundreds of thousands of other settlers.

The outposts received a new burst of life in 1998 when Ariel Sharon, fearing that the Oslo Accords might shatter his dreams of a Greater Israel, famously told his followers: 'Everyone there should move, should run, should grab more hills, expand the territory. Everything that's grabbed will be in our hands. Everything we don't grab will be in their hands.'[75] By the time Sharon became prime minister in 2001, there were some fifty outposts on hilltops across the West Bank; with him in power, the number doubled within months. Sharon appointed a settler leader and colonel in the reserves, Ron Schechner, to oversee the settlement enterprise, including the outposts, from 2002. Schechner and the Civil Administration ensured that the outposts, despite their official illegality, were rapidly connected to the electricity and water grids.[76] The Housing Ministry provided mobile homes, and the Education Ministry provided funds for schooling. Even state firms like the Egged bus company got involved: it runs regular services to these isolated and sparsely populated locations.[77] 'From the settlers' perspective, the outposts are a natural outgrowth of tower-and-stockade Zionism', wrote Nadav Shragai, a reporter sympathetic to the settlers, in early 2008. 'Every branch of the establishment helped the settlers set up outposts. Nothing was official, but everything was official.'[78]

However, public support for the outposts is even more problematic for Israeli governments than it is in the case of the main settlements. Under the terms of the Road Map, Israel is committed, in addition to freezing settlement expansion, to dismantling the outposts set up after Sharon became prime minister in spring 2001. According to the government, this covers twenty-five outposts, while Peace Now, which regularly records settlement activity by flying over the West Bank, puts the true number at more than fifty.[79] Israel has staged several very public confrontations with the inhabitants of the most isolated outposts, often referred to as 'hilltop youth', but has done almost nothing to reduce the number of outposts to date. The few that have been successfully dismantled are known as 'decoys' by the hilltop youth: empty caravans set up to offer the authorities the chance to look as if they are taking action.[80]

The fact that the growth in the number of outposts has been secretly sanctioned by successive governments and the army was revealed in early 2005 with the publication of the Sasson report. Talia Sasson, a former lawyer in the State Prosecutors' Office, was given six months by Sharon to investigate the outposts. She documented government collusion since Yitzhak Rabin's government in the mid-1990s in establishing some 105 unauthorized outposts (though she admitted the total could be far higher as she had not been given access to all the documents held by the Civil Administration).[81] She found that 61 of these outposts were built on land that did not belong to the state, and 15 were on land registered to Palestinian landowners.[82] The settlers had been chiefly assisted by the Housing and Education Ministries, the Civil Administration and the World Zionist Organization. In Sasson's words:

> No one seriously intended to enforce the law [against the settlers]. It seems as if the violation of the law has become institutional and institutionalized. There is blatant violation of the law by certain national authorities, public authorities, regional councils ... and the settlers.[83]

A ministerial committee to investigate the outposts was immediately set up by Sharon, but on the few occasions it sat no significant progress was made on curbing the growth of the outposts.

Why did Sharon, given his role as one of the fathers of the settlement enterprise, allow official complicity in the outposts to be made public? One Israeli analyst suggested that, in the run-up to the disengagement from Gaza, Washington had been considering 'sending a team of its own to do the work' and that, armed with the Sasson report, Sharon had managed to get the US 'off his back'.[84] There were other significant reasons. As already noted, by highlighting the illegality of the outposts, at a time when Israel was preparing to evacuate settlements in Gaza, Sharon deflected attention from the main settlements in the West Bank.[85] He created a consensus on the 'blocs' that Bush had agreed to back. He also set up a momentum of regular, though ineffectual, clashes over the outposts, with police confronting large numbers of their supporters, that satisfied domestic and international demands for action against the settlers. He appeared to be implementing his commitments without actually ever doing so. And finally Sharon fixed the number of outposts in the public imagination at 105 even though the evidence is that, rather than being reduced, their number has actually grown since. Peace Now believes there may now be more than 150 outposts.[86] In one of their latest moves, the settlers' leaders are offering to dismantle some of these outposts in return for approval of expanding the established settlements.[87] If history is a guide, they will get their way, and the evacuated outposts will simply be re-established at a later date.

At the end of 2007, the head of the Civil Administration, Brigadier-General Yoav Mordechai, was called to testify before the ministerial committee on outposts set up in the wake of the Sasson report. The meeting was given minimal coverage even in the Israeli media. He told the ministers that there were probably thousands of planned housing units in the West Bank for which building permits had already been issued and which did not need any further government approval before construction began. Sasson, also present, warned that the Justice Ministry was working on a proposal to overhaul the current planning procedures so that in future it would be possible to build in the settlements, and possibly in the outposts too, without the need for government approval.[88] Was this the future: a kind of privatization of the settlements, in which developers and sympathetic officials would be able to expand them with little control or oversight from the state? And, if the state was not directly involved, who could then hold it to account for the ever increasing theft of Palestinian land by the settlements?

4

Disappearing Palestine

We now moved in our own country surreptitiously, like unwanted strangers, constantly harassed, never feeling safe. We had become temporary residents of Greater Israel, living on Israel's sufferance, subject to the most abusive treatment at the hands of young male and female soldiers controlling the checkpoints, deciding on whim whether to keep us waiting for hours or allowing us passage. But worse than that was the nagging feeling that our days in Palestine were numbered and one day we were going to be victims of another mass expulsion.

Raja Shehadeh, Palestinian lawyer in Ramallah, 2007[1]

More than seven years after Israeli prime minister Ehud Barak first promoted the myth of his generosity to the Palestinians at Camp David in July 2000, a revealing document from that period came to light. In December 2007 *Ha'aretz* published details of a leaked 26-page paper entitled 'The Status of the Diplomatic Process with the Palestinians'. The document had been prepared by Israeli officials in the immediate aftermath of the failed negotiations in an attempt to brief whoever won Israel's general election a few months later, in

February 2001.[2] Laying out Israel's diplomatic bottom lines at Camp David, the document surfaced again in late 2007 only because it was shown to the incumbent prime minister, Ehud Olmert, before he headed off to the US for the Annapolis conference, called by President George W. Bush. Annapolis was the first official talks between Israel and the Palestinians, with other Arab leaders in attendance, since the collapse of the Oslo process in late 2000. Israeli officials, it seems, did not want there to be any danger of Olmert making greater concessions to the Palestinians than those offered by his predecessor. He did not disappoint.[3]

The negotiations at Camp David were Barak's attempt at wrapping up all the outstanding points of conflict between Israel and the Palestinians that had not been addressed during a series of Israeli withdrawals from the occupied territories specified in the Oslo agreements. Barak, backed by the US president of the time, Bill Clinton, pushed Palestinian Authority president Yasser Arafat into the hurried final-status talks, even though the Palestinian leader believed more time was needed to build confidence between the two sides. Contrary to the spirit of the Oslo agreements, Israel had doubled the number of illegal settlers in the occupied territories through the 1990s and failed to carry out the promised withdrawals in full. So what were the terms Barak offered Arafat? The document reveals that the Israeli prime minister insisted on three main principles in agreeing to end the occupation and establish a Palestinian state.

First, Israel's illegal 'settlement blocs' would be kept, with 80 per cent of the settlers remaining in the West Bank on land annexed to Israel. According to the document, it was proposed that Israel annex some 8 per cent of the territory; in return the Palestinians would be compensated with a much smaller wedge of Israeli land of much less value, probably in the Negev desert. This arrangement required leaving nearly 400,000 Jews living inside the West Bank and East Jerusalem in fortified communities connected by settler roads, creating a labyrinth of Israeli land corridors to consolidate a set of Palestinian ghettoes rather than the Palestinian state supposedly promised by Barak.

Second, a wide 'security zone', supervised by the Israeli army, was to be maintained along the Jordan Valley in the West Bank, from the Dead Sea to the northern Jewish settlement of Meholah. Such a security zone exists already, so we do not need to speculate on what it would look like. A few thousand settlers in the Jordan Valley have ensured that the area, nearly a fifth of the West Bank, has been all but annexed to Israel for decades. Most Palestinians, apart from the few permitted to live in the Valley itself, are barred from entering it. The Jordan Valley is one of the most fertile areas of the West Bank, its huge agricultural potential currently exploited mainly by Israel. Under Barak's offer, the Palestinians were to be deprived of both territorial and economic control over the Valley and the benefits that would accrue to any future Palestinian state.

And third, Israel demanded massive territorial concessions on East Jerusalem, in line with its illegal annexation of the half of the city occupied in 1967. Barak wanted to maintain territorial contiguity for the illegal settlements in the city, with the Palestinian inhabitants forced as a result into a series of what *Ha'aretz* referred to as 'bubbles'. Israel's current expanded municipal borders for Jerusalem would be maintained, severing the city, the economic and tourist hub of any future Palestinian state, from the rest of the West Bank. The large settlements of Ma'ale Adumim and Har Homa, controlling territory that runs down from East Jerusalem as far as the Jordan Valley, would have remained under Israeli sovereignty, thereby cutting the West Bank in half.

There were other significant Israeli conditions. In the Old City of Jerusalem, Israel wanted the Jewish and Armenian quarters and parts of the so-called 'sacred basin' outside the city walls to be annexed to Israel. The mosques of the Noble Sanctuary (known as Temple Mount to Jews) would be placed under an 'ambiguous' sovereignty – doubtless later to be exploited by the stronger party, Israel. These and the other Israeli demands for East Jerusalem would ensure that Palestinian areas were carved up into a series of ghettoes, a mirror image of Israel's policies in the West Bank. Israel also insisted it would keep absolute control over the land corridor connecting the two main parts of a future Palestinian state, the West Bank and Gaza Strip, allowing it the opportunity to sever the link should it choose to. Barak refused to concede the usual trappings of statehood, such as an army, wanted by Arafat. And Israel expected its illegal annexation and ethnic cleansing in 1967 of an area of the West Bank close to Jerusalem called the Latrun Salient, today known as Canada Park, to be recognized by the Palestinians.

Forgotten by Barak and Clinton in the negotiations, it seems, was the fact that more than a decade earlier, in the late 1980s, the Palestinians had made a major and largely unacknowledged concession to Israel. Arafat and the PLO had officially abandoned any hope of overturning their national dispossession in 1948 and instead restricted their territorial claim to the reversal of their dispossession in the West Bank and Gaza in 1967. In sum, the Palestinians had resigned themselves to a state on only 22 per cent of Mandatory Palestine. If that was the Palestinians' more than generous offer to Israel, how did Barak's proposal to the Palestinians compare? The document reveals that Barak was offering far less territory than the Palestinians' 22 per cent bottom line. Arafat was being asked to subtract from a state in Gaza and the West Bank large parts of the expanded municipality of Jerusalem, as well as the Latrun Salient, 8 per cent of the West Bank to accommodate the settlements and up to 20 per cent more for a security zone in the Jordan Valley. In other words, the Palestinians were being required to sign on to a deal that would give them a very compromised sovereignty over no more than about 14 per cent of their historic homeland. That was the extent of Barak's offer, according to Israel's own briefing paper.

Despite Barak's claims of generosity, we know from the *Ha'aretz* leak that he had strong doubts prior to Camp David that the Palestinians would be persuaded by his terms. The document reveals that, in parallel to his preparations for the talks, Barak was working on a unilaterally imposed 'separation' plan if the negotiations failed. His scheme was ready by June 2000, a month before the talks, and was approved for implementation by the cabinet in the immediate wake of the intifada, in October 2000. According to *Ha'aretz*, Barak's separation proposal encompassed all aspects of Palestinian life and was to be implemented over several years. Though apparently not mentioned in the briefing paper, Barak's deputy defence minister, Ephraim Sneh, had drawn up what was called a 'separation map' as the basis for Israel's offer to the Palestinians.[4] Barak's chief negotiator at Camp David, Shlomo Ben-Ami, observed later of Barak's preparations for the talks: 'He was very proud of the fact that his map would leave Israel with about a third of the [West Bank] territory.' According to Ben-Ami, the prime minister said of the ghettoes he intended to create for the Palestinians: 'Look, this is a state; to all its intents and purposes, it looks like a state.'[5]

The purpose of Camp David, we can infer from these various revelations, is that Barak hoped to win Arafat's approval for separation according to his distinctly ungenerous map. But, if he failed, as he expected to do, he was ready to impose it by force.

Separation versus Transfer

Like the Zionists who would follow in his path, Herzl did not favour sharing Palestine with the natives. Better, he confided in his diary, to 'try to spirit the penniless [Palestinian] population across the border by … denying it any employment in our own country'.[6] Zionism has debated the threat to Jewish statehood posed by a significant Palestinian presence ever since. In the pre-state era, as Jewish institution-building began, two camps formed around different, though closely related, strategies for dealing with the natives. The first, the Labor Zionism of David Ben-Gurion, gradually came to accept that the creation of a Jewish state would be impossible unless most of the indigenous population was cleared from Palestine. The historian Benny Morris explains that the need for 'transfer' – or ethnic cleansing – had been accepted by Ben-Gurion even before the 1948 war: 'He understood that there could be no Jewish state with a large and hostile Arab minority in its midst.'[7] In fact, Ben-Gurion felt confident to speak more openly about transfer from 1937, after Britain's Peel Commission recommended exchanges of populations as a prelude to Palestine's partition.[8] As we have already noted, Ben-Gurion developed a plan for ethnic cleansing under cover of war, compiling detailed dossiers on the communities that needed to be driven out and then passing on the order, in Plan Dalet, to commanders in the field. In this way he emptied the new state of Israel of at least 80 per cent of its indigenous population.

The other camp, the Revisionists, the intellectual forebears of today's right-wing Likud Party, had a far more ambivalent attitude to the native Palestinian population. Paradoxically, given their uncompromising claim to a Greater Israel embracing both banks of the Jordan river, they contemplated allowing many of the natives to remain where they were. Vladimir Jabotinsky, the leader of the Revisionist movement, observed in 1938 – possibly in a rebuff to Ben-Gurion, who had begun espousing transfer policies – that 'it must be hateful for any Jew to think that the rebirth of a Jewish state should ever be linked with such an odious suggestion as the removal of non-Jewish citizens'.[9] The Revisionists, it seems, were resigned to the fact that the enlarged territory they desired would inevitably include a significant number of Palestinians. They were therefore less concerned with removing the natives than finding a way to make them accept Jewish rule. In 1923, Jabotinsky formulated his answer, one that implicitly included the notion of separation: an 'iron wall' of unremitting force to cow the natives into submission. In his words, the agreement of the Palestinians to their subjugation could be reached only 'through the iron wall, that is to say, the establishment in Palestine of a force that will in no way be influenced by Arab pressure'.[10] An enthusiast of British imperial rule, Jabotinsky envisioned the future Jewish state in colonial terms, as a European elite ruling over the native population.

These two ideas, of separation and transfer, were far from mutually exclusive, and have been espoused in different situations and at different times by both the right and the left. In fact, they have existed in uneasy juxtaposition in the thinking of most Zionists.

One of Jabotinsky's disciples, Menachem Begin, who would later become a Likud prime minister, was leader in 1948 of the Irgun militia that committed one of the worst atrocities of the war. He led his fighters into the Palestinian village of Deir Yassin, where they massacred over 100 inhabitants, including women and children. Begin and his followers inflated the death toll to more than 250, repeated most famously in the pages of the *New York Times*, in a conscious effort to spread terror among the wider Palestinian population and encourage them to flee. He happily noted later: 'Arabs throughout the country, induced to believe wild tales of "Irgun butchery", were seized with limitless panic and started to flee for their lives. This mass flight soon developed into a maddened, uncontrollable stampede.'[11] Other prominent figures on the right have openly supported ethnic cleansing too, including the late General Rehavam Ze'evi, whose Moledet Party campaigned in elections under the symbol of the Hebrew character 'tet', for transfer. His successor, Benny Elon, a settler leader and rabbi, adopted a similar platform: 'Only population transfer can bring peace.'[12]

Despite Ben-Gurion's devotion to ethnic cleansing before and during the 1948 war, Labor Zionism has had a long tradition of supporting policies of separation too. For example, it adopted the principle of 'Hebrew labour', an uncompromising version of Jewish self-reliance that expected businesses to employ only other Jews. Although separation of Jews and Arabs was the immediate goal of this practice, an additional benefit, as Herzl hoped, might be encouragement of destitute Palestinians to emigrate. 'Hebrew labour' culminated in the creation in Palestine of a Jewish trade-union federation, the Histadrut, that for decades barred Palestinians from membership. On Israel's establishment, the Histadrut was the country's second largest employer after the government but still refused admission to Israel's Palestinian citizens. When they were finally allowed to join more than a decade later, they were restricted to a separate Arab department of the union. To this day they still have no influence on Histadrut decision-making.[13] Shmuel Toledano, a former Labor Party government adviser on Arab affairs, observed in 1977: 'All the economic positions in this country are filled by Jews, the Jews control all the banks, all the corporations. In politics and the Histadrut, they have all the power.'[14]

Another principle of Labor Zionism, 'redemption of the land', also took as its premiss ideas of separation and transfer, denying the Palestinian population any role in Jewish nation-building. 'Redemption' referred not only to the land – cleansing it of its tainted past under the illegitimate ownership of the natives – but also to the transformed character of the Jews who came to the Promised Land to toil its fields. By turning their backs on their supposedly weak and compromised Diaspora natures, Jews could reconnect to their ancient past and their true selves, returning to the land and becoming once again tough, muscular and independent 'Sabra' Jews. There was no room in the mythology of redemption for either cooperation or sharing the land with the natives.

Sharon's Conversion to *Hafrada*

Ehud Barak never got the chance to implement his plan for 'unilateral separation' – or *hafrada* in Hebrew. A few months after the failed Camp David talks, he was voted out of office and his political rival, Ariel Sharon, took power. Sharon, leader of the Likud Party, was known to have a strong attachment to the idea of Greater Israel, and had nurtured extremist groups among the settlers for many years, though his colonial reasons for wanting the occupied territories settled differed from their fanatical belief that they were fulfilling God's commandment. As he took over directing Israel's military response to the second intifada, he adopted the opposite approach to Barak's plan for 'unilateral separation': he sent the army back into the areas of the West Bank under nominal Palestinian rule, effectively tearing up the Oslo Accords. Sharon appeared to favour a return to direct occupation.

However, by summer 2002 there were the first hints that Sharon was changing course and moving towards Barak's position. Certainly, the Labor Party ministers in his national unity government put great pressure on him to adopt Barak's separation plan and begin work on the central pillar of its programme: a concrete and steel wall stretching the length of the West Bank. Polls showed the Israeli public overwhelmingly behind the construction of a wall too, believing it would prevent suicide attacks by the Palestinians. At first it looked as if Sharon had been manoeuvred unwillingly into backing the wall, but later evidence suggests he was quickly converted to its cause. Several factors, it seems, conspired to change his mind – and none of them was related to stopping suicide bombers. First, after the initial success in crushing the resurgence of Palestinian nationalism driving the intifada, Israel's direct reoccupation of the territories was proving costly both financially and in terms of soldiers' lives. Second, Sharon found it politically expedient to steal Labor's key policy, particularly given its popular support, and leave the rival party searching for a new platform. And third, and most decisively, Sharon was persuaded by his advisers, particularly his heir apparent, Ehud Olmert, that Israel's image as a democracy was under threat from the growing Palestinian populations in the occupied territories and inside Israel. These two groups living under Israeli rule were about to reach numerical parity with the Jewish population.[15] Sharon started to fear that Israel's rule over a Palestinian majority might look like apartheid.

As Barak had done before him, Sharon, therefore, turned to the experiences of South Africa for a solution. Ideas of separation promoted by and embodied in the apartheid regime had long proved attractive to Israel's leaders; connections between the two countries were intimate, if largely covert, for decades, even when white South Africa had become a pariah nation. The two countries' militaries, in particular, had worked closely together on developing weapons systems, and even on research into nuclear arms.[16] Apartheid's abiding influence on Sharon's thinking was explained by Avi Primor, vice-president of Tel Aviv University, in September 2002. He noted that Sharon and his generation of generals had always harboured an especial fondness for South Africa's solution to its own demographic problem: a series of sham black homelands known as Bantustans. In these small homelands, termed 'independent states' by white South Africans, the country's black population was supposed to exercise its political and civil rights. Writing two years after Camp David, when construction of the wall was just beginning, Primor argued that Israel was intending to establish, in line with apartheid policies, a set of bogus homelands for the Palestinians:

> A process is under way establishing a 'Palestinian state' limited to the Palestinian cities, a 'state' comprised of a number of separate, sovereign-less enclaves, with no resources for self-sustenance. The territories of the West Bank and Gaza remain in Israeli hands, and its Palestinian residents are being turned into 'citizens' of that 'foreign country'.[17]

Primor was not alone in noting Sharon's affection for the Bantustans. The influential journalist Akiva Eldar reported that Sharon had long dreamt of an independent state of 'Hamastan' in Gaza. 'In his house, they called it a bantustan, after the South African protectorates designed to perpetuate apartheid.' Eldar pointed out that Massimo D'Alema recalled a meeting a few years before Sharon was elected prime minister in which he confided that the Bantustan model was the right one for the Palestinians. What appealed to him was the fact that the Bantustans were designed not only to separate the white minority from the black majority to the latter's detriment, but also to divide the blacks from each other, isolating them in a series of separate and potentially antagonistic 'states'. Following Camp David, Eldar added, the Israeli leadership had agreed on a programme to cantonise the Palestinians, breaking up the putative Palestinian state into a series of disconnected ghettoes.

> Alongside the severance of Gaza from the West Bank, a policy now called 'isolation,' the Sharon–Peres government and the Olmert–Peres government that succeeded it carried out the bantustan program in the West Bank. The Jordan Valley was separated from the rest of the West Bank; the south was severed from the north; and all three areas were severed from East Jerusalem. The 'two states for two peoples' plan gave way to a 'five states for two peoples' plan: one contiguous state, surrounded by settlement blocs, for Israel, and four isolated enclaves for the Palestinians.[18]

Sharon's vision of separation quickly took shape in the West Bank. The 800 km wall snaking along its western length was designed to annex to Israel the settlement blocs and to strip Palestinians in rural areas of as much agricultural land as possible, forcing them to seek sanctuary deeper in the West Bank, in their 'city-states'. By late 2007, it was reported that the route of the wall was annexing at least 12 per cent of the West Bank – up significantly from the 8 per cent Barak had hoped to persuade Arafat to accept at Camp David.[19] Plans for a wall along the eastern edge of the West Bank, effectively annexing the Jordan Valley, were much discussed in 2002 but subsequently filed away quietly, presumably awaiting US approval and finance.[20] Meanwhile, Palestinians confined to their fledgling 'homelands', whose outlines were taking shape along the hilly spine of the West Bank, were being forced to come to terms with the curfews, checkpoints and roadblocks that now dominated their lives. The Palestinians were being sealed into their ghettoes, out of sight not only of Israelis but also increasingly of journalists and aid workers, who found it ever harder to reach their communities.[21]

It should have come as no surprise that Sharon, while building these Palestinian cages, also adapted the language he used about the conflict. For many years he had been known to favour, along with many other Israeli political and military leaders, creating a Palestinian state not in the occupied territories but in Jordan, by helping to overthrow the Hashemite king there and allow Jordan's Palestinian majority – refugees from the 1948 and 1967 wars – to take over. But in summer 2003, in a speech that shocked his Likud Party delegates, he told them it was time to give up at least parts of the occupied territories:

> The idea that it is possible to continue keeping 3.5 million Palestinians under occupation – yes, it is occupation, you might not like the word, but what is happening is occupation – is bad for Israel, and bad for the Palestinians, and bad for the Israeli economy. Controlling 3.5 million Palestinians cannot go on forever. You want to remain in Jenin, Nablus, Ramallah and Bethlehem?[22]

The only reasonable interpretation of his words was that he was advocating some kind of Palestinian 'state' in the occupied territories, probably centred on the main population centres. The evolution in his thinking would become clearer six months later, in early 2004, when he announced yet another step in his philosophy of separation: a unilateral withdrawal of all the Jewish settlers from Gaza, in what he called a 'disengagement'. Sharon hoped to persuade the international community that withdrawal would constitute an end to Israel's occupation of Gaza, even though the Israeli army would continue to have absolute control over all its borders and its airspace. Sharon's goal was to win approval for the establishment of the first of his Bantustans. In April 2005, a few months before the evacuation, President George W. Bush did just that by claiming disengagement would create the opportunity for 'a democratic state in Gaza'.[23] The US pushed this idea further by insisting on Palestinian elections in early 2006. A majority chose Hamas over the Fatah ruling party, which had been increasingly discredited during the Oslo period by its collaboration with the occupation.

Sharon's lapse into a coma in the short interval between disengagement and the Palestinian elections left Olmert in charge of Sharon's new party, Kadima. Drawing into its ranks representatives from both Labor and Likud, Kadima was founded as a centre party, embodying the new consensus around imposed separation from the Palestinians and Sharon's as-still-unclear vision of Palestinian statehood. Olmert carried on in much the same direction as Sharon, developing a 'convergence' plan that adapted the principle of disengagement for the West Bank. From Olmert's many speeches on the subject, convergence sounded much like Barak's proposal at Camp David: most of the half a million settlers would be left in place, significant areas of the West Bank would be annexed to Israel, and whatever was left over – disconnected ghettoes – would be called a Palestinian state.

Ruling through Division

One of the abiding concerns of Israel's leaders since the 1948 war has been the threat posed by a strongman emerging to lead the Palestinians in their struggle – either for the return of their homeland or for a secular democratic state embracing both peoples as equals. The

Palestinians were therefore subjected to a series of policies designed to deprive them of effective leadership. That was relatively easy after 1948, when the urban elites either fled or were driven from the new Jewish state, along with the overwhelming majority of the native population, leaving behind only isolated rural communities of mostly uneducated peasants. In addition, the creation of the military government, the banning of independent Palestinian political activity, and Israel's increasingly rigorous border controls ensured that it was difficult for the PLO to get a foothold inside these Palestinian communities. Instead Israel accentuated a series of divisions: between Muslims, Christians and Druze; between internal refugees and non-refugees; between the cities and villages; between those serving in the army and those not; between recognized and unrecognized communities; and so on.

The situation in the territories occupied in 1967 was rather different. There, a significant proportion of the educated elites in the cities remained. In addition, first Palestinian resistance groups and then the PLO had enjoyed nearly twenty years of relatively unfettered access to the West Bank and Gaza populations, developing awareness of Palestinian nationalism and recruiting strongly inside the refugee camps. After the 1967 war, therefore, Israel concentrated on intimidating, imprisoning and expelling anyone it identified as an independent leader, while seeking to 'manage' the rural population by co-opting its local leaders along family and communal lines. A landslide victory for the PLO in municipal elections in 1976, however, proved these policies were failing, and that a different approach was needed. In 1981 Sharon, then defence minister, organized a new system of control, renaming the military government a Civil Administration (though it was still run by military officers). The administration nurtured local anti-PLO groups, known as the Village Leagues, that were supposed to represent the rural regions as a way to marginalize the influence of the cities and the PLO. The Leagues proved unpopular from the outset, and to bolster their position Israel needed to arm them. At the time, Knesset member Uri Avnery noted that 'the West Bank is being transformed into a small-scale Lebanon'.[24] The system was aborted after the Jordanian government, which still had a lingering influence in the territory, threatened to put the Leagues' leaders on trial for 'treason'.

Israel experimented with another approach to undermining Palestinian nationalism, sanctioning the re-establishment of the Muslim Brotherhood in the occupied territories. An offshoot of the Islamic movement for social and moral reform born in Egypt in the late 1920s, the Brotherhood had branches in both Gaza and the West Bank after 1948, when the territories fell respectively under Egyptian and Jordanian rule. In 1973, six years after the occupation began, Israel licensed the Brotherhood again and allowed it to set up a network of charities and welfare societies, funded by the Gulf states. Israel hoped that the Muslim Brotherhood would dissipate Palestinian nationalism and support for the PLO among the local population and encourage a social and moral conservatism that would make the Palestinians more 'moderate'. Israel's thinking was explained by the late Israeli sociologist Baruch Kimmerling: 'Israelis administering the occupied territories and acting on the advice of orientalist experts supported traditional Islamic elements because they were considered more easily managed and submissive to the Israelis than the PLO nationalists.'[25]

However, just as the Village Leagues failed in the West Bank, Israel's new policy backfired too, in Gaza in particular. There the Brotherhood under the leadership of Sheikh Ahmed Yassin quickly metamorphosed into Hamas when the first intifada erupted in late 1987. Rather than promoting division, Hamas stood alongside Fatah in resisting Israel's harsh military response.

Only in the early 1990s, as the first intifada showed that Israel had no answer to the grassroots nationalism that had been unleashed in the occupied territories, did the Israeli leadership change tack again. They turned to Yasser Arafat, the long-time leader of the Palestinian national movement and head of the Fatah Party. Arafat had just emerged from a diplomatically disastrous decision to back the Iraqi leader, Saddam Hussein, during the first Gulf War. His international standing was at its lowest ebb ever, his bases of political support were gone, and the PLO was on the verge of bankruptcy after the Gulf states had withdrawn their financial aid. It was at this moment of profound Palestinian crisis that Israel finally agreed to deal with him, signing the Oslo Accords that allowed him to set up his 'Palestinian Authority' – what Arafat mistakenly assumed was a government-in-waiting – in the occupied territories.

Israel derived a major benefit from Arafat's presence in the territories. In his new role as head of the Palestinian Authority he represented only a fraction of the Palestinian population: those living in the West Bank and Gaza. His other role, as head of the PLO, in which he represented all Palestinians, including those inside Israel and in the refugee camps of the Middle East, was fatally compromised by his return on Israel's terms. Using the Oslo process, Israel successfully marginalized the question of justice for the entire Palestinian people by concentrating on the far more limited question of justice for Palestinians living under direct occupation.

His power entirely dependent on Israeli goodwill, Arafat's task as leader of the Palestinian Authority would soon become clear: to enforce Israel's security in the West Bank and Gaza, just as dozens of other Arab rulers had done before in their own territories on behalf of Western colonial powers. He was, in essence, Israel's security contractor. Arafat was doomed to fail in this task. Pulled between the pressures from Israel to crack down on any signs of resistance to its occupation and his own need to remain credible with his populations in the West Bank and Gaza, Arafat hedged his bets. He arrested Hamas leaders, as Israel demanded, only to release them soon afterwards in what Israel termed a 'revolving door' policy. Foolishly, Arafat trusted that Israel would honour its Oslo commitments to withdraw in stages from the occupied territories; instead, as we have already noted several times, the number of settlers increased dramatically during the 1990s.

But shortly before Arafat was allowed to return from exile, a massacre of twenty-nine worshippers in the Ibrahimi mosque in Hebron committed by a militant settler, Baruch Goldstein, tipped the balance in favour of his political opponents. While Arafat could do little more than bluster from Tunis, Hamas took decisive retaliatory action, striking in Israeli cities with a new tactic – the suicide bomber. Once in the occupied territories, the coterie around Arafat, rather than challenging the occupation, took advantage of their new-found status and privileged links to the Israeli military command. Corruption among the Fatah elite was soon rife. When in 2000 Camp David exposed Israel's bad faith, and Arafat's years of concessions to Israel, as worthless, the streets of the occupied territories exploded in anger. Arafat rode the wave of violence unleashed by the second intifada as best he could.

The significance of Israel's decision to imprison Arafat in his compound in Ramallah for most of the intifada, until his mysterious death in late 2004, has been little understood. Arafat had proved himself a dismal failure in the role he had been assigned by Oslo. He had neither signed off on the final dispossession of the Palestinians at Camp David, nor crushed all signs of Palestinian resistance, particularly by Hamas, before the negotiations. His failure to rein in the second intifada was the final proof that he had outlived his usefulness. His death was only a matter of time. Israel, with the US now acting almost as a branch of the government in Jerusalem, approved Arafat's replacement, Mahmoud Abbas, a weak and uncharismatic member of the Fatah old guard. They may have assumed that, as one of the Palestinians closely involved in drafting the Oslo Accords, Abbas would be more prepared than Arafat to abandon the dream of Palestinian statehood.

The policy of keeping the Palestinians fragmented, and its leadership compromised, faced its biggest challenge in early 2006, when the US forced Israel to approve national elections in the occupied territories in the hope of bolstering Abbas's barely existent mandate. The result was apparently not foreseen by either the US or the international community, though Israel's military intelligence may have had its doubts. Hamas stormed to victory in both Gaza and the West Bank, exploiting the popular disillusionment with a Fatah Party that had shown itself incapable of resisting Israel's malevolent designs. Much to Abbas's embarrassment, Hamas formed a new government with a popular mandate for organized and violent resistance to the occupation. Determined to overturn Hamas's election promptly, Israel and the US, backed by Western governments, imposed a suffocating boycott of the Hamas-led Palestinian Authority, based in Gaza. Aid was cut off and salaries of government workers went unpaid as Israel held back hundreds of millions of dollars in tax revenues it had collected on behalf of the PA under the Oslo Accords. A blockade of Gaza also prevented food and medicines from reaching the local population.

The stage, Israel and the US hoped, was set for a Palestinian civil war. The US began building up Fatah's forces for the time when Hamas could be challenged in a power struggle, while Israel rounded up Hamas legislators in the West Bank, including some well-known moderates. In late 2006, the occupied territories finally sank into feuding and fighting of a kind that seemed to have been Israel's goal for several decades. A short time later, in early 2007, tensions briefly dissipated when the Arab states intervened to help the two rival factions create a national unity government. Israel and the US made little effort to conceal their hostility to this new arrangement. According to one of Condoleezza Rice's officials in the State Department, she 'was apoplectic' at the news.[26] Plans were quickly drawn up to disrupt the agreement by publicly bolstering Abbas loyalists in Gaza with training and weapons in an attempt to undermine Hamas. A leaked report from Alvaro de Soto, the retiring UN envoy for the Middle East peace process, highlighted the American mood as Hamas and Fatah prepared to meet in Mecca over forging a national unity government:

> The US clearly pushed for a confrontation between Fatah and Hamas, so much so that, a week before Mecca, the US envoy [David Welch] declared twice in an envoys meeting in Washington how much 'I like this violence', referring to the near-civil war that was erupting in Gaza in which civilians were being regularly killed and injured because 'it means that other Palestinians are resisting Hamas'.[27]

In June 2007 the unity government collapsed when Hamas launched what it claimed was a pre-emptive strike in Gaza against a coup planned by forces loyal to a Fatah strongman, Mohammed Dahlan. According to Hamas, Dahlan, who had been cultivated by US officials for several years, was plotting with Washington to overthrow the elected government. Hamas was widely condemned for its violent actions, though six months later its claims that it had foiled a Fatah coup were finally confirmed. Drawing on official US documents, an article in *Vanity Fair* revealed that the White House had been conspiring with Dahlan to topple the Hamas government. According to the plan, Washington's 'desired outcome' was to give Abbas 'the capability to take the required strategic political decisions ... such as dismissing the [Hamas] cabinet [and] establishing an emergency cabinet'.[28] A budget of more than $1 billion over five years had been set aside for salaries, training and arms to support a Fatah putsch. Hamas was alerted to the plan when the Israeli media reported that shipments of arms were arriving from Egypt for Fatah fighters. Hamas decided to strike first.

Abbas responded to Hamas's triumphant reassertion of power in Gaza by creating a rival government in the West Bank, along the lines of the Fatah 'emergency government' wanted by Washington. The US and Israel appeared to agree that this division offered a further opportunity to entrench what was already a geographic division between Gaza and the West Bank into a political separation too. Or, as the Israeli foreign minister, Tzipi Livini, observed: 'We should take advantage of this split to the end. It differentiates between the moderates and the extremists.'[29] The US approved lifting the economic blockade of Abbas's government in the West Bank, while Israel declared that Hamas-controlled Gaza would be treated as a 'hostile entity'. The potential state of Palestine appeared now permanently riven – in the words of Israel's propagandists – into a Hamastan and a Fatahland.

Revival of the Jordanian Option

The comparison between Israeli rule of the occupied territories and apartheid South Africa has not been lost on Israel's more liberal commentators. In spring 2008, an editorial in the *Ha'aretz* newspaper backed former US president Jimmy Carter, who was then visiting the region, for considering

> the system of separate roads for Jews and Arabs, the lack of freedom of movement, Israel's control over Palestinian lands and their confiscation, and especially the continued settlement activity, which contravenes all promises Israel made and signed, a matter that cannot be accepted. The interim political situation in the territories has crystallized into a kind of apartheid that has been ongoing for 40 years.[30]

Nonetheless, Azmi Bishara, a former Knesset member and a Palestinian citizen of Israel forced into exile, observes that Zionism's hankering for separation from the Palestinians is of a special quality that needs to be differentiated from standard apartheid.

> In South Africa, that pioneer of apartheid, racial segregation was not absolute. It took place within a framework of political unity. The racist regime saw blacks as part of the system, an ingredient of the whole. The whites created a racist hierarchy within the unity.[31]

Whites in apartheid South Africa needed the black population, relying on it as a labour force to preserve white privilege. Much like Jabotinsky, most white South Africans assumed they would always be a minority, and therefore concentrated on manipulating the country's system of government so that it would appear as democratic as possible, thereby legitimizing their rule. Labor Zionism, on the other hand, has tended to treat the native population of Palestine with greater hostility. The principles of 'Hebrew labour' and 'redemption of the land' promoted ethnic self-reliance over colonial exploitation. Or as Ben-Gurion explained in 1934:

> We do not want to create a situation like that which exists in South Africa, where the whites are the owners and rulers, and the blacks are the workers. If we do not do all kinds of work, easy and hard, skilled and unskilled, if we become merely landlords, then this will not be our homeland.[32]

Israel's supporters have tended to assume that this statement meant Ben-Gurion envisioned a utopia in which Jews would share the burden equally with the natives. That seems an inadequate interpretation. If Ben-Gurion expected the Jews in his planned Jewish state to do all kinds of work, more likely it was because he intended to dispense with the services for most of the natives. Such reasoning was simple. The presence of a significant proportion of Palestinians, let alone a majority, in Palestine contradicted one of Zionism's fundamental tenets: it undermined Israel's status as a sanctuary for Jews, a state where they enjoyed undisputed sovereignty.

In 1948 Ben-Gurion decided that Israel's craving for acceptance among the democratic nations required not separation within political unity, an apartheid system, but ethnic cleansing to ensure an overwhelming Jewish majority. Ariel Sharon summed up the problem for Zionism in his typically blunt manner: 'The intention of Zionism was not to bring democracy, needless to say. It was solely motivated by the creation in Eretz-Israel of a Jewish state belonging to all the Jewish people and to the Jewish people alone.'[33] But if Zionism was not primarily concerned that the Jewish state *be* democratic, it was concerned that it *appear* democratic. The lack of political decisiveness that uncharacteristically gripped Israel following the capture of the West Bank and Gaza in 1967 reflected the fact that the country's leaders had no solution equivalent to Ben-Gurion's when confronted with the same demographic problem. Unable to find a pretext for expelling most of the Palestinian population from the occupied territories, and unwilling to offer them citizenship, Israel has searched in vain for another policy it can present as democratic.

Bishara describes the distinctive features of Zionism in relation to Palestine's indigenous inhabitants:

> This unique type of colonialism does not seek to 'develop' the [native] inhabitants, as other colonialists once did in homage to the 'white man's burden'. This colonialism displaces people, confiscates their land or bypasses them (the term, often applied to roads, is pertinent). It 'develops' the land for settlement, but not for the inhabitants. Because of this Moshe Dayan and his aides adopted a policy of open bridges after the 1967 war. They wanted the Palestinians to have an economic and demographic outlet to Jordan, the Gulf countries, and other parts

of the region, so as to free Israel from the economic and other responsibilities commonly assumed by occupying authorities.[34]

From the moment the occupation began in 1967, the Israeli cabinet engaged in a series of debates that lasted several months about what kind of separation plan to impose on the occupied territories. The main territorial problem, it was understood even then, related to the much-prized West Bank rather than Gaza. Dayan, almost alone at this early stage, favoured 'digesting' the West Bank. He argued that Israel should settle the area with Jews, fragment it territorially so that the Palestinians could not gain independence, and offer its inhabitants employment in the Israeli economy. Dayan wanted funds to improve the quality of life of the natives by investing in their hospitals, water system and power lines. As we have seen, he hoped 'to bind the two economies so that it will be difficult to separate them again.'[35] But, Dayan was adamant that in his scheme the Palestinians would not become citizens of Israel.

Dayan's proposal smacked too obviously of colonialism, and apartheid, for most of his colleagues. (Although, in the absence of a decision either to annex the occupied territories or to withdraw, the journalist Gershom Gorenberg notes that for many years Dayan's plan was implemented by default. More and more Palestinians would come to depend on Israel for employment as their own economy was crushed – at least until the Oslo Accords initiated a process of actual physical separation.[36]) Formal annexation too was rejected, as we have seen, because it would have entitled the Palestinians in the territories to citizenship. Two other solutions were discussed instead. Known as the Palestinian and Jordanian options, each was considered in the context of the Allon Plan's goal of settling strategically important areas of the West Bank with Jews while not taking responsibility for the native population. The first option would give the Palestinians limited self-rule in areas not annexed by Israel, while the second option would transfer to the Jordanian monarch those parts of the unannexed West Bank.

Early on, the Palestinian option seemed the most attractive. Yigal Allon favoured the establishment of what he termed a Palestinian state. 'Not a canton, not an autonomous region, but an independent Arab state agreed on between us and them in an enclave surrounded by Israeli territory.' Allon's small Palestinian state in a sea of Israeli territory was the most generous vision on offer – 'the maximum possibility' as he called it. The prime minister, Levi Eshkol, wanted to hold on to the whole of the West Bank militarily, although he appreciated the danger that this might lead to demands for a bi-national state. He therefore proposed 'a quasi-independent region' for the Palestinians. 'I don't care if they eventually want representation in the United Nations. I started with an autonomous region, but if it turns out that this is impossible, they will get independence.'[37]

In early 1968 Eshkol began clandestine talks with sympathetic leaders in the occupied territories about creating an autonomous region in the West Bank. Their response was that none of them would be able to make a deal with Israel unless the wider Arab world gave its backing first. Eshkol reportedly replied: 'If you claim that you can't act as Palestinians, then we have reached deadlock.'[38] As a result, Eshkol switched tracks, approaching Israel's only reliable ally in the Arab world, King Hussein of Jordan. Allon reformulated his plan too, keeping the same settlement map but arguing now that the parts of the territory left after Israeli annexation would be handed over to Hussein. Palestinian autonomy under Israeli rule, he added, 'would be identified as … some kind of South African Bantustan'.[39] After tacit approval from the Americans, Eshkol met with Hussein several times to discuss such an arrangement. Eventually the king declined, aware that his rule inside his kingdom was too precarious to survive a deal on these terms with Israel. The Jordanian option was revived a few times over the years, either by Hussein himself or by Israel, but an agreement was never reached.

As the occupied territories sank into deep division between Hamas and Fatah in 2007, the idea of a 'Jordanian option' in the West Bank – as well as an 'Egyptian option' in Gaza – was resurrected by Israel. In fact, analysts had been speculating about just such a move back in 2005, in the immediate wake of the disengagement. Aluf Benn, the diplomatic editor of *Ha'aretz*, reported that Sharon was trying to create a Palestinian state of two halves, or what he referred to as two Palestinian mini-states: an 'Eastern Palestine' in the West Bank and a 'Western Palestine' in Gaza. Sharon hoped to achieve this by giving the two territories a different status, and by blocking any political and physical connection between them. Each mini-state would be encouraged instead to identify with its Arab hinterland: in the case of the West Bank with Jordan, and in the case of Gaza with Egypt. Benn noted:

> Figures in the Israeli defense establishment speak of their desire to reinstate the pre-1967 situation, when Egypt took care of the Gaza Strip and Jordan took care of the West Bank. They are encouraged by Egypt's willingness to take responsibility for the Philadelphi route [the effective border between Gaza and Egypt] and to train the Palestinian defense forces in the Gaza Strip, which would enable Cairo to supervise the area indirectly.[40]

Reuven Pedatzur, a leading scholar on Israel's strategic policies in the Middle East, noted similar developments in summer 2007. He reported that senior figures in the Jordanian regime were considering a 'confederation' between Jordan and the Palestinians. If Israel agreed to the creation of a Palestinian state, they argued, the two neighbours could be run by a federal government presided over by the Jordanian king. Joint security services would also come under the control of the federal government – a move designed to placate both Israeli and Jordanian concerns about the creation of a Palestinian army on their doorsteps. Pedatzur pointed out that a former Jordanian prime minister, Abdel Salaam Majali, apparently with the blessing of the late Hussein's son, King Abdullah, had been sounding out support in the US for the plan. Amman was reported to have shown renewed interest because it feared that the simmering tensions between Fatah and Hamas might eventually spill over into Jordan: either parallel struggles might develop inside its own borders among the Palestinian population there or fighting in the West Bank might lead to a large exodus of refugees pouring across the Jordan river. Fatah officials in Ramallah, meanwhile, were reported to be keen on Jordanian involvement, believing that Amman's support might win them a Palestinian state and revive their flagging fortunes against Hamas.

Although Israeli officials did not comment publicly on the proposal, Pedatzur observed that Shimon Peres, Israel's new president, had already expressed his support for a similar arrangement: 'We have to seek a new structure with the Palestinians. In my heart, I have returned to the conclusion that I always held in life: we must bring in the Jordanians. We cannot make peace only with the Palestinians.'[41] Others shared his view. The Israeli security establishment had been concerned since the Gaza disengagement that the 'Palestinian option' – creating a bogus Palestinian state in the ghettoes left behind after the annexation of their land – would simply encourage more resistance of the kind Hamas was mastering in Gaza. In particular, it was feared that rockets being fired over the walls of the prison Israel had created for Gaza would grow in number, accuracy and distance. Israel could do little to prevent such developments without direct occupation of the kind that even Sharon had been persuaded to abandon.

Shortly after Hamas's strike against the Fatah plotters in summer 2007, Olmert attended a summit in the Sinai resort of Sharm el-Sheikh to meet with Abbas and his counterparts in Egypt and Jordan. As he headed off, he announced that he wanted to 'jointly work to create the platform that may lead to a new beginning between us and the Palestinians'. Did he mean a partnership with Jordan and Egypt? A spokesman in his office explained the purpose of the meeting. 'These are the four parties directly impacted by what is happening right now, and what is needed is a different level of cooperation between them.'[42] Thus far the involvement of the 'friendly' neighbouring Arab states had been strictly limited by Israel to minor roles such as mediating with the Palestinians and securing their borders against smuggling. Now hints were growing that Israel might ask Jordan and Egypt to start policing the Palestinian areas too, effectively replacing the Palestinian Authority as Israel's security contractor. In late June 2007 the opposition leader, Binyamin Netanyahu, suggested deploying the Jordanian army in the West Bank.[43] A month later *Ha'aretz* reported that Olmert had 'raised the possibility of introducing regular forces from the Jordanian Army. He has said this could be an effective way to help Abbas create a semblance of security in the West Bank'.[44]

The incentive for Jordan and Egypt to get involved was explained by a senior official in the Israeli Foreign Affairs Ministry:

> Hamas rule in the Gaza Strip has posed a new challenge not only for Israel but also for Jordan and Egypt, in both of which the Muslim Brotherhood, Hamas' mother movement, constitutes opposition to the regime. The inspiration that the Hamas victory in Gaza could provide the radical Islamic movements in Jordan, Egypt, the Gulf and North African states is obvious to their rulers.[45]

The Americans too appeared to favour greater involvement from Israel's two neighbours. Aluf Benn reported in summer 2007:

> Bush called Jordan and Egypt 'natural gateways for Palestinian exports' and urged them to be open to trade with their neighbors in the West Bank and Gaza Strip. ... [He] has accepted Israel's position, that the Arabs must look after their kinfolk, and the trade in the territories must go through the Rafah crossing [to Egypt] and Allenby Bridge [to Jordan].[46]

In other words, it looked as though Israel might be returning to its original strategy for frustrating the Palestinian ambition for meaningful statehood. As the finishing touches were put to the 'separation wall', to seal the Palestinians into a series of small prisons masquerading as a state, Israel and the US hoped to find new jailers for the Palestinians in the shape of the Arab world.

Fruits of Occupation

It hardly needs stating that Israel has held on to the occupied territories for so long, and settled them so intensively, because the advantages of remaining there were seen as great. Like other colonial regimes, Israel has exploited the resources, both material and human, of another people for its own benefit. Shlomo Gazit, an adviser to Moshe Dayan when the occupation began, wrote many years later: 'At the end of the sixties, the world was already watching the end of the era of colonialism, and precisely then Israel found itself marching in the opposite direction.[47]

The benefits of occupying the Palestinian territories – and the West Bank in particular – were many. Most obviously, Israel acquired large areas of extra territory, including farmland and quarries, and the water under it. The decision to locate settlement blocs along the hilly ridge of the West Bank was not accidental: they sat atop the territory's plentiful aquifers, justifying Israel preventing the Palestinians from drilling wells on their own land. Meanwhile, the sparsely populated settlements along the Jordan Valley staked Israel's claim to the aquifer there, as well as the Valley's rich agricultural land. Today Israel controls 80 per cent of the West Bank's water sources, and diverts most of that supply to its own citizens, inside Israel and the settlements. Only a fifth of the West Bank's water goes to its Palestinian inhabitants, who as a result consume far less than the 100 litres each recommended by the World Health Organization as the daily minimum. On average, Palestinians consume just 60 litres each a day, including for their industry, and in some places, such as Hebron, they consume only 15 litres.[48] While Mekorot, Israel's national water company, supplies each settler with nearly 1,500 cubic metres of water per year, it provides each Palestinian with just 83 cubic metres. More than 200,000 rural Palestinians, most living in Area C under Israeli control, have no running water at all and have to buy water from Israeli tanker-trucks.[49] Israel has also systematically destroyed wells in West Bank villages, and forbidden Palestinians from collecting rainwater.

The West Bank's sources of water have become increasingly vital to Israel as its own supplies – mainly from the coastal aquifers – have become polluted with sea water from overdrilling.[50] In March 2008, the situation had become so dire that Israel's National Water Authority warned that the country was facing a 'water crisis'. The head of the Authority, Uri Shani, said he was 'afraid of what will happen in 2009 if we go on another year like this'.[51]

Exploitation of the West Bank's material resources has driven, and continues to drive, Israel's programme of creeping annexation. But the policy of unilateral separation implemented since Oslo has required a dramatic rethinking of Israel's exploitation of the occupied territories' other main resource: its people. For several decades Israel benefited both from the pool of cheap labour available in the occupied territories and from the captive market the Palestinians provided for Israeli products. Separation has forced Israel to make hard choices about redefining its economic priorities. For more than a decade now, Israel has been reducing its reliance on cheap Palestinian labour, turning instead to 'foreign workers', little more than slave labourers imported from countries like China, Thailand and Romania.[52] Today, almost all Palestinian workers are banned from entering Israel; Israeli industrial zones – often polluting and poorly regulated – linked to West Bank settlements have been cutting back on their dependence on Palestinian workers too.

But Israel's other main economic relationship with the Palestinians has not been shed so easily. Until very recently Israel continued to rely heavily on the economic benefits of exporting its goods and produce to a captive market of nearly 4 million Palestinians under occupation. In 2006, for example, some 6 per cent of all Israel's exports – excluding diamonds – went to the territories, a trade worth some $2 billion, making the Palestinian Authority Israel's second biggest customer after the United States. According to Ilan Eshel, head of the Israeli Fruit Growers' Association, 10 per cent of all Israeli fruit was exported to Gaza, usually third-class produce that could not be sold elsewhere. He explains why the 1.5 million people in Gaza have provided such a reliable market: 'They are hungry and they have hardly any orchards. The citrus groves have almost completely disappeared because of the Israel Defense Forces' activities [cutting down their trees and bulldozing their land on the pretext of Israel's security needs]. We are the only source of food for them.'[53] Given that Israel has sealed Gaza off on all sides and controls the crossing points into the Strip, and has nearly completed the same process in the West Bank, Palestinians must rely on Israel for satisfying their basic needs, from milk and medicine to nappies and cement. Even imports from abroad come through Israeli middlemen who take their cut, while the

Israeli tax authorities collect the customs fees – hundreds of millions of dollars a year – that are supposed to be transferred to the PA but rarely are.[54]

Nonetheless, Israel finally appears to be turning its back on this market. The change of policy was hinted at back in 2006, immediately after Hamas's election victory, by Dov Weisglass, an adviser to Ehud Olmert. He explained Israel's new approach: 'It's like an appointment with a dietician. The Palestinians will get a lot thinner, but won't die.'[55] He was referring to Israel's imposition of an economic blockade on Gaza, backed by an aid boycott by Western governments, that has pushed the Strip's population into a profound state of destitution. Eyad al-Sarraj, of the Gaza Community Mental Health Programme, and Harvard scholar Sara Roy reported in early 2008 that Israel had reduced the number of basic commodities it allows into Gaza from some 9,000 before Hamas's election victory in 2006 to just 20. Even supplies that are getting through have been severely reduced in quantity. For example, although Gaza requires 340 tons of flour daily to feed its population, by November 2007 Israel had cut supplies of this staple to 90 tons per day – a reduction of 73 per cent.[56] In February 2008, after eight months of continuous Israeli closures of the crossings, the UN under-secretary general for humanitarian affairs, John Holmes, reported that life in Gaza was 'grim and miserable' and that its people were receiving only a tenth of the supplies that they had depended on a year earlier.[57]

The Palestinians have precious little local industry, and barely more than subsistence farming, to fall back on. This state of affairs was intended by Israel, explains the peace activist Jeff Halper:

> the economy of the territories had to be kept under strict control lest [the Palestinians'] cheap products and labor undermine or compete with Israel's own market – and lest a feeling of economic strength and independence create demands for political independence as well.[58]

With Palestinians unable to work inside Israel, and few surviving Palestinian businesses able to reach external markets, unemployment and poverty have risen relentlessly. Even before the blockade of Gaza, in 2002, a survey by the Johns Hopkins University showed that nearly a fifth of the Strip's children under the age of 5 were suffering long-term malnutrition because of Israel's regular closure of the crossings.[59] By 2007 the situation had deteriorated further, with 87 per cent of Gazans living below the poverty line, more than a tripling of the percentage in 2000.[60] In early 2008 a coalition of eight British human rights organizations produced a report calling the humanitarian situation in Gaza the worst in forty years of occupation: 80 per cent of residents were dependent on food aid; unemployment in the private sector was close to 70 per cent; hospitals were suffering power cuts of up to 12 hours a day; and the water and sewerage systems were close to collapse.[61] The Palestinians' physical infrastructure was also being wrecked by regular Israeli bombardments and military incursions. Al-Sarraj and Roy noted that in the three years before the disengagement some $2 billion of damage had been inflicted by the Israeli army on the Palestinians' environment, with more than half the destruction targeting agricultural land. According to Karen Koning AbuZayd, the commissioner-general of UN refugee agency UNRWA: 'Gaza is on the threshold of becoming the first territory to be intentionally reduced to a state of abject destitution, with the knowledge, acquiescence and – some would say – encouragement of the international community.'[62]

There was, however, one financial advantage to ruling over the Palestinians that Israel appeared to want to continue exploiting. This benefit, which has reinforced a trend towards absolute separation, largely offsets the losses suffered to Israeli exporters. The country's hi-tech and military industries have come to depend on the West Bank and Gaza as laboratories for developing new kinds of technologies for urban warfare, counter-terrorism, crowd control and surveillance. Yossi Sarid, the former leader of the dovish Meretz Party, observed in early 2008:

> Gaza is a dream laboratory for experiments on human beings, to discover the precise point when a dependent person transfers from one situation to another – when does he keep up the struggle and when does he stop and become acclimated? Or when is the horse's breaking

point – when does it only continue to lose weight and when does it flop and breathe its last?[63]

In her book *The Shock Doctrine* Naomi Klein singles Israel out as a country that has pioneered the booming 'homeland security industries' that are the bedrock of US national security in the post 9/11 world. According to the Israeli Export Institute, nearly 400 local corporations were dedicated to selling homeland security products in 2007.[64] The companies, invariably run by former senior military officers, draw on the experience gained by their staff during army service to develop new products. In 2006 Israel's defence exports reached $3.4 billion, making it the fourth largest arms dealer in the world; it also had more tech patents registered in the US than China and India combined.[65] A Middle East analyst, Steve Niva, has noted the growing similarities in the Israeli and American occupations, respectively, of Palestine and Iraq. The US has been persuaded to model its own occupation on Israel's strategy in the occupied territories, which 'seeks to control Palestinians from beyond their walled-off enclosures by selectively controlling access to life essentials and relying on air-strikes to quell resistance'. Techniques of domination, points out Niva, are increasingly moving away from direct applications of violence 'to indirect spatial incarceration, multiplying archipelagos of externally alienated and internally homogenous ethno-national enclaves through walls and checkpoints, under a blanket of aerial surveillance'.[66]

With economic growth surging at 8 per cent in 2006, in a situation of war with Lebanon and low-level hostilities with the Palestinians, Israel had small incentive to make peace. Echoing Bishara's earlier point about the difference between Israel's approach to its native population and apartheid's, Klein observed:

> South Africa's Bantustans were essentially work camps, a way to keep African laborers under tight surveillance and control so they would work cheaply in the mines. What Israel has constructed is a system designed to do the opposite: to keep workers from working, a network of open holding pens for millions of people who have been categorized as surplus to humanity.[67]

The Meaning of Shoah

In February 2008 Israel's deputy defence minister, Matan Vilnai, was interviewed during one of the intermittent bouts of bloodletting that nowadays punctuate the Israeli army's relations with the inhabitants of the Gaza Strip. Israel had unleashed a series of air and ground strikes on populated areas of Gaza that over the course of a few days had killed more than 100 Palestinians – at least half of whom were civilians and 25 of whom were children, according to the human rights group B'Tselem.[68] Vilnai's radio interview also took place in the wake of rockets fired from Gaza that killed a mature student in Sderot and for the first time hit the centre of the southern city of Ashkelon.

Vilnai told the interviewer: 'The more Qassam fire intensifies and the rockets reach a longer range, they [the Palestinians of Gaza] will bring upon themselves a bigger shoah because we will use all our might to defend ourselves.'[69] The comment was picked up by the news agency Reuters because the word 'Shoah' – literally 'disaster' in Hebrew – was long ago reserved for the Holocaust in which millions of European Jews were murdered by the Nazis. Its use in any other context is virtually taboo. Appreciating the potential damage the remark could do, Israel's Foreign Ministry immediately launched a *hasbara* (propaganda) offensive to persuade the world's media that Vilnai was only referring to a 'disaster' not a holocaust.[70] Few Israelis were deceived. For example, *Ha'aretz*'s cultural commentator Michael Handelzalts noted that 'whatever connotations the word [Shoah] had before the Nazis embarked on their systematic extermination of the Jews, today it means – with quotation marks or without them, with "the" preceding it or without it – just that.'[71] But why would Vilnai select this extremely provocative and troubling word to frame his threat to the Palestinians?

There is one problem with Klein's otherwise apposite description, quoted above, of the areas of the occupied territories not yet annexed to Israel as 'holding pens'. Rather than quietly waiting to expire, the Palestinians – or, more especially, Hamas and the Gazans – have been refusing to go quietly. Unlike Fatah, which is prepared to cooperate with an interminable peace process (designed to give Israel the time it needs to annex yet more of the West Bank), Hamas has refused so far to compromise. It has proved itself both immune to Israeli and US machinations to topple it and potentially capable of organizing resistance on several fronts damaging to Israel.

The most obvious resistance from Hamas, in a form that poses the most immediate threat to Israel, is the regular rocket fire out of Gaza. Although the Qassams have a short range and rarely cause casualties (by early 2008 fourteen Israelis had died from the rockets over seven years),[72] the Palestinians are acquiring ever better technology. The range and accuracy of the rockets is likely to grow, as the attack on Ashkelon demonstrated. But more significantly, as Hizbullah's month-long barrage of rockets on northern Israel during the war in summer 2006 showed, the Israeli public's resolve can crumble quickly in the face of sustained attack. It has not gone unnoticed by the Israeli leadership, for example, that in Sderot, which has been the target of rocket attacks for years, the mayor, Eli Moyal, has broken ranks to call for talks with Hamas.[73] A poll published in the *Ha'aretz* daily in February 2008 showed the rocket attacks are having a wider impact: 64 per cent of Israelis agreed with Moyal's view,[74] an abrupt reversal of Israel's motto throughout the second intifada that 'There is no one to talk to'. Not surprisingly, the defence minister, Ehud Barak, has been investing major effort and money in developing a 'shield' against the rockets.[75] The fear among Israel's leaders is that the 'holding pens' created for the Palestinians cannot be preserved if the Israeli public starts demanding that Hamas be brought to the negotiating table.

Another form of resistance that is still in its infancy but could yet develop into a major threat to Israel's policy is mass civil disobedience, especially if Israeli left-wingers participate in significant numbers. So far, much to Israel's relief, neither Hamas nor Fatah has invested much effort in organizing this kind of resistance; and as Israel completes its wall, the opportunities for Israelis to struggle alongside Palestinians is rapidly shrinking. Incidents of mass non-violent protest have mainly taken place in the West Bank, such as the weekly march towards the

wall stealing farmland from the village of Bilin. But these demonstrations are organized locally, are small scale and have faced obstruction
rather than support from the Fatah leadership. Israel, fearful that such
protests might catch on, has greeted the demonstrators at Bilin with
regular displays of violent overreaction from its soldiers. Israelis participating alongside Palestinians have also been targeted, apparently
in an attempt to deter others from following in their path.[76]

But if Fatah appears incapable of organizing acts of mass resistance,
Hamas does not. In January it grabbed the initiative from Israel by
blowing up sections of the wall between Gaza and Egypt, giving tens
of thousands of Gazans a brief respite from their captivity and the
chance to flood into the Sinai.[77] Hamas's stunt demonstrated to Israel's
politicians and generals alike that the Islamic movement has the ability, as yet unrealized, to launch a focused mass non-violent protest
against the military siege of Gaza. As Meron Benvenisti, a former
deputy mayor of Jerusalem, notes, this scenario 'frightens the army
more than a violent conflict with armed Palestinians'.[78] Israel fears
that the sight of unarmed women and children being executed for the
crime of trying to free themselves from their prison may give the lie
to the idea that the disengagement ended Israel's brutal occupation
or that the Israeli army is the most moral in the world.

Hamas failed to capitalize on its success a short time later when
Gazan activists arranged for several thousand Palestinians to create
a human chain along part of Gaza's fence with Israel to highlight
their suffering and the world's silence.[79] In the end, the turnout was
low after Hamas failed to get involved. Nonetheless, the Israeli army
could barely contain its panic, fearing that large numbers of women
and children might turn up and try to break out of the Strip. Heavy
artillery was brought to the perimeter and snipers were ordered to
shoot protesters' legs if they approached the fence. As Amira Hass,
Ha'aretz's long-time reporter in the occupied territories, observed,
Israel has so far managed to terrorize most ordinary Gazans into
a paralysed inactivity on this front. In the main Palestinians have
refused to take the 'suicidal' course of directly challenging their imprisonment by Israel, even peacefully: 'The Palestinians do not need

warnings or reports to know that Israeli soldiers shoot the unarmed as well, and they also kill women and children.'[80]

But increasingly, it seems, Israeli officials are starting to suspect that, if Gaza's misery grows, the fear of confronting the Israeli army may dissipate and the pressure for direct action from Palestinians grow. If Hamas can harness that popular energy it could become a formidable foe.

The final threat posed by the Palestinians is one that has been preying on Israeli minds for several years. Veteran reporter Danny Rubinstein explains the concern in the following terms:

> There will be increasingly strong demands by Palestinian Arabs, who constitute almost half the inhabitants of this land, who will say: Under the present conditions we cannot establish a state of our own, and what remains for us is to demand civil rights in the country that is our homeland. They will adopt the slogans of the struggle of the Arabs who are Israeli citizens, who demand equality and the definition of Israel as a state of all its citizens. That won't happen tomorrow morning, but there doesn't seem to be any option to its happening eventually. If there aren't two states for the two nations, in the end there will be one state.[81]

Olmert himself expressed this worry back in late 2003 when he warned that Israel was facing a switch by the Palestinians from 'a struggle against "occupation", in their parlance, to a struggle for one-man-one-vote. That is, of course, a much cleaner struggle, a much more popular struggle – and ultimately a much more powerful one. For us, it would mean the end of the Jewish state.'[82] He has repeated the point many times, not least in 2007 as the Annapolis peace conference ended: 'If the day comes when the two-state solution collapses, and we face a South African-style struggle for equal voting rights ... then, as soon as that happens, the State of Israel is finished.'[83]

So how has Israel chosen to pre-empt these threats? It is worth examining the direction Vilnai and his boss, defence minister Ehud Barak, started pushing government policy towards a Hamas-run Gaza. In summer 2007 the Israeli cabinet agreed to declare the Strip a 'hostile territory'[84] – a significant evolution of the policy of separation initiated by Sharon's disengagement. At the same time Barak announced that essential services, including electricity and fuel, supplied by Israel – as long-time occupier – would be cut. (In December 2005, shortly before he fell into a coma, Sharon contemplated cutting electricity for a few hours after each rocket was fired from Gaza. At that time the Israeli army was opposed, arguing that it was collective punishment and would be hard to justify.[85]) Several legal petitions were launched by human rights groups, but in late 2007 the Israeli courts gave their blessing to this policy.[86]

Under international law, Israel as the occupying power has an obligation to guarantee the welfare of the civilian population in Gaza. Barak therefore claimed tendentiously that the humanitarian needs of Gazans were still being safeguarded by the limited services and supplies of fuel being allowed through. Behind the scenes, however, he and Vilnai sought a way to neutralize international law so that the army would not be bound by its provisions. In October 2007, after a meeting of defence officials, Vilnai said there was no obligation on Israel to supply electricity 'beyond the minimum required to prevent a crisis'.[87] Three months later he went further, arguing that Israel should cut off 'all responsibility' for Gaza.[88] Disengagement, he added, should be taken to its logical conclusion: 'We want to stop supplying electricity to them, stop supplying them with water and medicine, so that it would come from another place.' He suggested that Egypt might be forced to take over responsibility.[89] Shortly afterwards, in March 2008, the Israeli media reported that Israel and Egypt had agreed that the latter would start supplying Gaza's electricity in two years' time, when a new power plant had been built in the Sinai, probably funded by Saudi Arabia. An official said: 'Ostensibly, we will lose our control of the Gaza power switch, but it also entails a huge advantage if we can transfer responsibility for electricity to Egypt.'[90] In Barak's view, apparently, if the world could be persuaded that the occupation of Gaza really was over, Israel's obligations under international law towards the civilian population of the Strip would end.

Vilnai and Barak's proposals did not surface in a political vacuum. They echoed an increasing number of statements from cabinet ministers advocating war crimes against Palestinian civilians as a way to stop the rocket fire from Gaza. Prime Minister Ehud Olmert, for example, declared that Gazans should not be allowed 'to live normal lives';[91] internal security minister Avi Dichter wanted Israel to take action 'irrespective of the cost to the Palestinians';[92] and the interior minister, Meir Sheetrit, suggested that the Israeli army should 'decide on a neighborhood in Gaza and level it' after each rocket attack.[93]

In the wake of Hamas's mass break-out from Gaza, Barak and Vilnai started formulating policies that matched the rhetoric. In March 2008 the Israeli media revealed that Barak's officials were working on a way to make it lawful for the army to direct artillery fire and air strikes at civilian neighbourhoods of Gaza in response to rocket fire. They were already doing this covertly, of course, but now, it seemed, they wanted to make it official policy, sanctioned by the international community.[94] At the same time Vilnai proposed a related idea, of declaring areas of Gaza 'combat zones' in which the army would have free rein and from which residents would have little choice but to flee. In practice, this would allow Israel to expel civilians from wide areas of the Strip, herding them into ever smaller spaces.[95]

'Palestine is finished'

'Genocide' is widely, and mistakenly, assumed to refer only to an act of mass extermination of a racial or ethnic group akin to the industrialized murder of Europe's Jews committed by the Nazis. In fact, the word's legal definition is far broader. The lawyer who coined the term, Raphael Lemkin, was a Polish Jew who fled to the United States during the Second World War. Lemkin's determination to alert the world to the horrors of genocide was prompted not just by the Holocaust but by earlier massacres: of the Armenians by the Turks during the First World War, and of the Assyrians in Iraq in 1933.[96] In 1943 Lemkin offered his definition of genocide:

> Generally speaking, genocide does not necessarily mean the im-
> mediate destruction of a nation, except when accomplished by mass

killings of all members of a nation. It is intended rather to signify a coordinated plan of different actions aiming at the destruction of essential foundations of the life of national groups, with the aim of annihilating the groups themselves. The objectives of such a plan would be the disintegration of the political and social institutions, of culture, language, national feelings, religion, and the economic existence of national groups, and the destruction of the personal security, liberty, health, dignity, and even the lives of the individuals belonging to such groups.[97]

Five years later, the United Nations adopted a Convention on the Prevention and Punishment of the Crime of Genocide, defined as:

any of the following acts committed with intent to destroy, in whole or in part, a national, ethnical, racial or religious group, as such:
a) Killing members of the group;
b) Causing serious bodily or mental harm to members of the group;
c) Deliberately inflicting on the group conditions of life calculated to bring about its physical destruction in whole or in part;
d) Imposing measures intended to prevent births within the group;
e) Forcibly transferring children of the group to another group.[98]

It is difficult not to consider Israel's current actions against the Palestinians as fitting the definitions offered by both Lemkin and the UN Convention. However, most critics of Israeli policy have been uncomfortable publicly reaching such a conclusion. The late Israeli sociologist Baruch Kimmerling, one of the country's foremost scholars of Israeli and Palestinian nationalism, invented a new word, 'politicide', rather than resort to the term 'genocide'. In 2003 he defined politicide as having two effects:

The first is the destruction of the Palestinian public sphere, including its leadership and social and material infrastructure. The second effect is to make everyday life for the Palestinians increasingly unbearable by destroying the private sphere and any possibility of normalcy and stability. ... All of these conditions are ... designed to lower Palestinian expectations, crush their resistance, isolate them, make them submit to any arrangement suggested by the Israelis, and eventually cause their voluntary mass emigration from the land.[99]

It hardly matters whether we describe the Israeli plan outlined by Kimmerling as genocide or politicide; he accurately presents Israel's monstrous vision of a half-life for Palestinians in the occupied territories in which they are stripped not only of their rights but also of their humanity. On this view, Palestinians are conceived of not as lesser beings, in the way that apartheid conceived of its black population, but as non-beings whose fate should not trouble us at all.

As early in the occupation as the mid-1970s Moshe Dayan observed that 'politically Palestine is finished'.[100] For the next three decades Israel's leaders made sure that his judgement was proved correct, while at the same time exploiting both sensitivities about anti-Semitism and the benefits of US patronage to ward off criticism. In partially defending Israel's record, Professor Yoram Shahar, of the influential Herzliya Interdisciplinary Centre, alludes to the guiding principle of Israeli policy in the occupied territories. So long as Israeli outrages can be presented as spontaneous, unsystematic and related to security needs, the international community will turn a blind eye.

> There has been no genocide here, no wholesale devastation of territory, no mass rapes, no concentration camps, no mass starvation and no systematic deportation of local residents. There has been no Kosovo or Rwanda here – the sort of situations that arouse the international community to act.[101]

In other words, as long as Israel ensures that politicide – a subtle, incremental war of attrition against Palestinian public and private life – does not look too much like the popular notion of genocide – concentration camps and butchery – Israel will be able to continue its policies unchecked. As long only dozens of Palestinians die each month from Israeli artillery fire or food blockades rather than hundreds or thousands, then the consciences of Western politicians can remain clear. The ultimate goal, however, as Kimmerling warns, will be the same: the disappearance of a Palestinian nation for good.

Back in September 2002, two years into the second intifada, General Eitan Ben Elyahu, a former head of Israel's air force, declared on Israeli television that 'eventually we will have to thin out the number of Palestinians living in the territories'.[102] His was a vision of ethnic cleansing that would have been familiar to Ben-Gurion: bombing, starving and maiming to terrorize the Palestinian population into flight, just as had occurred in 1948. More than five years later, Gaza's inmates are staring at a future in which they are supposed to return to the Stone Age, without fuel, electricity, medicines and even basic foodstuffs. The ghettoes in the West Bank are not far behind. Eyad al-Sarraj, of Gaza's Community Mental Health Programme, wrote an email in early 2008 warning that eventually Israel's policy would leave Egypt with no choice but to open its border with Gaza. What would happen then? 'Wait for the exodus', he warned.[103]

PART II

5

Zionism and Its Meanings

Despite waves of Jewish immigration, the proportion of Palestinian citizens in Israel has barely altered over six decades, remaining at approximately a fifth of the population. With a far higher birth rate, and no visible new sources of Jewish immigrants, Palestinian citizens – more usually referred to as 'Israeli Arabs' – are now widely regarded as a long-term threat to the state's Jewishness. In these three essays I explore different aspects of that problem.

In 'Finishing the Job' I examine a feud between Zionism's two main camps, commonly seen as representing the left and right, over the nature of a Jewish state. Should it be a sanctuary within Israel's existing and accepted borders, or the reclaiming of a biblical birthright that includes all of historic Palestine and possibly more? I argue that the differences between these camps are more apparent than real, and that both ultimately see the country's Palestinian citizens as the Jewish state's Achilles heel and hence in need of expulsion.

The political rise of Avigdor Lieberman, an immigrant from Moldova who leads a far-right party, is considered in 'Minister of

Strategic Threats'. Lieberman, I argue, is the likely face of Israel's
political future. He has been publicly promoting, and garnering
support for, the expulsion of Israel's Palestinian minority, a policy
that has been secretly formulated by more mainstream leaders for
some time.

Finally, in 'The Persecution of Azmi Bishara', I investigate
the first major casualty of the renewed atmosphere of expulsion.
Bishara, the most articulate critic of the Jewish state among the Palestinian minority and a proponent of wide-ranging political reforms
to end Israel's ethnic basis, has been hounded by the security
services for years. In spring 2007, while he was out of the country,
this campaign culminated in threats that he would be tried for
treason on his return. Although no serious evidence has yet been
produced, Bishara has been silenced and many in the Palestinian
minority sufficiently intimidated to end their demands for Israel's
democratization.

Finishing the Job
(*November 2002*)

What caused Benny Morris's recent conversion to the racist ideology
of transfer? The 'new historian' who began unravelling Israel's narrative of the war of 1948 – that the Palestinians fled rather than the
truth that most were expelled or terrorized from their homes – says
he now believes David Ben-Gurion, the country's first prime minister,
made a grievous mistake in not finishing the job of clearing the land
of Arabs between the Mediterranean Sea and the Jordan river. In
Britain's *Guardian* newspaper, Morris argues that peace in the Middle
East might have been possible had the entire Arab population been
removed from historic Palestine to make way for a Greater Israel.[1] Not
only does Morris believe that the nearly 4 million Palestinians in the
West Bank and Gaza are a permanent obstacle to peace, but so too,
he says, are Israel's 1 million Palestinian citizens – the descendants of

the 150,000 Palestinians (out of an original 900,000) who managed to remain on the land declared Israel in 1948. In the interests of peace, he now suggests that all Palestinians should have been transferred east to what is now Jordan at Israel's founding. Reflecting on this historic failure, Morris concludes:

> One wonders what Ben-Gurion – who probably could have engineered a comprehensive rather than a partial transfer in 1948, but refrained – would have made of all this, were he somehow resurrected. Perhaps he would now regret his restraint. Perhaps, had he gone the whole hog, today's Middle East would be a healthier, less violent place.

Morris is one of a growing number of Israelis espousing this hard-line policy of expulsion, or 'transfer' as it is more commonly, and coyly, referred to. Opinion polls consistently show that up to 60 per cent of Israeli Jews support schemes to encourage or force Arabs to leave both the occupied territories and Israel.[2] It is worth pausing to reflect on what might have brought a man of Morris's stature to the point where he becomes a high-profile recruit to the cause of transfer. Why are so many Israelis convinced that there is only one way to ease the 'existential fear' they are experiencing, and that is by committing the crime of ethnic cleansing? To explain this phenomenon, one needs to understand the overarching but unspoken role of Zionism in shaping Israelis' world-view. It is a frame of ideological reference that prefaces every argument, every thought, every action. It completely dictates public opinion and state policy.

There are many ideological strands to Zionism: from the national-religious settlers of the occupied territories, some of whom would happily transfer every Arab they meet, to secular, left-wing Zionists who demand withdrawal from the West Bank and Gaza and agonize over Israel's treatment of its own Palestinian citizens. But these variations are a reflection of fundamental disagreements about survival strategies for the Jewish state, not about the basic tenets of Zionism or the morality of its world-view.

So what do we mean by Zionism? For an ideology that has caused such misery, both to Israelis and Arabs in the Middle East, it is surprising that its goals are so rarely articulated beyond simplistic slogans. Few who examine the history and development of the ideology look beyond the intentions of its nineteenth-century prophet, Theodor Herzl, and its pre-state ideologues, men like Ben-Gurion, Vladimir Jabotinsky and Martin Buber.[3] The practical expression of Zionism in statehood, a project of more than five decades' duration, is barely mentioned.

Zionists take as their starting point the idea that the Jews deserve, as a political and moral right, a homeland. From this thesis flows another, less spoken, assumption: that no other people's claim to this land is equivalent to the Jewish claim. Others must therefore be required to make sacrifices to ensure the continuing survival of the Jewish state. Zionism is, in essence, a reinvention for the secular modern era of the idea that the Jews are a chosen people. But the practice as well as the preaching must be analysed. How did Zionism as a nation-building ideology evolve from its earliest days to the establishment of Israel and beyond?

Zionism's original goal may have been honourable enough: the creation of a sanctuary for the much-persecuted Jewish people. Herzl, in particular, was not overly concerned about where this sanctuary would be: in fact, there was a time when it might have been established in Argentina or Uganda. But over time the Zionists' focus shifted to the Holy Land. Early immigrants to Palestine, mainly East Europeans fleeing the pogroms, were helped by Zionist organizations such as the Jewish Agency and the Jewish National Fund to settle on land bought from the indigenous population, the Palestinians. But the migration to Palestine only took off with the rise of Hitler and the consequent flight of Jews from most of Europe, combined with the refusal of the United States, the preferred destination of European Jews, to accept many of these refugees. With the horror of the Holocaust, Zionism's arguments about the need for a sanctuary for the Jews grew more urgent.

The incontrovertible truth about the war of 1948, in which some 750,000 Palestinians were expelled or forced to flee their homes, has come to light only over the past two decades, after academics like

Benny Morris trawled the Israeli archives. They showed that Israelis' traditional account of their 'War of Independence' – one presenting it as a battle for survival – were far from plausible. In fact, according to Morris and others, the Jewish militias and the army often met little or no resistance from the local population – mainly rural, peasant farmers – but nonetheless drove Palestinians from their homes and land.[4] The sanctuary that was left the Israelis after 1948, however, was far from satisfactory from a Zionist point of view. The project of creating a safe Jewish homeland in the Promised Land was incomplete because some 150,000 Palestinians remained in pockets across the country. During the period of the military government imposed on these unwelcome citizens until 1966, there was much dark plotting about how to expel the 'Israeli Arabs', as they were now called. None of the schemes, however, could be fully implemented without risking the wrath of the international community.

The Zionists hoped another strategy – bringing waves of Jewish immigrants to Israel – might eventually swamp the rump indigenous population. After the slaughter of European Jewry in the Holocaust, Israel's founders feared there were no longer enough Ashkenazi Jews to ensure the success of their project and so reluctantly also brought to the new state Jews from the Arab countries, a group that would come to be known as the Mizrahim.[5] But the Palestinian minority's higher birth rate meant that over many decades they held steady at about a fifth of the population, despite the waves of Jewish immigration. The state's failure to dilute the Palestinian presence in Israel provoked ever greater concern that one day the Jewish state would be destroyed from within by this 'demographic timebomb'. The sanctuary idea remained an unrealized dream. Hundreds of thousands of Palestinians remained within the borders of the Jewish state with ties to millions more in the region.

Zionism, however, had a chance to reinvent itself after the 1967 war, when the movement split into two camps with very different conceptions of the role of the Jewish state. Some, including Ben-Gurion, clung to the idea of sanctuary and urged an immediate withdrawal from the West Bank and Gaza.[6] But others, either elated by the seemingly miraculous nature of Israel's victory or enticed by the prospect of further colonial expansion, posited a different objective. They argued that Israel had been presented with an opportunity to reclaim a biblical birthright: the return of the Jewish people to all of its homeland. It was a strange argument for a supposedly secular state but it had several advantages over the discredited sanctuary idea.

First, whereas the goal of a sanctuary highlighted the internal flaws in the idea of a Jewish state, the goal of a biblical return was a unifying project: it reinforced the Jews' sense of themselves as an ethnic and religious nation. For this reason, one of the driving forces – at least publicly – for territorial expansion in Palestinian areas was the reclaiming of Jewish holy sites, from Joseph's tomb near Nablus and Rachel's near Bethlehem to the Tomb of the Patriarchs in Hebron.

Second, unlike the goal of sanctuary which could only be realized by overtly immoral means (ethnic cleansing), the goal of return could be implemented through silent but aggressive settlement beyond Israel's recognized borders. At first small groups of zealots, backed by the government and army, set up encampments on hilltops overlooking Palestinian towns and villages. They looked to the world like mavericks, people who were happy to live in caravans without water or services. But soon, as the 1948 Zionists lost the argument in government, the national-religious extremists were joined by construction companies that bulldozed vast tracts of land and laid foundation stones for high-rise blocks of flats. Within two decades East Jerusalem, the Palestinian half of the city before the 1967 war, was surrounded by great housing estates, all illegally built on occupied land. The Jordan Valley too was dotted with small Israeli settlements along a main highway that made Jerusalem and Israel a quick drive away. All this happened in a way designed not to disturb the West until the 'facts on the ground' made reversing the settlement programme all but impossible.

And third, and most importantly, the new territorial acquisitiveness became a successful justification for demanding ever greater subsidies from Israel's chief sponsor, the United States. As Norman Finkelstein documents in his book *The Holocaust Industry*, links between American Jewry and Israel were tenuous before the 1967 war. But after Israel proved its credentials on the battlefield, the United States began rethinking Israel's role, seeing it as a powerful client state in the region and a useful destabilizing influence on its Arab neighbours that might prevent the emergence of an Arab unity that would interfere with its imperial designs.[7] Equally, American Jewry began to see Israel – and Palestinian and Arab attacks on the Jewish state – as the perfect way to advance its own causes and influence. Thus the awesome Zionist lobby, compulsively seeking out anti-Semitism, was born in the States, with offshoots in Europe. The benefit to Jewry in America, as Finkelstein notes, was the 'Holocaust Industry' itself: huge sums to be claimed from European states ostensibly to compensate Holocaust victims but in practice to pay the inflated salaries of Jewish lawyers and promote the projects of Jewish businessmen in America and Israel.

The regional instability caused by the Israeli army's continuing occupation of Palestinian and Syrian land, its invasion of south Lebanon and the unresolved status of millions of refugees provided the perfect setting for crying 'security' and 'existential threat' every time an Arab leader sneezed. The US Congress approved ever larger disbursements of military aid to Israel. By the end of the first Gulf War, Israel was receiving nearly $5 billion of aid annually from the American taxpayer – almost $1,000 for every man, woman and child.[8] The Israeli economy, and its military might, was effectively propped up by America.

Shortly after the 1967 war, arguments about the goals of Zionism raged.[9] Those preaching the 1948 idea of sanctuary wanted a small but defensible homeland in the Middle East for the Jewish people. A more vociferous group, however, demanded Israel become a muscular, regional superpower wired into the financial and military heart of the West. Thus was born the unholy alliance between the religious extremist settlers and the country's military, political and business elites.[10] The image of Israel that predominates in the international community, however, is refracted solely through this first prism:

Israel as a weak state fighting for its life. But in Israel the second vision quickly became more compelling. Most Israelis, including left-wingers, wanted the huge benefits of Western support. The alternative was Middle Eastern anonymity, Israel struggling against its Arab neighbours for international attention but without the bonus of Iraqi and Saudi oil fields. It was not an appealing prospect.

Success did not go in one direction only. The sanctuary-Zionists scored victories of a kind in their peace agreements with Egypt in 1978 and Jordan in 1994, curbing the excesses of the expansionists. But although the colonial settlement project was made more manageable, it continued apace in the West Bank and Gaza. The invasion of south Lebanon, the expansionists' most ambitious and aggressive project, spawned a peace movement, led by Peace Now, in the early 1980s. But it was the first intifada, between 1987 and 1993, that really polarized Israeli society. For the first time in a generation the peaceniks clearly articulated the sanctuary idea of the Jewish state and argued for withdrawal from the West Bank and Gaza.

Oslo happened for many reasons. The Americans needed a public relations coup in the Arab world after the savagery of its attack on Iraq during the first Gulf War. Israel also realized that Yasser Arafat's PLO was bankrupt and internationally isolated after siding with Saddam Hussein in the same war. Arafat was in no position for hard bargaining. Another consideration, according to Shlomo Ben-Ami, a historian and former government minister, was that, after six years in which the Israeli army had been unable to crush the first intifada, an uprising that consisted mainly of women and children throwing stones at heavily armed soldiers, Rabin believed that bringing Arafat into the territories might 'stop the uprising the IDF had failed to suppress'.[11] Arafat would be Israel's security contractor. But, just as importantly, the Israeli leadership needed to dampen down the combustible tensions within Israeli society between the two oppositional Zionisms, tensions that had been exacerbated by the first intifada. The Oslo peace process was one way to do it.

Nonetheless, the Oslo agreements encapsulated everything that was misjudged in the international debates about Israel. It was assumed that Israel was at the signing ceremony on the White House lawn in 1993 because it wanted to carve out a peaceful space for itself in a hostile Arab environment. In practice, however, Oslo was a sophisticated attempt to legitimize the main thrust of the expansion programme. Israel continued to control ever more Palestinian territory through its settlement projects while at the same time handing over the poisoned chalice of the West Bank cities and large refugee camps to the new Palestinian Authority. Now Arafat could do the messy job of guaranteeing Israelis' security and he could take the blame when an Islamic extremist slipped into Israel to turn human bomb. Meanwhile, Israel quietly continued confiscating land and subsidizing more and more settlers to move to the West Bank and Gaza.

Israelis, from the peace movement to Yitzhak Rabin's assassin Yigal Amir, entirely failed to grasp the extent of the sham of Oslo, or the causal connection between it and the growing popularity among Palestinians of the Islamic militant factions, Hamas and Islamic Jihad, and the wave of suicide attacks on Israeli cities that followed from the mid-1990s. Palestinian disillusionment culminated in the second uprising, which erupted in late 2000, as both the leadership and masses finally gave up hope that the Oslo agreements would ever bring them statehood. Unlike the first intifada, which had accentuated the tensions in Zionism, the second intifada encouraged a new 'Jewish consensus': that peace – or at least a peace that Israel could live with – would never come from negotiations or dialogue. The mantra of 'There is no one to talk to' came to dominate Israeli politics. The fudging, many Israelis decided, had to end; a permanent, and imposed, solution was required. What form this imposed solution should take, of course, depended on one's view of Zionism, whether one wanted a Jewish nation 'like other nations' or a voracious, settler state. The current debates raging among Israelis about how to respond to the second intifada posit two unilateral options: to withdraw (either completely or partially) or to invade. To build a fence or to build a Greater Israel. These alternatives reflect the differences between the 1948 idea of a Jewish sanctuary with fixed and defensible borders, and the 1967 idea of an expansionist state that refuses to define its territorial limits or the preconditions for a peace agreement.

A common error in the West is to interpret these two political positions in simple moral terms. We create a facile dichotomy: the Oslo peace process vs Operation Defensive Shield; Israeli refuseniks vs West Bank settlers; Yossi Beilin vs Ariel Sharon. But these are not polar opposites, they are two sides of the same coin.[12] They represent differing visions, the first deriving from 1948, the second from 1967, but Zionism is the constant. For all Israelis, bar a minuscule number of non-Zionists, the arguments assume as their starting point that Israel's primary political objective is the maintenance of exclusive ethnic privileges for Jews. It is certainly not about correcting historic injustices, helping the Palestinians create a viable state, or contributing to a Middle Eastern peace. The divide between Beilin or Shimon Peres and Sharon is not a moral one but one of differing conceptions about how to protect the long-term interests of Israel as an ethnic state. Both strands of Zionism have accepted the idea of Israel as an aggressive, ethnic, colonizing nation. They differ only in their view of the limits of Israel's sphere of action. For the sanctuary-Zionists, Jewish privilege over non-Jews essentially extends to the 1948 borders of the state. For the expansionist-Zionists, on the other hand, Palestinians and Arabs must submit to Jewish authority within Israel proper, in the occupied territories and potentially anywhere else needed for Israel's 'security' (or promised by God). The implied threat in both positions, however, is that if the Palestinian populations refuse to accept their fate to live as subjugated peoples, they will face retribution or worse.

(Sharon's breakaway party, Kadima, cleverly created common ground for these two camps by fusing the idea of sanctuary, through the adoption of the Labor Party's programme of unilateral separation, with that of a Greater Israel, embodied in the Likud Party's ideology of expanded borders and unlimited control over the Palestinian ghettoes left behind after separation. In short, Kadima's limited withdrawals promised a diminished Greater Israel.)

These are large criticisms of Israel and Zionism. What is the evidence? The case against 1967 Zionism is not difficult to make.

It has been Israeli orthodoxy since the late 1970s. All governments, Labor and Likud, have promoted settlement on Palestinian land to the point where 42 per cent of the West Bank is now directly controlled by settlers. Even now settlements like Har Homa, near Jerusalem, are being opened and families offered huge incentives to move in. A report earlier this year by the Adva Centre, a Tel Aviv think-tank dedicated to examining issues of inequality in Israeli society, showed huge economic and social discrimination in favour of the settlers throughout the 1990s. House-building rates in the occupied territories through the Oslo period were 63 per cent higher than in Israel proper, and families received double the subsidy on buying a property. Spending on municipal services was also 50 per cent higher for settlers, even after security expenditure was excluded.[13] Palestinian areas in the West Bank are now such a patchwork that even the PLO's negotiating department recently admitted that disentangling them from Jewish-controlled areas would be nigh impossible. A two-state solution is starting to look fanciful.

For a country obsessed with demographic and security threats, Israel's ever greater implantation of its Jewish population into the West Bank seems more than illogical; it looks suicidal. If Israel rules over what is effectively a single state, it will within a few years face a combined population of Palestinians inside the West Bank, Gaza and Israel that outnumbers Jews. But the approach is not suicidal if the real intention is to replicate the apartheid model of South Africa, to make Bantustans of the Palestinian cities in a sea of Israeli-dominated territory, leaving settlers to control the arable land and vital water resources. The besieging of West Bank cities looks suspiciously like a push in this direction.

The apartheid model is unlikely to be the end of the story, how-ever. Palestinians, obstinately refusing to submit, will continue the terror attacks.[14] And the longer it takes to divide the West Bank into a series of ghettoes, the harder it will be to persuade the world that this is not in practice what has been done. The grey will start to look more like sharply differentiated black and white. Another solu-tion – transfer – will be needed. The Israeli public is already being softened up, with government ministers openly subscribing to it.[15] Palestinians will have to be encouraged, or made, to leave their homes and land. The destruction of the West Bank's physical and economic infrastructure in the Israeli army's 'Operation Defensive Shield' is the beginning of this process.

But increasingly the Sharon view of Zionism is under attack, if only from the ragged remains of the Labor Party and Peace Now. Can Israel be steered off the depraved course being taken by the 1967 Zionists? Can a Zionism that seeks only a sanctuary for the Jewish people be made more morally clear-sighted than its later upstart? Can Beilin and his ilk not save us from the moral quagmire into which Sharon and his settler friends wish to drag us? The answer, if it is not already clear, is a resounding no. Israel's Eden was always a mirage. In fact, the Zionism of expansion emerged precisely out of the failures of the Zionism of sanctuary. The strategies facing 1948 Zionists are essentially the same as those facing 1967 Zionists: the difference is the arena. If Sharon will have to consolidate apartheid in the West Bank, a left-wing successor who withdraws from the occupied territories will have to do the same inside Israel with the country's Palestinian minority.

Since the end of the military government for Palestinian citizens in 1966, Israel has maintained a largely benevolent apartheid system inside Israel. Arab citizens are barred from Jewish communities, Arab municipalities are starved of funds, the separate education system is a pale reflection of the Jewish one, Arabs cannot work in many sectors of the economy. Although Arabs have the vote, their parties are never allowed to take part in government. And strict enforcement of religious marriage ceremonies, combined with even stricter rules for conversion, makes intermarriage between Palestinians and Jews all but impossible. But, nonetheless, Israel's Palestinian citizens can sit on buses next to Jews and eat with them in restaurants. They can study at university, even if language and other barriers make it harder for them to gain entry. They can speak out relatively freely too.

But even these partial equalities are being rapidly eroded as the 1 million Palestinian citizens become as assertive of their rights as their ethnic kin in the occupied territories. The first two cases of 'Israeli Arabs' having their citizenship revoked signals a dangerous precedent,[16] and newly passed laws have stripped Arab politicians of the right to criticize either the ethnic character of the state or government policies towards the Palestinians. Several of the Arab parties are at risk of being banned before the next election.[17] This new climate is producing a much harsher apartheid system, one much less benevolent.

If Israelis turn their back on the Zionism of expansion and choose the sanctuary model of 1948 Zionism, if the wall being built in the West Bank actually becomes a border, this process of delegitimization and segregation inside Israel will gather pace. But it too cannot be the end of the story. As Benny Morris reminds us, the sanctuary inside Israel proper will be as meaningless as it was in 1948 unless it is cleared of its Arabs, of those who are perceived to threaten the Jewish state from within. Belatedly, the job of 1948 will have to be finished. Today a military government will not be enough to keep the indigenous population in line; priority will have to be given to 'redeeming' the land by cleansing it of its non-Jewish inhabitants. What Morris and many other Israeli Jews now understand is that whether Israel expands or contracts, invades or withdraws, it will face the same choice: it will have to transfer Palestinians, either those in the West Bank and Gaza or those in Israel itself. It must choose between the big war crime and the smaller one. Either direction Israel jumps is sure to send it – as a Jewish state – plummeting into the depths of the abyss. Either way lies the crime of transfer.

Minister of Strategic Threats
(October 2006)

The furore that briefly flared this week at the decision of Israel's prime minister, Ehud Olmert, to invite Avigdor Lieberman and his Yisrael Beiteinu Party into the government coalition is revealing, but not in quite the way many observers assume. Lieberman, a Jewish immigrant from Moldova, is every bit the populist and racist politician he is portrayed as.[18] Like many of his fellow politicians, he harbours a strong desire to see the Palestinians of the occupied territories expelled, ideally to neighbouring Arab states or Europe. Lieberman, however, is more outspoken than most in publicly advocating for this position.

Where he is seen as overstepping the mark is in arguing that the state should strip up to a quarter of a million Palestinians living inside Israel of their citizenship and seal them and their homes into the Palestinian ghettoes being created inside the West Bank (presumably in preparation for the moment when they will all be expelled to Jordan). He believes any remaining Arab citizens should be required to sign a loyalty oath to Israel as a 'Jewish and democratic state' – loyalty to a democratic state alone will not suffice. Any who refuse will be physically expelled from Israel. And, as a *coup de grâce*, he has recently demanded the execution for treason of any Arab parliamentarian who talks to the Palestinian leadership in the occupied territories or commemorates Nakba Day, which marks the expulsion and permanent dispossession of the Palestinian people in 1948.[19] In practice, that includes every elected representative of Israel's Arab population.

These are Lieberman's official positions. Apparently unofficially he wants even worse measures taken against Palestinians, both inside Israel and in the occupied territories. In May 2004, for example, he told a crowd of his supporters, in Russian, that 90 per cent of the country's Arab citizens should be expelled. 'They have no place here. They can take their bundles and get lost.'[20]

Despite Lieberman's well-known political platform, Olmert has been courting him ever since Yisrael Beiteinu (Israel is Our Home) upset the expected three-way struggle between Olmert's Kadima Party, Labor and Likud in the March elections. Lieberman romped home with eleven seats in the Knesset, making his party a sparring partner of both Likud and the popular religious fundamentalist party Shas. According to reports in the Israeli media, Lieberman has not joined the coalition until now because he has been playing hard to get, making increasing demands of Olmert before agreeing to sign up for the government. His hand has grown stronger too: according to opinion polls, he is now the most popular politician in Israel after Binyamin Netanyahu, leader of the Likud Party.[21] In the newly established post of deputy prime minister and minister for strategic threats, Lieberman – the avowed Arab hater – will shape Israel's response to Iran. After that, he will presumably help the government decide what other 'strategic threats' it faces.

While Olmert enthuses over Lieberman, most in the Labor Party seem quietly resigned to his inclusion.[22] Labor's elder statesman and former leader, Shimon Peres, says he has no objections, so long as Lieberman does not challenge the core policies agreed by Kadima and Labor. This, of course, is precisely what Lieberman is doing – it was the price of the bargain he struck with Olmert. Lieberman wants no peace overtures to the Palestinians, and favours the hard-line neoliberal economic policies pursued by Kadima. On Wednesday the Labor leader Amir Peretz, a supposed socialist and former head of the Israeli trade-union movement, accepted Lieberman's entry to the coalition, as Olmert surely knew he would. In typical Labor style, Peretz bought off his conscience by insisting on a package of modest benefits for Arab citizens, the same Arab citizens Lieberman wants expelled.[23] The last time the government made a similar promise to its Arab minority back in late 2001 – when the prime minister of the day, Ehud Barak, needed their votes – the $1 billion pledge was broken immediately after the election.[24]

So why are Israel's politicians, of the left and right, so comfortable sitting with Lieberman, the leader of Israel's only unquestionably fascist party? Because, in truth, Lieberman is not the maverick politician of popular imagination, even if he is every bit the racist – a Jewish version of Austria's Jorg Haider or France's Jean-Marie Le Pen. In reality, Lieberman is entirely a creature of the Israeli political establishment, his policies sinister reflections of the principles and ideas he learnt in the inner sanctums of the Likud Party, a young hopeful immigrant rubbing shoulders with the likes of Ariel Sharon, Binyamin Netanyahu and, of course, Ehud Olmert. From their political infancy, the latter three were schooled in the minor arts of Israeli diplomacy:

feel free to speak plainly in the womb of the party; speak firmly but cautiously in Hebrew to other Israelis; and speak in another tongue entirely when using English, the language of the *goyim*, the non-Jews. But Lieberman, who arrived in Israel as a 21-year-old, was not around for those lessons. He imbibed nothing of the principles of *hasbara*, the 'advocacy for Israel' industry that has its unpaid battalions of propagandists regularly assaulting the phone lines and email inboxes of the Western media. He tells it exactly as he sees it, even if mostly in Russian.

Inside the Likud Party, Lieberman's political training ground, that hardly mattered. He rapidly rose through the ranks to become director general of Likud from 1993 to 1996 and soon afterwards to head the office of Prime Minister Binyamin Netanyahu. For many years he was the darling of the Likud, a party that today exists in two halves: its original incarnation, once again led by Netanyahu; and the renovated, sleeker model, Kadima, created by Sharon. But it was in breaking from Likud and founding his own party, Yisrael Beiteinu, in 1999 that Lieberman finally found his voice outside the Likud's smoke-filled rooms. The audience for his message was as untutored in the deceits of Israeli politicking as Lieberman himself.

Lieberman emigrated to Israel in 1978, leading the vanguard of a wave of immigration from Russia and its satellite states that reached a peak in the early 1990s as the Soviet empire broke up. By the time most Russian speakers began pouring into Israel, Lieberman was already well ensconced in the Israeli political system. Yisrael Beiteinu's openly racist agenda spoke to the darkest instincts of these 1 million newly arrived Russian speakers, many of whom profoundly distrusted left-wing politics and at the same time lusted after strongmen as leaders. Poor and struggling to adapt to Israeli culture, most live far from the prosperous centre of the country in their own neglected ghettos, Little Moscows, where the signs and street language are, more than a decade later, still in Russian. They feel little affinity for the Jewish state – apart from a loathing for everything Arab. And the state has found it easy to manipulate these immigrants' emotions. They have little understanding of the historic reasons for Israel's conflict with the Palestinians, and, like other Israelis, learn almost nothing more at school. With no context for appreciating why the Palestinians might carry out suicide attacks, Russian speakers assume the Palestinians are simply the hate-filled barbarians described to them by their politicians and media.

When young Russian men do their three years of active duty in the occupied territories, all these prejudices are confirmed. Now one of the largest blocs of Israel's citizen army, the Russians are assigned some of the toughest spots in the West Bank and Gaza, often their first experience of meeting 'Arabs'. They return home after their tours of duty, finding it hard to make sense of Israeli officialdom's lip service in distinguishing between Arab citizens, who have some rights in the Jewish state, and the 'Arabs' of the occupied territories, who have none. Many Russian speakers wonder why Israel does not simply kill or expel the lot of them. And this is where Lieberman steps in. Because usefully this is exactly what he not only believes but also openly declares. Lieberman can tap the support of nearly a million voters, a huge reservoir of support for any prime ministerial hopeful trying to assemble the coalition needed to form a government under Israel's fractious political system.

Neither Olmert nor Netanyahu can afford to say what is really on their minds: that they want to cleanse the region of as many Palestinians as they can manage – most certainly those in the oc-cupied territories, and later the even bigger nuisance of the ones who have citizenship and undermine Israel's Jewishness. But instead they can let a Lieberman, the charismatic leader of a popular party who does dare to say these things, join the government with minimal damage to their own reputations. They can also let him use the platform provided by a cabinet position to shape a new coarser politi-cal language in which ideas of expulsion and transfer become ever more mainstream. Until one day the policies Lieberman advocates, reflections of the values he imbibed during his long years spent in Likud, become acceptable enough that a prime minister – Olmert or Netanyahu or Lieberman himself – will be able to put them in the government's programme. Instead of using words like 'disengagement', 'convergence' or 'realignment', Israel's politicians of the near future may simply call for the expulsion of Arabs, all Arabs.

Even now Israeli leaders do little to conceal the fact that such thoughts are uppermost in their minds. Netanyahu, currently Israel's most popular politician and leader of the opposition, has repeatedly called the 1.2 million Arab citizens of the country a 'demographic timebomb'. Back in 2002, for example, he told an audience of policymakers: 'If there is a demographic problem, and there is, it is with the Israeli Arabs who will remain Israeli citizens. We therefore need a policy that will first of all guarantee a Jewish majority.'[25] Unlike Lieberman, Netanyahu never spells out what policies he is advocating. But most Israelis understand that in practice, if he felt free to speak his mind, his platform would not look much different from Yisrael Beiteinu's.

Olmert too uses code words readily understood by his Israeli audiences. In late 2004, in an interview with the *Ha'aretz* newspaper, he said Israel needed to find a 'solution' to its problem of Palestinian demographic growth in both the occupied territories and Israel, which might 'mean the end of the Jewish state.'[26] What 'solution' was Olmert referring to? Israelis know only too well. Every year since 2000 Olmert, Netanyahu, Peres and other senior policymakers have been meeting at the Herzliya conference, near Tel Aviv, to draw up ideas about how to deal with the demographic threat: the rapidly approaching moment when the Palestinians, either those with Israeli citizenship or the non-citizens living under military occupation in the West Bank and Gaza, will outnumber Jews. The solutions they have proposed have been similar to Lieberman's. Both the disengagement from Gaza and the planned limited withdrawals from the West Bank came out of Herzliya. But so did a range of measures to deal with the country's Arab citizens: land swaps to lose areas of Israel densely populated with Arabs in return for the settlements in the West Bank; loyalty oaths as a condition of citizenship; stripping the Arab population of their right to vote; and forcing all political parties to subscribe to Zionist ideals.[27]

These are not fanciful ideas; they are now firmly in the mainstream. Israel already has legislation requiring all parties running for the Knesset to support Israel remaining a 'Jewish and democratic state'. Technically, the only non-Zionist parties – two Arab parties and the small joint Jewish and Arab Communist Party – could quite legally be disqualified from all general elections under the current legislation. They expect that at some point in the future they will be too. The two previous prime ministers, Ehud Barak and Ariel Sharon, both secretly favoured land swaps in which large numbers of Arab citizens would be removed from the Jewish state. Barak proposed such a scheme at Camp David in the summer of 2000, as several participants later confirmed.[28] And in February 2004 Sharon floated the same idea during an interview in the *Ma'ariv* newspaper. When it caused a storm, he backtracked, but investigations by the paper revealed that he had been formulating a land swap for some time with his advisers and had even consulted the then Labor leader and his foreign minister, Shimon Peres, on its feasibility.[29]

At the top of Lieberman's list of demands before agreeing to enter Olmert's coalition were major changes to the Israeli constitution, including the introduction of a presidential system to replace the current parliamentary system. Israel already has a president, but the post is entirely symbolic. Lieberman wants a president who has the authority to make major legislative changes, even constitutional ones, without having to make the backroom compromises to keep together the coalition governments that characterize Israel's current political system. The president Lieberman has in mind would be more on the lines of an autocratic ruler. Olmert is apparently sympathetic to these plans. It is not difficult to understand why.

The Persecution of Azmi Bishara
(*June 2007*)

The second Palestinian intifada has been crushed. The 700 km wall is sealing the occupied population of the West Bank into a series of prisons. The 'demographic timebomb' – the fear that Palestinians, through higher birth rates, will soon outnumber Jews in the Holy Land and that Israel's continuing rule over them risks being compared to apartheid – has been safely defused through the disengagement from Gaza and its 1.4 million inhabitants. On the fortieth anniversary of Israel's occupation of the West Bank and Gaza, the security establishment is quietly satisfied with its successes. So, with these achievements under its belt, where next for the Jewish state?

It should come as no surprise that we are witnessing the first moves in Israel's next phase of the Palestinians' conquest. With nearly 4 million Palestinians in the occupied territories caged inside their ghettos, the turn has come of Israel's Palestinian citizens. Today nearly a fifth of Israel's population, these citizens are the legacy of an oversight by the country's Jewish leaders during the ethnic cleansing campaign of the 1948 war. Ever since, Israel has been pondering what to do with them. Israel's founders, men such as the first prime minister, David Ben-Gurion, preferred that they be marginalized and eventually expelled.[30] The question has been when and how to do the deed. The time appears to be drawing nearer, and the crushing of these more than 1 million unwanted citizens currently inside the walls of the fortress – the Achilles heel of the Jewish state – is likely to be just as ruthless as that of the Palestinians under occupation.[31]

I have charted the preparations for this crackdown before.[32] Israel has been secretly devising a land-swap scheme that would force up to a quarter of a million Palestinian citizens (but hardly any territory) into the Palestinian ghettoes being crafted next door – in return Israel will annex swathes of the West Bank on which the illegal Jewish settlements sit. The Bedouin in the Negev are being reclassified as trespassers on state land so that they can be treated as guest workers rather than citizens. And lawyers in the Justice Ministry are toiling over a loyalty scheme to deal with the remaining Palestinians: pledge an oath to Israel as a Jewish and democratic state (that is, one in which you are not wanted) or face being stripped of your rights and possibly expelled. There will be no resistance to these moves from Israel's Jewish public.

But these measures cannot be implemented until an important first battle has been waged and won in the Knesset, the Israeli parliament. One of Israel's gurus of the so-called 'demographic threat', Arnon Sofer, a professor at Haifa University, has explained the problem posed by the presence of a growing number of Palestinian voters: 'In their hands lies the power to determine the right of return [of Palestinian refugees] or to decide who is a Jew. In another few years, they will be able to decide whether the state of Israel should continue to be a Jewish-Zionist state.'[33]

The warning signs about how Israel might defend itself from this 'threat' have been clear for some time. In *Silencing Dissent*, a report published in 2002 by the Human Rights Association based in Nazareth, the treatment of Israel's ten Palestinian Knesset members was documented: over the previous two years, nine had been assaulted by the security services, some on several occasions, and seven hospitalized. The report also found that the state had launched twenty-five investigations of the ten MKs in the same period.[34] All this abuse was reserved for the representatives of a community the Israeli general Moshe Dayan once referred to as 'the quietest minority in the world'.[35] But the state's violence towards, and intimidation of, Palestinian Knesset members – until now largely the reflex actions of officials offended by the presence of legislators refusing to bow before the principles of Zionism and privileges for Jews – is entering a new, more dangerous phase.[36]

The problem for Israel is that for the past two decades Palestinian legislators have been entering the Knesset not as members of Zionist parties, as was the case for many decades, but as representatives of independent Palestinian parties. (A state claiming to be Jewish and democratic has to make some concessions to its own propaganda, after all.) The result has been the emergence of an unexpected political platform: the demand for Israel's constitutional reform. Palestinian political parties have been calling for Israel's transformation from a Jewish state into a 'state of all its citizens' – or what the rest of us would call a liberal democracy. The figurehead of this political struggle has been the legislator Azmi Bishara. A former philosophy professor, Bishara has been running rings around Jewish politicians in the Knesset for more than a decade, as well as exposing to outsiders the sham of Israel's self-definition as a 'Jewish and democratic' state. Even more worryingly he has also been making an increasingly convincing case to his constituency of 1.2 million Palestinian citizens that, rather than challenging the hundreds of forms of discrimination they face one law at a time, they should confront the system that props up the discrimination: the Jewish state itself. He has started to persuade a growing number that they will never enjoy equality with Jews as long as they live in an ethnic state.

Bishara's campaign for a state of all its citizens has faced an uphill struggle. Palestinian citizens spent the first two decades after Israel's creation living under martial law, a time during which their identity, history and memories were all but crushed. Even today the minority has no control over its educational curriculum, which is set by officials charged with promoting Zionism, and its schools are effectively run by the secret police, the Shin Bet, through a network of collaborators among the teachers and pupils.[37]

Given this climate, it may not be surprising that – even allowing for the dubious phrasing of their question – in a recent poll conducted by the Israel Democracy Institute 75 per cent of Palestinian citizens said they would support the drafting of a constitution defining Israel as a Jewish and democratic state. Interestingly, however, what concerned commentators was the survey's small print: only a third of the respondents felt strongly about their position compared to more than half of those questioned in a similar survey three years ago. Also, 72 per cent of Palestinian citizens believed the principle of 'equality' should be prominently featured in such a constitution.[38] Even more 'worrying' views from Israel's Palestinian citizens have been noted in another survey, this one conducted by the Adenauer Foundation at Tel Aviv University. It found that 68 per cent supported the establishment of an elected representative national body for Israel's Palestinian citizens; 86 per cent supported the return of refugees living in Israel to their original villages; and 40 per cent wanted to see Israel transformed into a 'state of all its citizens'.[39]

These shifts of opinion are at least partly a result of Bishara's political work. He has been trying to persuade Israel's Palestinian minority – most of whom, whatever the spin tells us, have had little practical experience of participating in a democracy other than casting a vote – that it is impossible for a Jewish state to enshrine equality in its laws. Israel's nearest thing to a Bill of Rights, the Basic Law on Freedom and Human Dignity, intentionally does not mention equality anywhere in its text.

It is in this light that the news about Bishara that broke in mid-April should be read. While he was abroad with his family, the Shin Bet announced that he would face charges of treason on his return.[40] Under the annually renewed emergency regulations, he could be executed if found guilty. Bishara so far has chosen not to return and has resigned from the Knesset. Coverage of the Bishara case has concentrated on the two main charges against him, which are only vaguely known as the security services have been trying to prevent disclosure of their evidence with a gagging order.

The first accusation – seemingly for the consumption of Israel's Jewish population – is that Bishara actively helped Hizbullah in its targeting of Israeli communities in the north during the war against Lebanon last summer. The Shin Bet claim this after months of listening in on his phone conversations – made possible by a change in the law in 2005 that allows the security services to bug legislators' phones.[41] The other Palestinian MKs suspect they are being subjected to the same eavesdropping after the attorney general Menachem Mazuz failed to respond to a question from one, Taleb a-Sana, on whether the Shin Bet was using this practice more widely.[42]

Few informed observers, however, take this allegation seriously. An editorial in Israel's leading newspaper *Ha'aretz* compared Bishara's case to that of the Israeli Jewish dissident Tali Fahima, who was jailed on trumped-up charges that she translated a military plan, a piece of paper dropped by the army in the Jenin refugee camp, on behalf of a Palestinian militant, Zacharia Zbeidi, even though it was widely known that Zbeidi was himself fluent in Hebrew. The editorial noted that it seemed likely the charge of treason against Bishara, will turn out to be a tendentious exaggeration of his telephone conversations and meetings with Lebanese and Syrian nationals, and possibly also of his expressions of support for their military activities. It seems very doubtful that MK Bishara even has access to defense-related secrets that he could sell to the enemy, and like in the Fahima case, the fact that he identified with the enemy during wartime appears to be what fueled the desire to seek and find an excuse for bringing him to trial.[43]

Such doubts were reinforced by reports in the Israeli media that the charge of treason was based on claims that Bishara had helped Hizbullah conduct 'psychological warfare through the media'.[44]

The other allegation made by the secret police has a different target audience. The Shin Bet claim that Bishara laundered money from terrorist organizations. The implication, though the specifics are unclear, is that Bishara both helped fund terror and squirrelled some of the money away, possibly hundreds of thousands of dollars, presumably for his own benefit. This is supposed to discredit him with his own constituency of Palestinian citizens. It should be noted that none of this money has been found in extensive searches of Bishara's home and office,[45] and the evidence is based on testimony from a far from reliable source: a family of money changers in East Jerusalem.

This second charge resembles allegations faced by the only other Palestinian of national prominence in Israel, Sheikh Raed Salah, head of the Islamic Movement and a spiritual leader of the Palestinian minority. He was arrested in 2003, originally on charges that he laundered money for the armed wing of Hamas, helping them buy guns and bombs.[46] As with Bishara, the Shin Bet had been bugging Salah's every phone call for many months and had supposedly accumulated mountains of evidence against him. Salah spent more than two years in jail, the judges repeatedly accepting the Shin Bet's advice that his requests for bail be refused, as this secret evidence was studied in minute detail at his lengthy trial.[47] In the closing stages, as it became clear that the Shin Bet's case was evaporating, the prosecution announced a plea bargain. Salah agreed (possibly unwisely, but understandably after two years in jail) to admit minor charges of financial impropriety in return for his release.[48] To this day, Salah does not know what he did wrong. His organization had funded social programmes for orphans, students and widows in the occupied territories and had submitted its accounts to the security services for approval. In a recent interview, Salah observed that in the new reality he and his party had discovered that it was 'as if helping orphans, sick persons, widows and students had now become illegal activities in support of terrorism'.[49]

Why was Salah targeted? In the same interview, he noted that shortly before his arrest the prime minister of the day, Ariel Sharon, had called for the outlawing of the Islamic Movement, whose popularity was greatly concerning the security establishment. Sharon was worried by what he regarded as Salah's interference in Israel's crushing of Palestinian nationalism. Sharon's concern was twofold: the Islamic Movement was raising funds for welfare organizations in the occupied territories at the very moment Israel was trying to isolate and starve the Palestinian population there; and Salah's main campaign, 'Al-Aqsa is in danger', was successfully rallying Palestinians inside Israel to visit the mosques of the Noble Sanctuary in the Old City of Jerusalem, the most important symbols of a future Palestinian state. Salah believed that responsibility fell to Palestinians inside Israel to protect these holy places as Israel's closure policies and its checkpoints were preventing Muslims in the occupied territories from reaching them. Salah also suspected that Israel was using the exclusion of Palestinians under occupation from East Jerusalem to assert its own claims to sovereignty over the site, known to Jews as Temple Mount. This was where Sharon had made his inflammatory visit backed by 1,000 armed guards that triggered the intifada; and it was Ehud Barak's insistence on absolute control over Temple Mount that 'blew up' the Camp David negotiations, according to one of his advisers.[50] Salah had become a nuisance, an obstacle to Israel realizing its goals in East Jerusalem and possibly in the intifada, and needed to be neutralized. The trial removed him from the scene at a key moment when he might have been able to make a difference. That now is the fate of Bishara.

Indications that the Shin Bet wanted Bishara's scalp over his campaign for Israel's reform to a state of all its citizens can be dated back to at least the start of the second intifada in 2000. That was when, as Israel prepared for a coming general election, the departing head of the Shin Bet observed: 'Bishara does not recognize the right of the Jewish people to a state and he has crossed the line. The decision to disqualify him [from standing for election] has been submitted to the attorney general.'[51] Who expressed that view? None other than Ami Ayalon, currently contesting the leadership of the Labor Party and hoping to become the official head of Israel's peace camp.[52] In the meantime, Bishara has been put on trial twice (unnoticed, the charges later fizzled out);[53] he has been called in for police interrogations on a regular basis; he has been warned by a state inquiry, the Or Commission; and the laws concerning Knesset immunity and travel to foreign states have been changed specifically to prevent Bishara from fulfilling his parliamentary duties.[54]

True to Ayalon's advice, Bishara and his political party, the National Democratic Assembly (NDA), were disqualified by the Central Elections Committee during the 2003 elections. The committee cited the 'expert' opinion of the Shin Bet:

> It is our opinion that the inclusion of the NDA in the Knesset has increased the threat inherent in the party. Evidence of this can also be found in the ideological progress [of its ideas] from the margins of Arab society (such as a limited circle of intellectuals who dealt with these ideas theoretically) to center stage. Today these ideas [concerning a state of all its citizens] have a discernible effect on the content of political discourse and on the public 'agenda' of the Arab sector.[55]

On this occasion, however, the Shin Bet failed to get its way. Bishara's disqualification was overturned on appeal by a wafer-thin majority of the Supreme Court's justices.[56]

The Shin Bet's fears of Bishara resurfaced with a vengeance in March this year, when the *Ma'ariv* newspaper reported on a closed meeting between the prime minister, Ehud Olmert, and senior Shin Bet officials 'concerning the issue of the Arab minority in Israel, the extent of its steadily decreasing identification with the State and the rise of subversive elements'. *Ma'ariv* quoted the assessment of the Shin Bet:

> Particularly disturbing is the growing phenomenon of 'visionary documents' among the various elites of Israeli Arabs. At this time, there are four different visionary documents sharing the perception of Israel as a state of all citizens and not as a Jewish state. The isolationist and subversive aims presented by the elites might determine a direction that will win over the masses.[57]

In other words, the secret police were worried that the influence of Bishara's political platform was spreading. The proof was to be found in the four recent documents cited by the Shin Bet and published by very different groups: the Democratic Constitution by the Adalah legal centre;[58] Ten Points by the Mossawa political lobbying group;[59] the Future Vision by the traditionally conservative political body comprising mostly mayors known as the High Follow-Up Committee;[60] and the Haifa Declaration, overseen by a group of academics known as Mada.[61] What all these documents have in common is two assumptions: first, that existing solutions to the Israeli–Palestinian conflict are based on two states and that in such an arrangement the Palestinian minority will continue living inside Israel as citizens; and second, that reforms of Israel are needed if the state is to realize equality for all citizens, as promised in its Declaration of Independence. Nothing too subversive there, one would have thought. But that was not the view of the Shin Bet.

Following the report in *Ma'ariv*, the editor of a weekly Arab newspaper wrote to the Shin Bet asking for more information. Did the Shin Bet's policy not constitute an undemocratic attempt to silence the Palestinian minority and its leaders, he asked. A reply from the Shin Bet was not long in coming. The secret police had a responsibility to guard Israel against 'strategic threats', it was noted. 'The Shin Bet security service will thwart the activity of any group or individual seeking to harm the Jewish and democratic character of the State of Israel, even if such activity is sanctioned by the law.' The letter added that the Shin Bet would carry out the task under 'the principle of a democracy that defends itself'.[62] Questioned by Israeli legal groups about this policy when it became public, the head of the Shin Bet, Yuval Diskin, wrote a letter clarifying what was meant. Israel had to be protected from anyone 'working toward changing the basic values of the state by obviating its democratic or Jewish character'. He was basing his opinion on a law passed in 2002 that charges the Shin Bet with safeguarding the country from 'terror threats, sabotage, subversion, espionage and the revelation of state secrets'.[63]

In other words, in the view of the Shin Bet, a Jewish and democratic state is democratic only if you are a Jew or a Zionist. If you try to use Israel's supposed democracy to challenge the privileges reserved for Jews inside a Jewish state, that same state is entitled to defend itself against you. The extension in the future of this principle from Bishara to the other Palestinian MKs and then on to the wider Palestinian community inside Israel should not be doubted. In the wake of the Bishara case, Israel Hasson, a former deputy director of the Shin Bet and now a right-wing Knesset member, described Israel's struggle against its Palestinian citizens as 'a second War of Independence'[64] – the war in 1948 that founded Israel by cleansing it of 80 per cent of its Palestinians.

The Shin Bet is not, admittedly, a democratic institution, even if it is operating in a supposedly democratic environment. So how do the state's more accountable officials view the Shin Bet's position? Diskin's reply had a covering letter from attorney general Menachem Mazuz, the country's most senior legal officer. Mazuz wrote: 'The letter of the Shin Bet director was written in coordination with the attorney general and with his agreement, and the stance detailed in it is acceptable to the attorney general.'[65] So now we know. As Israel's Palestinian politicians have long been claiming, a Jewish and democratic state is intended as a democracy for Jews only. No one else is allowed an opinion.

6

Life under Occupation

Israel's corralling of the Palestinian population into ever-shrinking ghettoes in the occupied territories has required the enforcement of severe restrictions on Palestinian movement – and the cornerstone of that policy has been the checkpoint. In 'Watching the Checkpoints' I join a team of Israeli women belonging to Machsom Watch who exploit, like the settlers, their privileges as Jews to move around the West Bank. In their case, however, they are there to witness and record some of the abuses committed by Israeli soldiers against the Palestinian population at a few of the hundreds of checkpoints and roadblocks that have created an apartheid road system in the West Bank. The women's actions, as they readily admit, are a drop in the ocean of Israel's oppression of the Palestinians; a few even fear that their very presence creates the false impression that the occupation is somehow accountable and well-intentioned.

The other three essays in this section deal with the occupation regime's determination to prevent resistance from the Palestinians to their imprisonment, including by blocking the emergence of any effective national leadership.

One minor but revealing method, which barely merited attention, is explained in 'Israel's Latest Bureaucratic Obscenity'. In early 2006 it was decided to begin expelling from the occupied territories those Palestinians who hold a foreign passport. In most cases Palestinians hold such a passport only because their right to reside in the occupied territories was revoked by Israel, in violation of international law, after an absence studying or living abroad. Many, including businessmen and academics, have been living in the territories for many years on tourist visas. They are almost uniformly people who have a great deal invested in a peaceful resolution of the conflict, who have been helping to create a fledgling civil society, and who possess an ability to communicate the Palestinian experience of occupation to the West. Their expulsion suggested yet again Israel's enduring bad faith.

In 'An Experiment in Human Despair' I examine the real reasons behind Israel's menacing of the population of the Gaza Strip, including bombing its only power station, and how its actions are designed to undermine the Palestinian leadership, provoke factionalism and encourage ordinary Palestinians to give up hope. 'The Struggle for Palestine's Soul' considers Israel's recent manipulation of these divisions to foment civil war between Fatah and Hamas and deflect both groups from their true purpose: resistance to the occupation.

Watching the Checkpoints
(*February 2007*)

The scene: a military checkpoint deep in Palestinian territory in the West Bank. A tall, thin elderly man, walking stick in hand, approaches a line of Palestinians, many of them young men, waiting obediently behind concrete barriers for permission from an Israeli soldier to leave one Palestinian area, the city of Nablus, to enter another Palestinian area, the neighbouring village of Huwara. The long queue is moving slowly, the soldier ostentatiously taking his time to check each person's papers. Impatient, the old man heads off purposefully down a parallel but empty lane reserved for vehicle inspections. A young soldier controlling the human traffic spots him and orders him back in line. The old man stops, fixes the soldier with a stare and refuses. The soldier looks startled, and uncomfortable at the unexpected show of defiance. He tells the old man more gently to go back to the queue. The old man stands his ground. After a few tense moments, the soldier relents and the old man passes.

Is the confrontation revealing of the soldier's humanity? That is not the way it looks – or feels – to the young Palestinians penned in behind the concrete barriers. They can only watch the scene in silence. None would dare to challenge the soldier in the manner of the old man – or to take his side had the Israeli been of a different disposition. An old man is unlikely to be detained or beaten at a checkpoint. Who, after all, would believe he attacked or threatened a soldier, or resisted arrest, or was carrying a weapon? But the young men know their own injuries or arrests would barely merit a mention in Israel's newspapers, let alone an investigation. And so, the checkpoints have made potential warriors of Palestine's grandfathers at the price of emasculating their sons and grandsons.

I observed this small indignity – such humiliations are now a staple of life for any Palestinian who needs to move around the West Bank – during a shift with Machsom Watch. The grassroots organization founded by Israeli women in 2001 monitors the behaviour of soldiers at a few dozen of the more accessible checkpoints (*machsom* in Hebrew).[1] The checkpoints came to dominate Palestinian life in the West Bank (and, before the disengagement, in Gaza too) long before the outbreak of the second intifada in late 2000, and even before the first Palestinian suicide bombings. They were Israel's response to the Oslo Accords, which created a Palestinian Authority to govern limited areas of the occupied territories. Israel began restricting Palestinians allowed to work in Israel to those issued with exit permits – a system enforced through a growing network of military roadblocks. Soon the checkpoints were limiting movement inside the occupied territories too, ostensibly to protect the Jewish settlements built illegally on Palestinian land.[2] By late 2006, according to the United Nations Office for the Coordination of Humanitarian Affairs, 528 checkpoints and roadblocks had been recorded in the West Bank, choking its roads every few miles.[3] Israel's daily *Ha'aretz* newspaper put the figure even higher: in January 2007 there were 75 permanently manned checkpoints, some 150 mobile checkpoints, and more than 400 places where roads have been blocked by obstacles.[4]

All these restrictions on movement for a place that is, according to the CIA's *World Factbook*, no larger than the tiny US state of Delaware.[5] As a result, moving goods and people from one place to the next in the West Bank has become a nightmare of logistics and costly delays. At the checkpoints, food spoils, patients die, and children are prevented from reaching their schools. The World Bank blames the checkpoints and roadblocks for strangling the Palestinian economy.[6] Embarrassed by publicity about the burgeoning number of checkpoints, the Israeli prime minister, Ehud Olmert, promised the Palestinian president, Mahmoud Abbas, in December 2006 that there would be an easing of travel restrictions in the West Bank – to little effect, according to reports in the Israeli media. Although the army announced a month later that 44 earth barriers had been removed in fulfilment of Olmert's pledge, it soon emerged that none of the roadblocks had actually been there in the first place.[7]

Contrary to the impression of most observers, the great majority of the checkpoints are not even near the Green Line, Israel's internationally recognized border until it occupied the West Bank and Gaza in 1967. Some are so deep inside Palestinian territory that the army refuses to allow Machsom Watch to visit them. There, the women say, no one knows what abuses are being perpetrated unseen on Palestinians. But at Huwara checkpoint, where the old man refused to submit, the soldiers at least know that most of the time they are being watched by fellow Israelis and that their behaviour is being recorded in monthly logs. Machsom Watch has a history of publishing embarrassing photographs and videos of the soldiers' actions. It showed, for example, a videotape in 2004 of a young Palestinian man being forced to play his violin at Beit Iba checkpoint, a story that gained worldwide attention because it echoed the indignities suffered by Jews at the hands of the Nazis.[8]

Machsom Watch has about 500 members, including reportedly Olmert's left-wing daughter, Dana. But only about 200 actively take part in checkpoint duties, an experience that has left many outspoken in denouncing the occupation. The organization is widely seen by the Israeli public as extremist, with pro-Israel groups accusing the women of 'demonizing' Israel.[9] It is the kind of criticism painfully familiar to Nomi Lalo, from Kfar Sava. A veteran of Machsom Watch, she is the mother of three children, two of whom have already served in the army while the youngest, aged 17, is due to join up later this year. 'He has been more exposed to my experiences in Machsom Watch and has some sympathy with my point of view', she says. 'But my oldest son has been very hostile about my activities. It has caused a lot of tension in the family.'

Most of the women do shifts at a single checkpoint, but I joined Nomi on 'patrol' duty in the central region, moving between the dozens of checkpoints west of Nablus. She started by showing me the separate road system in the West Bank, with unrestricted and high-quality roads set aside for Jewish settlers while Palestinians are forced to make difficult and lengthy journeys over hills and through valleys on what are often little more than dirt tracks. Machsom Watch calls this 'apartheid', a judgement shared by Amira Hass, a veteran reporter in the occupied territories for the *Ha'aretz* newspaper, who recently wrote that Israeli parents ought to 'be very worried about their country sending their sons and daughters on an apartheid mission: to restrict Palestinian mobility within the occupied territory in order to enable Jews to move freely.'[10]

We leave the small Palestinian town of Azzoun, close by the city of Qalqilya, and head directly north towards another city, Tulkarm. A trip that should take little more than a quarter of an hour is now all but impossible for most Palestinians. 'This road is virtually empty, even though it is the main route between two of the West Bank's largest cities', Nomi points out. 'That is because most Palestinians cannot get the permits they need to use these roads. Without a permit they can't get through the checkpoints, so either they stay in their villages or they have to seek circuitous and dangerous routes off the main roads.' We soon reach one of the checkpoints Nomi is talking about. At Aras, two soldiers sit in a small concrete bunker in the centre of the main junction between Tulkarm and Nablus. The bored soldiers are killing time waiting for the next car and the driver whose papers they will need to inspect. A young Palestinian man, in woollen cap to protect him from the cold, stands by a telegraph post close by the junction. Bilal, aged 26, has been 'detained' at the same spot for three hours by the soldiers. Nervously he tells us that he is trying to reach his ill father in hospital in Tulkarm. Nomi looks unconvinced and, after a talk with the soldiers and calls on her mobile phone to their commanders, she has a clearer picture.

> He has been working illegally in Israel and they have caught him trying to get back to his home in the West Bank. The soldiers are holding him here to punish him. They could imprison him but, given the dire state of the Palestinian economy, the Israeli prisons would soon be overflowing with jobseekers. So holding him here all day is a way of making him suffer. It's illegal but, unless someone from Machsom Watch turns up, who will ever know?

Is it not good that the military commanders are willing to talk to her? 'They know we can present their activities in the West Bank in a very harsh light and so they cooperate. They don't want bad publicity. I never forget that fact when I am speaking to them. When they are being helpful, I remind myself their primary motive is to protect the occupation's image.'

Nomi sees proof in cases like Bilal's that the checkpoints and Israel's steel and concrete barrier in the West Bank – or fence, as she calls it – are not working in the way Israel claims.

> First, the fence is built on Palestinian land, not on the Green Line, and it cuts Palestinians off from their farmland and their chances of employment. It forces them to try to get into Israel to work. It is self-defeating. And second, thousands of Palestinians like Bilal reach

Israel from the West Bank each day in search of work. Any one of them could be a suicide bomber. The fence simply isn't effective in terms of stopping them. If Palestinians who are determined enough to work in Israel can avoid the checkpoints, those who want to attack Israel can certainly avoid them. No one straps a bomb on and marches up to a checkpoint. It is ordinary Palestinians who suffer instead.

The other day, says Nomi, she found a professor of English from Bir Zeit University held at this checkpoint, just like Bilal. He had tried to sneak out of Tulkarm during a curfew to teach a class at the university near the city of Ramallah, some 40 km south of here. Nomi's intervention eventually got him released. 'He was sent back to Tulkarm. He thanked me profusely, but really what did we do for him or his students? We certainly didn't get him to the university.'

After Nomi's round of calls, Bilal is called over by one of the soldiers. Wagging his finger reprovingly, the soldier lectures Bilal for several minutes before sending him on his way with a dismissive wave of the hand. Another small indignity.

As we leave, Nomi receives a call from a Machsom Watch group at Jitt checkpoint, a few miles away. The team of women say that, when they turned up to begin their shift, the soldiers punished the Palestinians by shutting the checkpoint. The women are panicking because a tailback of cars – mainly taxis and trucks driven by Palestinians with special permits – is building. After some discussion with Nomi, it is decided that the women should leave. Meanwhile, we head uphill to another checkpoint, some 500 metres from Aras, guarding the entrance to Jabara, a village whose educated population includes many teachers and school inspectors. Nowadays, however, the villagers are among several thousand Palestinians living in a legal twilight zone, trapped on the Israeli side of the wall. Cut off from the rest of the West Bank, the villagers are not allowed to receive guests and need special permits to leave their village to reach the schools where they work. (According to the United Nations, an additional quarter of a million Palestinians have been sealed off from both Israel and the West Bank in their own ghettoes.[11]) 'Children who have married out of Jabara are not even allowed to visit their parents here', says Nomi. 'Family life has been torn apart, with people unable to attend funerals and weddings. I cannot imagine what it is like for them. The Supreme Court has demanded the fence be moved but the state says it does not have the money for the time being to make the changes.'[12] Jabara's children have a checkpoint named after them through which they have to pass each day to reach their schools nearby in the West Bank.

At the far end of Jabara we have to pass through a locked gate to leave the village. There we are greeted by yet another checkpoint, this one closer to the Green Line on a road the settlers use to reach Israel. It is one of a growing number that look suspiciously like border crossings, with special booths and lanes for the soldiers to inspect vehicles, even though these checkpoints are not located on the Green Line. The soldiers see our yellow number plate, distinguishing us from the green plates of the Palestinians, and wave us through. Nomi is using a settlers' map she bought from a petrol station inside Israel to navigate our way to the next checkpoint, Anabta, close by an isolated Jewish settlement called Enav. Although this was once a busy main road, the checkpoint is empty and the soldiers mill around with nothing to do. An old Palestinian man wearing the black and white *keffiyah* (head scarf) popularized by Yasser Arafat approaches them trying to sell socks. There are no detained Palestinians, so we move on.

Nomi is as sceptical of claims she hears in the Israeli media about the checkpoints foiling suicide attacks as she is about the army's claims that they have been removing the roadblocks. 'I spend all day monitoring a checkpoint and come home in the evening, turn on the TV and hear that four suicide bombers were caught at the checkpoint where I have been working. It happens just too often. I stopped believing the army a long time ago.' We arrive at another settlement, comprising a couple of dozen Jewish families, called Shavei Shomron. It is located next to Road 60, once the main route between Nablus and the most northerly Palestinian city, Jenin. Now the road is empty and leads nowhere; it has been blocked by the army, supposedly to protect Shomron. 'Palestinians have to drive for hours across country to reach Jenin just because a handful of settlers want to live here by the main road', observes Nomi.

A short distance away, also on Road 60, is one of the larger and busier checkpoints: Beit Iba, the site where the Palestinian was forced to play his violin. A few kilometres west of Nablus, the checkpoint has been built in the most unlikely of places: a working quarry that has covered everything in the area with a fine white dust. 'I look at this place and think the army at least has a sense of humour', Nomi says. Yellow Palestinian taxis are waiting at one end of the quarry to pick up Palestinians allowed to leave Nablus on foot through the checkpoint. At the vehicle inspection point, a donkey and cart stacked so high with boxes of medicines that they look permanently on the verge of tipping over is being checked alongside ambulances and trucks. Close by is the familiar corridor of metal gates, turnstiles and concrete barriers through which Palestinians must pass one at a time to be inspected. On a battered table, a young man is emptying the contents of his small suitcase, presumably after a stay in Nablus. He is made to unfold his underwear and hold it up for the soldiers in front of the Palestinian onlookers. Another small indignity.

Here at least the Palestinians wait under a metal awning that protects them from the sun and rain. 'The roof and the table are our doing,' says Nomi. 'Before the Palestinians had to empty their bags on to the ground.' Machsom Watch is also responsible for a small Portakabin office nearby, up a narrow flight of concrete steps, with the ostentatious sign 'Humanitarian Post' by the door. 'After we complained about women with babies being made to wait for hours in line, the army put up this cabin with baby-changing facilities, diapers and formula milk. Then they invited the media to come and film it.' The experiment was short-lived apparently. After two weeks the army claimed the Palestinians were not using the post and removed the facilities. I go up and take a look. It's entirely bare: just four walls and a very dusty basin.

How effective does she feel Machsom Watch is? Does it really help the Palestinians or merely add a veneer of legitimacy to the checkpoints by suggesting, like the humanitarian post, that Israel cares about its occupied subjects? It is, Nomi admits, a question that troubles her a great deal.

It's a dilemma. The Palestinians here used to have to queue under the sun without shelter or water. Now that we have got them a roof, maybe we have made the occupation look a little more humane, a little more acceptable. There are some women [in Machsom Watch] who argue we should only watch, and not interfere, even if we see Palestinians being abused or beaten.

Which happens, as Machsom Watch's monthly reports document in detail. Even the Israeli media are starting to report uncomfortably about the soldier's behaviour, from assaults to soldiers urinating in front of religious women.[13] At Beit Iba in October 2006, says Nomi, a Palestinian youngster was badly beaten by soldiers after he panicked in the queue and shinned up a pole shouting that he couldn't breathe. *Ha'aretz* later reported that the soldiers beat him with their rifle butts and smashed his glasses. He was then thrown in a detention cell at the checkpoint.[14] And a month later, Haitem Yassin, aged 25, made the mistake of arguing with a soldier at a small checkpoint near Beit Iba called Asira al-Shamalia. He was upset when the soldiers forced the religious women he was sharing a taxi with to pat their bodies as a security measure. According to Amira Hass, Yassin was then shoved by one of the soldiers. He made the mistake of pushing back. Yassin was shot in the stomach, handcuffed and beaten with rifle butts while other soldiers blocked an ambulance from coming to his aid. Yassin remained unconscious for several days in hospital.[15]

We leave Beit Iba and within a few minutes we are at another roadblock, at Jitt. This is where the soldiers shut the checkpoint to traffic when the Machsom Watch team showed up earlier. Nomi wants to talk to them. We park some distance away, behind the queue of Palestinian cars, and she walks towards them. There is a brief discussion and she is back. Meanwhile, one of the soldiers takes out a megaphone and calls to the taxi driver at the front of the queue. He is told to leave his car at the wait sign and approach the checkpoint 100 metres away on foot. 'They are not happy. Now they are punishing the drivers because I have turned up. It's exactly the same response as this morning.' Nomi decides Machsom Watch should retreat again. We leave as the queue of cars starts to build up.

The notorious Huwara checkpoint, guarding the main road to Nablus from the south, is our next destination. Early in the intifada, there were regular stories of soldiers abusing Palestinians here. Today, Machsom Watch has an almost permanent presence at the checkpoint, as do army officers concerned about bad publicity. It is a surreal scene. We are deep in the West Bank, with Palestinians everywhere, but two young Jews – sporting a hippy look fashionable among the more extreme religious settlers – are lounging by the side of the road waiting for a lift to take them to one of the more militant settlements that encircle Nablus. A soldier, there to protect them, stands chatting. 'There used to be a taxi rank here waiting for Palestinians as they came through the checkpoint', says Nomi, 'but it has been moved much further away so the settlers have a safer pickup point. The convenience of the settlers means that each day thousands of Palestinians, including pregnant women and the disabled, must walk more than an extra hundred yards to reach the taxis.' As I am photographing the checkpoint, a soldier wearing red-brown boots – the sign of a paratrooper, according to Nomi – confronts me, warning that he will confiscate my camera. Nomi knows her, and my, rights and asks him by what authority he is making such a threat. They argue in Hebrew for a few minutes before he apologizes, saying he mistook me for a Palestinian. 'Are only Palestinians not allowed to photograph the checkpoints?' Nomi scolds him, adding as an afterthought: 'Didn't you hear that modern mobile phones have cameras? How can you stop a checkpoint being photographed?'

The army's pleasant face at Huwara is Micha, an officer from the District Coordination Office who oversees the soldiers. When he shows up in his car, Nomi engages him in conversation. Micha tells us that yesterday a teenager was stopped at the checkpoint carrying a knife and bomb-making equipment. Though the two are friendly, Nomi cannot help but scoff, much to Micha's annoyance. 'Why is it always teenagers being stopped at the checkpoints?' she asks him. 'You know as well as I do that the Shin Bet [Israel's domestic security service] puts these youngsters up to it to justify the checkpoints' existence. Why would anyone leave Nablus with a knife and bring it to Huwara checkpoint? For God's sake, you can buy swords on the other side of the checkpoint, in Huwara village.'

We leave Huwara and go deeper into the West Bank, along a 'sterile road' – army parlance for one the Palestinians cannot use – that today services settlers reaching Elon Moreh and Itimar. Once Palestinians travelled the road to the village of Beit Furik but not any more. 'Israel does not put up signs telling you that two road systems exist here. Instead it is the responsibility of Palestinians to know that they cannot drive on this road. Any that make a mistake are arrested.' South-east of Nablus we pass the village of Beit Furik itself, the entrance to which has a large metal gate that can be locked by the army at will. A short distance on and we reach Beit Furik checkpoint and beyond it, tantalizingly in view, the grey cinderblock homes of the city of Nablus.[16] Again, when I try to take a photo, a soldier storms towards me barely concealing his anger. Nomi remonstrates with him, but he is in a foul mood. Away from him, she confides: 'They know that these checkpoints violate international law and that they are complicit in war crimes. Many of the soldiers are scared of being photographed.'

Faced with the hostile soldier, we soon abandon Beit Furik and head back to Huwara. Less than a minute on from Huwara (Nomi makes me check my watch), we have hit another checkpoint: Yitzhar. A snarl-up of taxis, trucks and a few private cars is blocking the Palestinian inspection lane. We overtake the queue in a separate lane reserved for cars with yellow plates (settlers) and reach the other side of the checkpoint. There we find a taxi driver waiting by the side of the road next to his yellow cab. Faek has been there for ninety minutes after an Israeli policeman confiscated both his ID and his driving licence, and then disappeared with them. Did Faek get the name of the policeman? No, he replies. 'Of course not', admits Nomi. 'What Palestinian would risk asking an Israeli official for his name?' Nomi makes more calls and is told that Faek can come to the police station in the nearby settlement of Ariel to collect his papers. But, in truth, Faek is trapped. He cannot get through the checkpoints separating him from Ariel without his ID card. And even if he could find a tortuous route around the checkpoints, he could still be arrested for not having a licence and issued a fine of a few hundred shekels, a small sum for Israelis but one he would struggle to pay. So quietly he carries on waiting in the hope that the policeman will return. Nomi is not hopeful. 'It is illegal to take his papers without giving him a receipt but this kind of thing happens all the time. What can the Palestinians do? They dare not argue. It's the Wild West out here.'

Some time later, as the sun lowers in the sky and a chill winter wind picks up, Faek is still waiting. Nomi's shift is coming to an end and we must head back to Israel. She promises to continue putting pressure by phone on the police to return his documents. Nearly two hours later, as I arrive home, Faek unexpectedly calls, saying he has finally got his papers back. But he is still not happy: he has been issued with a fine of 500 shekels ($115) by the police. Nomi's phone is busy, he says. Can I help get the fine reduced?

Israel's Latest Bureaucratic Obscenity
(*July 2006*)

The same malign intent from Israel towards the Palestinians is stamped through its history like the lettering in a child's stick of seaside rock. But despite the consistent aim of Israeli policy, generation after generation of Western politicians, diplomats and journalists has shown a repeated inability to grasp what is happening before its very eyes.

The Palestinian historian Rashid Khalidi once noted that the first goal of Israel's founders as they prepared to establish their Jewish state on a large swathe of the Palestinian homeland in 1948 was to empty Palestine's urban heartlands of their educated elites. Even before Israel's Declaration of Independence on 15 May 1948, most Palestinians had been terrified away from the two wealthiest cities in coastal Palestine: Jaffa and Haifa. Other Palestinian cities soon fell during the war of 1948: Israeli forces mostly cleansed Lydd, Ramla,

Acre, Safad, Tiberias, Bisan and Beersheva of their native populations. Today all these cities have been repopulated with Jews – as well as renamed. Khalidi has written: 'These refugees from the urban areas of the country generally tended to be those Palestinians with the highest levels of literacy, skills, wealth, and education.'[17] Or, in other words, the small number of Palestinians that managed to remain in their homeland were peasant families living in isolated rural communities. These Palestinians posed little threat to the new Jewish state: they lacked the education and tools to resist both the wholesale dispossession of their people and their own personal loss as their farmlands were expropriated by the state to establish the Jewish farming communes of the kibbutz and moshav movements.

And so history repeats itself. As Israel's violent siege of Gaza continues, the Associated Press reported that dozens of Palestinians with American passports have left Gaza, escorted out of the Strip in a convoy of United Nations vehicles. One Palestinian American mother said she and her children could no longer stand the terrifying sonic booms produced by Israeli aircraft flying overhead during the night.[18] These fleeing Palestinians have two things that most of their kin in Gaza lack: they have lots of money that they might have invested in rebuilding Gaza's economy were Israel not intent on destroying it; and they are familiar with a language and ideas that might have conveyed very effectively to Western audiences the horror currently being endured by Gaza's civilian population. They are also among the least radicalized elements of Gaza's population and might have been the ones most willing to start a dialogue with Israel – had Israel shown any interest in negotiating. But of course their absence from Gaza, and flight to America, will not be mourned by Israel.

How much Israel fears the presence in the occupied territories of Palestinians who have lived in the West – those who have money and influence, and speak in a language the non-Arab world can understand – was highlighted in another, related piece of news that went mostly unnoticed. According to the *Ha'aretz* newspaper, Israel's Interior Ministry has been quietly implementing a new rule since April 2006 that allows it to refuse entry into both Israel and the occupied territories to Palestinians holding foreign passports.[19] Most of those affected are Palestinians who are today citizens of either America or Europe. Israel has this power over these Palestinians because, since its capture of the West Bank and Gaza in 1967, it has controlled both entry into the occupied territories and the Palestinian Population Registry, even after the Palestinian Authority was established.[20] In another sign of how mistaken Western observers are in believing that the occupation of Gaza somehow ended with the withdrawal of Jewish settlers last year, Israel has continued restricting access to the Strip, as well as the West Bank, since the disengagement.

The new exclusion policy affects thousands of the wealthiest and most educated Palestinians, some of whom have been living in the occupied territories for a decade or more investing in the economy as entrepreneurs, teaching in the universities or establishing desperately needed civil society organizations. In another irony, many of these Palestinians have a foreign passport only because Israel stripped them of their rights to residency in the occupied territories in violation of international law. Using its control of the area's borders since 1967, Israel revoked the residency of many Palestinians while they were studying or working abroad. As the Israeli journalist Amira Hass documented in a recent dispatch, some of these Palestinians eventually came back to the occupied territories after marrying a local Palestinian resident but were refused rights of residency they should be entitled to according to Israel's laws of family unification.[21] Instead they remained in the occupied territories at Israel's discretion. As long as they renewed their tourist visa every three months by crossing the border into Jordan or Egypt, they were left in relative peace.

But Israel is now unilaterally changing the rules (as it always does), even if it has been too embarrassed to declare the fact openly. Apparently the US embassy has been aware of the change for some time but did not think it should intervene in the 'sovereign decisions' of another country – or, more accurately, in the decisions of a sovereign country, Israel, that violate the rights of an occupied people, the Palestinians.[22] Palestinians with US passports have been told by Israel that, when their three-month visas expire, they will no longer be entitled to enter the occupied territories to visit their families – except in rare 'humanitarian cases' such as a close relative dying. Some will be separated from their spouse and children, while others will lose their businesses and everything they have invested in them. With foreign passport holders forced to leave the occupied territories, the pressure is sure to grow on their families left behind in Gaza and the West Bank to seek ways to emigrate abroad to be with them again. The purpose of Israel's current bureaucratic obscenity is the same as it was in 1948, when the highest priority was clearing Palestinian cities of their elites to make way for the establishment of the Jewish state.

This time Israel needs to empty the ghettoes it is crafting for the Palestinians of the most educated and well-connected of their number so that it can more credibly claim that there is no one 'moderate' to talk to. Any Palestinian with a stake in peace, even an Israeli-imposed one that damages Palestinian national interests, will have been forced out by Israel's policies long before. Those who remain behind, trapped by walls of concrete and steel, will be powerless to resist the unilateral and illegal expansion of Israel's borders explicit in Ehud Olmert's convergence plan and the building of the wall. When the only noise heard from the Palestinians in their cages is the occasional whine of a home-made Qassam rocket flying out of the ghetto into the Jewish state, we will be told by Israel and its US ally that terror is the only language the Palestinians know. But, in truth, it may be the only language the Palestinians have been left to speak.

An Experiment in Human Despair
(*July 2006*)

One needed only to watch the interview on British television this week with Israel's deputy ambassador to the UK to realize that the Israeli army's tightening of the siege on Gaza, its invasion of the northern parts of the Strip, and the looming humanitarian crisis across the territory have nothing to do with the recent capture of an Israeli soldier – or even the feeble home-made Qassam rockets fired, usually ineffectually, into Israel by Palestinian militants. Under questioning from presenter Jon Snow of Channel Four News on the reasons behind Israel's bombing of Gaza's only power station – thereby cutting off electricity to more than half of the Strip's 1.4 million inhabitants for many months ahead, as well as threatening the water supply that depends on electricity generation – Zvi Ravner denied this action amounted to collective punishment of the civilian population.[23] Rather, he claimed, the electricity station had to be disabled to prevent the soldier's captors from having the light needed to smuggle him out of Gaza at night. It was left to a bemused Jon Snow to point out that smugglers usually prefer to do their work in the dark and that Israel's actions were more likely to assist his captors than disadvantage them.

The *Alice through the Looking Glass* quality of Israeli disinformation over the combined siege and invasion of Gaza – and its widespread and credulous repetition by the Western media – is successfully distracting attention from Israel's real goals in this one-sided war of attrition. The current destruction of Gaza's civilian and administrative infrastructure is reminiscent of the Israeli army's cruel rampages through the streets of West Bank cities in the repeated invasions of 2002 and 2003, and the Jewish settlers' malicious attacks on Palestinian farmers trying to collect their olive harvests. The relative absence today of these horror stories from the West Bank is simply a reflection of the terrible success of the wall Israel has built across Palestinian farmland and around Palestinian population centres. Settlers no longer need to plunder the olive harvest when the fruit is being left to rot on the trees because farmers can no longer reach their groves.

In the case of the West Bank invasions, Israeli tanks rolled easily into Palestinian cities that had already been isolated and crippled by the stranglehold of checkpoints and roadblocks all over the territory. Israeli heavy armour knocked down electricity pylons as though it was playing a game of ten-pin bowling, snipers shot up the water tanks on people's roofs, soldiers defecated into office photocopiers and the army sought out Palestinian ministries so that their confidential records and documents could be destroyed or stolen.[24] Notably, only in the warren of alleys in the overcrowded refugee camps of Jenin and Nablus did the army find the going far tougher and suffer relatively high casualties. Which may explain the military caution exercised by Prime Minister Ehud Olmert in launching a ground invasion of Gaza. The tiny Strip, besieged on its land borders by the Israeli army behind an electronic fence and on the seafront by the Israeli navy, is one giant, overcrowded refugee camp. The past week has seen Gaza 'softened up' with airstrikes on its infrastructure and government ministries.

Three long-standing motives are discernible in Israel's current menacing of Gaza. First, Israel is determined to continue its campaign of impairing the Palestinian Authority's ability to govern. This has nothing to do with the recent election of Hamas to run the Palestinian Authority. Israel's official policy of unilateralism – ignoring the wishes of the Palestinian people – began long before, when Yasser Arafat was in charge. It has continued through the presidency of Mahmoud Abbas, a leader who is about as close to a quisling as Israel is likely to find. Hamas's electoral success has merely supplied Israel with the pretext it needs for launching its invasion and the grounds for demanding international support as it chokes the life out of Gaza. Israel doubtless hopes that at the end of this process it will be left with Abbas, a figurehead president backed into a corner and ready to put his name to whatever agreement Israel imposes.

Second, the attack on Gaza – as ever – is partly a distraction from the real battle. It was widely recognized that Ariel Sharon's dogged pursuit of his Gaza disengagement policy last year was designed to free his hand for the annexation of large chunks of a greater prize, the West Bank, and for securing the biggest prize of all, East Jerusalem. Nothing has changed on this front. As Israel keeps all eyes directed towards the suffering in Gaza, it continues the creeping process of annexation in the West Bank and Jerusalem. Particularly significant are the overlooked manoeuvres Israel is undertaking in East Jerusalem. Last week Israel stripped four Hamas MPs of their right to live in East Jerusalem, effectively expelling them to the West Bank. It also showed that it could lock up them and dozens of other democratically elected Palestinian representatives with barely a peep from the international community.[25] Few in the media bothered to note that the MPs are being deprived of even their most basic rights, such as meeting with a lawyer.[26] As the four Jerusalem MPs' legal advisers have argued, it is a nonsense that Israel allowed these Hamas politicians to stand in the recent elections and now, after their victory, calls their membership of the party 'support for terrorism'. It is also a disturbing sign of how easily Israel will be able to begin ethnically cleansing East Jerusalem of its Palestinian inhabitants using the flimsiest of excuses.

And third, and perhaps most significantly of all, Israel is using the siege and invasion of Gaza as a laboratory for testing policies it also intends to apply to the West Bank after completion of the wall. Gazans are the guinea pigs on whom Olmert can try out the 'extreme action' he has been boasting of.[27] The destruction of Gaza's power plant and loss of electricity to some 700,000 people; the consequent scarcity of water, build-up of sewage that cannot be disposed of, and inevitable spread of disease; the shortages of fuel and threats to the running of vital services such as hospitals; the sonic booms of Israeli aircraft that terrify Gaza's children and unpredictable air strikes that terrify everyone; the inability of Palestinian officials to run bombed ministries and provide services; the constant threat of invasion by massed Israeli troops on the 'border'; and the breakdown of law and order as Fatah and Hamas gunmen are encouraged to turn on each other. All these factors are designed to one end: the slow demand by Palestinians, civilians and militants alike, to clear out of the hell-hole of Gaza.

One day the traffic through the tunnels that have served Gaza's smugglers will change direction: where once cigarettes and arms came into Gaza, the likelihood is that soon it will be people passing through those underground passages to leave Gaza and seek a life outside. If this experiment in human despair works in the small Gaza Strip, its lessons can be applied to much bigger effect in the West Bank ghettoes being created. This is how ethnic cleansing looks when it is designed not by butchers in uniforms but by technocrats in suits.

The Struggle for Palestine's Soul
(*October 2006*)

The message delivered to US Secretary of State Condoleezza Rice this week by Israeli officials is that the humanitarian and economic disaster befalling Gaza has a single, reversible cause: the capture by Palestinian fighters of an Israeli soldier, Gilad Shalit, in late June from a perimeter artillery position that had been shelling Gaza. When Shalit is returned, negotiations can start – or so Rice was told by Israel's defence minister, Amir Peretz.[28] If Peretz and others are to be believed, the gunmen could have done themselves and the 1.4 million people of Gaza a favour and simply executed Shalit weeks ago. Israel doubtless would have inflicted terrible retribution, such as the bombing of the Strip's only power station – except, of course, it had already done that to avenge Shalit's capture. But according to Peretz's logic, with the Israeli soldier dead, there would have been no obstacle to sitting down and talking. Yet, as we all know, there would have been. Because Israel's refusal to negotiate – and its crushing of Gaza – long predates the capture of Shalit.

Israel's occupation began four decades ago, long before anyone had heard, or dreamt, of Hamas. Israel's rampages through Gaza have continued unabated, even though Hamas's military wing refrained from retaliating to Israeli provocations and maintained a ceasefire for more than a year and a half. Shalit is the current pretext, but there are a host of others that can be adopted should the need arise. And that is because as far as Israel and its American patron are concerned, any Palestinian resistance to the illegal occupation of Gaza and the West Bank is unacceptable. Whatever the Palestinians do – apart from submitting willingly to occupation and permanently renouncing their right to statehood – is justification for Israeli 'retaliation'. Absolute political and military inactivity is the only approved option for the Palestinians, both because it implies acceptance of the occupation and because then the world can quietly forget about the suffering in Gaza and the West Bank. On the other hand, Palestinian activity of any kind – and especially in pursuit of goals like national liberation – must be punished.

All this provides the context for decoding the latest events unfolding in Gaza, as rival fighters from Fatah and Hamas confront each other violently on the streets. This is the moment Israel has long been waiting for, from the moment a Likud government that included Ariel Sharon began seriously meddling in internal Palestinian politics by helping to establish the Muslim Brotherhood organization that later became Hamas. Israel hoped that an Islamist party would be a bulwark against the growing popularity of Yasser Arafat's exiled Fatah party and its secular Palestinian nationalism. Things, of course, did not go quite to plan. In the first intifada that erupted in 1987, Hamas adopted the same assertive agenda of Palestinian national liberation (with added Islamic trimmings) as Fatah. The two groups' goals complemented each other rather than conflicted. Later, after Israel finally allowed Arafat to return to the occupied territories under the terms of the Oslo Accords, the Palestinian president avoided as far as possible carrying out Israeli demands to crack down on Hamas, understanding that this risked provoking a civil war that would damage Palestinian society and weaken the chances of eventual statehood.

Similarly, Arafat's successor, Mahmoud Abbas, resisted confronting Hamas almost as studiously as he has avoided challenging Israeli diktats. Instead, until recently at least, we saw fighters from Hamas and Fatah in Gaza cooperating on several attacks on Israeli military positions.[29] But this week's clashes in Gaza are the first sign that Israel may be succeeding in its designs to deflect the Palestinian resistance from its common goal of national liberation – to achieve a state – by redirecting its energies into fratricidal war. Or as Zeev Schiff, a veteran *Ha'aretz* commentator with exceptional contacts in the military, observed: 'Lesson number 1 is that the international financial and economic siege of the Hamas government, which is being led by the United States, is succeeding.'[30]

Certainly the economic blockade has nothing to do with securing the return of Shalit, as even a senior Israeli army officer and self-styled 'counter-terrorism expert' warned this week. 'Due to the disagreements between the two sides [Hamas and Fatah], the soldier's release is not in sight', Col. Moshe Marzouk told the website of the Israeli daily *Yediot Aharonot.*[31] Instead, the economic strangulation of Gaza has been the catalyst for internal Palestinian conflict. Inevitably, social bonds grow weak and fragile, even tear, when nearly half the population is unemployed and more than three-quarters are living in poverty. If children are hungry, parents will contemplate opposing their government – even if they agree with its goals – to put food on the table. But the immiseration of Gaza does not, of itself, explain why the clashes are taking place, or what is motivating the factions. This is not just about who will get the scraps from the master's table, or even a struggle between two parties – Hamas and Fatah – for control of the government. It is now no less than a battle for the very soul of Palestinian nationalism.

It is no coincidence that the international community, at Israel's behest, has been making three demands of the Hamas government that supposedly justify the throttling of Gaza's economy. The conditions are now well known: recognizing Israel, renouncing violence, and abiding by previous agreements. Let us put aside Israel's worse failure – as the stronger party – to honour any of these conditions itself. But more strangely, observers have also failed to note both that Fatah, under Arafat, agreed to all three conditions years ago and that Fatah's compliance to Israeli demands never helped advance the struggle for statehood by one inch. Arafat and the PLO recognized Israel back in the late 1980s, and the Palestinian leader put his signature to this recognition again in the Oslo Accords.[32] In returning to the occupied territories as head of the Palestinian Authority, Arafat also renounced violence against Israel. He headed the new security forces whose job was to crack down on Palestinian dissent, not respond to Israel's many military provocations or fight the occupation. And of course, Arafat and Fatah, unlike Israel, had every reason to want previous agreements honoured: they mistakenly believed that they were their best hope of winning statehood. They did not factor in Israel's bad faith, and its continuation and intensification of the settlement project. So the lesson learnt by Hamas from the Fatah years of rule is that these conditions were and are only a trap, and that they were imposed by Israel to win Palestinian obeisance to the occupation, not national liberation. During the Oslo years, the benefits of accepting Israeli conditions accrued not in a peace dividend that led to Palestinian statehood but in rewards that flowed from collaboration with the occupation, a stealthy corruption that enriched many of Fatah's leaders and kept its followers in the large government bureaucracy at a basic standard of living.

Following the outbreak of the second intifada, a majority of ordinary Palestinian voters began to understand how terminally damaging Fatah's complicity with the occupation had become. For example, as Palestinian, Israeli and international activists tried to demonstrate against the building of Israel's wall across the West Bank, and the subsequent annexation of large swathes of Palestinian land to Israel, the protesters found obstacles placed in their way at every turn by the ruling Fatah party. Its leaders did not want to jeopardize their cement and building contracts with Israel by ending the wall's progress. Liberation was delayed for the more immediate prize of remuneration.[33] By signing up to the same conditions as Fatah, Hamas would be as good as abandoning its goal of national liberation, as well as forsaking the majority of voters who realized that Fatah's corrupt relationship with Israel had to end. Hamas would self-destruct, which is reason enough why Israel is making such strenuous demands of the international community to force Hamas to comply.

The struggle on the streets of Gaza is a defining moment, one that may eventually decide whether a real national unity government – one seeking Palestinian statehood – is possible. The question is: will Fatah force Hamas to cave in to Israeli demands and co-opt it, or will Hamas force Fatah to abandon its collaboration and return to the original path of national liberation? The stakes could not be higher. If Hamas wins, then the Palestinians will have the chance to re-energize the intifada, launch a proper, consensual fight to end the occupation, one that unites the secular and religious, and try to face down the bullying of the international community. As with most national liberation struggles, the price in lives and suffering is likely to be steep. If Fatah wins and Hamas falls, we will be back to the Oslo process of official Palestinian collaboration with Israel and consent to the ghettoization of the population – this time behind walls. Such an arrangement may be done under Fatah rule or, more likely, under the favoured international option of government by Palestinian technocrats, presumably vetted by Israel and the United States.[34] The consequences are not difficult to divine. If the hopes of ordinary Palestinians for national liberation are dashed again, if Hamas falters just as Fatah did before it, these frustrated popular energies will resurface, finding a new release and one likely to have a different agenda from either Hamas or Fatah. If the goal of establishing a Palestinian state cannot be realized, then the danger is that many Palestinians will look elsewhere for their liberation, not necessarily in national but in wider regional and religious terms. The Islamic component of the struggle – at the moment a gloss, even for Hamas, on what is still a national liberation movement – will grow and deepen. National liberation will take a back seat to religious jihad.[35]

Do Israel and the United States not understand this? Or maybe, like serial felons who cannot de diverted from the path of crime, they are simply incapable of changing their ways.

7

Compromised Critics

Settler colonialism is distinguished from traditional colonialism (which is primarily concerned with the indigenous population's exploitation) by its intention to replace the natives with members of the colonizing group. In these circumstances, the colonized have historically sought the solidarity and active assistance of dissident members of the settler community in the struggle to liberate themselves. The black population under apartheid, for example, came to rely on a growing number of white South Africans whose support contributed to the erosion of apartheid's legitimacy. In the case of Palestine, such solidarity is even more crucial given the success the colonizer, Israel, has enjoyed in exploiting its people's historic oppression, which culminated in the Holocaust, to shield itself from criticism of its policies towards the Palestinians. In these essays I reflect on the failure of most Israeli left-wingers and human rights activists to offer such solidarity and break out of the intellectual straitjacket of Zionism.

In 'Hollow Visions of the Future' I argue that two prominent members of the Israeli left, David Grossman and Uri Avnery, share as their central concern the continued existence of Israel as a Jewish state. Rather than identifying with the oppressed, they search for convoluted ways – often mistaken as sensitivity on their part – to grant legitimacy to an ethnic state and its ideology of settler colonialism.

Such intellectual compromises sometimes also taint the work of Israeli human rights groups such as B'Tselem, as I explain in 'Bad Faith'. Israel's malevolent bombing of Gaza's power station, for example, was harshly criticized in a B'Tselem report that referred to it as an 'act of vengeance' for the earlier capture of an Israeli soldier. At a deeper level, however, B'Tselem's characterization of the power station's destruction concealed rather than illuminated the nature of Israeli policy towards the victims of its settler colonialism. The bombing was not an emotional overreaction to a specific event but part of a consistent and systematic policy designed to make life unbearable for Gazans.

In 'No Right to Non-violent Resistance' I consider a related failure to hold accountable the colonizer by the internationally respected Human Rights Watch. In a particularly egregious example of taking the trend of 'blaming the victim' to its appalling logical conclusion, as well as of identifying with the colonizer, HRW produced a report that effectively denied Palestinians a right not only to resist their occupation but to organize non-violently as well.

Hollow Visions of the Future
(*November 2006*)

David Grossman's speech at the annual memorial rally for Yitzhak Rabin earlier this month was widely publicized.[1] One of Israel's foremost writers and a figurehead for its main peace movement, Peace Now, Grossman personifies the caring, tortured face of Zionism that so many of the country's apologists – in Israel and abroad, trenchant and wavering alike – desperately want to believe survives, despite the evidence. Grossman makes it possible to believe, for a moment, that the Ariel Sharons and Ehud Olmerts are not the real upholders of Zionism's legacy, merely a temporary deviation from its true path.

In reality, of course, Grossman draws from the same ideological wellspring as Israel's founders and its greatest warriors. He embodies the same anguished values of Labor Zionism that won Israel international legitimacy just as it was carrying out one of history's great acts of ethnic cleansing: the expulsion of some 750,000 Palestinians, or 80 per cent of the native population, from the borders of the newly established Jewish state. Remove the halo with which he has been crowned by the world's liberal media and Grossman is little different from Zionism's most distinguished statesmen, those who also ostentatiously displayed their hand-wringing or peace credentials as, first, they dispossessed the Palestinian people of most of their homeland in 1948; then dispossessed them of the rest in 1967; and today are working on the slow genocide of the Palestinians, through a combined strategy of their physical destruction and their dispersion as a people.

David Ben-Gurion, for example, masterminded the ethnic cleansing of Palestine in 1948 before very publicly agonizing over the occupation of the West Bank and Gaza – because of the demographic damage that would be done to the Jewish state as a result. Golda Meir refused to recognize the existence of the Palestinian people as she launched the settlement enterprise in the occupied territories, but did recognize the anguish of Jewish soldiers forced to 'shoot and cry' to defend the occupation. Or as she put it: 'We can forgive you [the Arabs] for killing our sons. But we will never forgive you for making us kill yours.'[2] Yitzhak Rabin, Grossman's most direct inspiration, may have initiated a 'peace process' at Oslo (even if only the terminally optimistic today believe that peace was really its goal), but as a soldier and politician he also personally oversaw the ethnic cleansing of Palestinian cities like Lydd in 1948; he ordered tanks into Arab villages inside Israel during the Land Day protests of 1976, leading to the deaths of six unarmed Palestinian citizens; and in 1988 he ordered his army to crush the first intifada by 'breaking the bones' of Palestinians, including women and children, who threw stones at the occupying troops.

Like them, Grossman conspires in these original war crimes by preferring to hold on to what Israel has, or even extend it further, rather than confront the genuinely painful truth of his responsibility for the fate of the Palestinians, including the hundreds of thousands of refugees and the millions of their descendants. Every day that Grossman denies a Right of Return for the Palestinians, even as he supports a Law of Return for the Jews, he excuses and maintains the act of ethnic cleansing that dispossessed the Palestinian refugees more than half a century ago. And every day that he sells a message of peace to Israelis who look to him for moral guidance that fails to offer the Palestinians a just solution – and that takes instead as its moral yardstick the primacy of Israel's survival as a Jewish state – then he perverts the meaning of peace.

Another Israeli peace activist, Uri Avnery, diagnoses the problem posed by Grossman and his ilk with acute insight in a recent article. Although Grossman wants peace in the abstract, Avnery observes, he offers no solutions as to how it might be secured in concrete terms and no clues about what sacrifices he or other Israelis will have to make to achieve it. His 'peace' is empty of content, a mere rhetorical device.[3] Rather than suggest what Israel should talk about to the Palestinians' elected leaders, Grossman argues that Israel should talk over their heads to the 'moderates', Palestinians with whom Israeli leaders can do business. The goal is to find Palestinians, any Palestinians, who will agree to Israel's 'peace'. The Oslo process in new clothes. Grossman's speech looks like a gesture towards a solution only because Israel's current leaders do not want to speak with anybody on the Palestinian side, whether 'moderate' or 'fanatic'. The only interlocutor is Washington, and a passive one at that.

If Grossman's words are as 'hollow' as those of Ehud Olmert, Avnery offers no clue as to the reasons for the author's evasiveness. In truth, Grossman cannot deal in solutions because there is almost no constituency in Israel for the kind of peace plan that might prove acceptable even to the Palestinian 'moderates' Grossman so wants his government to talk to. Were Grossman to set out the terms of his vision of peace, it might become clear to all that the problem is not Palestinian, but Israeli, intransigence.

Although surveys regularly show that a majority of Israelis support a Palestinian state, they are conducted by pollsters who never specify to their sampling audience what might be entailed by the creation of the state posited in their question. Equally the pollsters do not require from their Israeli respondents any information about what kind of Palestinian state each envisages. This makes the nature of the Palestinian state being talked about by Israelis almost as empty of content as the alluring word 'peace'. After all, according to most Israelis, Gazans are enjoying the fruits of the end of Israel's occupation. And according to Olmert, his proposed 'convergence' – a very limited withdrawal from the West Bank to behind the lines created by the 'separation wall' – will establish the basis for a Palestinian state there too. When Israelis are asked about their view of more specific peace plans, their responses are overwhelmingly negative. In 2003, for example, 78 per cent of Israeli Jews said they favoured a two-state solution, but when asked if they supported the Geneva Initiative – which envisions a very circumscribed Palestinian state on less than all of the West Bank and Gaza – only a quarter did so. Barely more than half of the supposedly left-wing voters of Labor backed the Geneva Initiative.[4] This low level of support for a barely viable Palestinian state contrasts with the consistently high levels of support among Israeli Jews for a concrete, but very different, solution to the conflict: 'transfer', or ethnic cleansing. In opinion polls, 60 per cent of Israeli Jews regularly favour the emigration of Arab citizens from the as-yet-undetermined borders of the Jewish state.

So when Grossman warns us that 'a peace of no choice' is inevitable and that 'the land will be divided, a Palestinian state will arise', we should not be lulled into false hopes. Grossman's state is almost certainly as 'hollow' as his audience's idea of peace. His refusal to confront the lack of sympathy among the Israeli public for the Palestinians, or challenge it with solutions that will require of Israelis that they make real sacrifices for peace, deserves our condemnation. He and the other gurus of Israel's mainstream peace movement, writers like Amos Oz and A.B. Yehoshua, have failed in their duty to articulate to Israelis a vision of a fair future and a lasting peace.

So what is the way out of the impasse created by the beatification of figures like Grossman? What other routes are open to those of us who refuse to believe that Grossman stands at the very precipice before which any sane peace activist would tremble? Can we look to other members of the Israeli left for inspiration? Uri Avnery again steps forward. He claims that there are only two peace camps in Israel: a Zionist one, based on a national consensus rooted in the Peace Now of David Grossman; and what he calls a 'radical peace camp' led by ... well, himself and his group of a few thousand Israelis known as Gush Shalom. By this, one might be tempted to infer that Avnery styles his own peace bloc as non-Zionist or even anti-Zionist. Nothing could be further from the truth, however. Avnery and most, though not all, of his supporters in Israel are staunchly in the Zionist camp. The bottom line in any peace for Avnery is the continued existence and success of Israel as a Jewish state. That rigidly limits his ideas about what sort of peace a 'radical' Israeli peace activist ought to be pursuing.

Like Grossman, Avnery supports a two-state solution because, in both their views, the future of the Jewish state cannot be guaranteed without a Palestinian state alongside it. This is why Avnery confesses to agreeing with 90 per cent of Grossman's speech. If the Jews are to prosper as a demographic (and democratic) majority in their state, then the non-Jews must have a state too, one in which they can exercise their own separate sovereign rights and, consequently, abandon any claims on the Jewish state. However, unlike Grossman, Avnery not only supports a Palestinian state in the abstract but a 'just' Palestinian state in the concrete, meaning for him the evacuation of all the settlers and a full withdrawal by the Israeli army to the 1967 lines. Avnery's peace plan would give back East Jerusalem and the whole of the West Bank and Gaza to the Palestinians. The difference between Grossman and Avnery on this point can be explained by their different understanding of what is needed to ensure the Jewish state's survival. Avnery believes that a lasting peace will hold only if the Palestinian state meets the minimal aspirations of the Palestinian people. In his view, the Palestinians can be persuaded under the right leadership to settle for 22 per cent of their historic homeland – and in that way the Jewish state will be saved.

Of itself, there is nothing wrong with Avnery's position. It has encouraged him to take a leading and impressive role in the Israeli peace movement for many decades. Bravely he has crossed national confrontation lines to visit the besieged Palestinian leadership when other Israelis have shied away. He has taken a courageous stand against the separation wall, facing down Israeli soldiers alongside Palestinian, Israeli and foreign peace activists. And through his journalism he has highlighted the Palestinian cause and educated Israelis, Palestinians and outside observers about the conflict. For all these reasons, Avnery should be praised as a genuine peacemaker. But there is a serious danger that, because Palestinian solidarity movements have misunderstood Avnery's motives, they may continue to be guided by him beyond the point where he is contributing to a peaceful solution or a just future for the Palestinians. In fact, that moment may be upon us.

During the Oslo years, Avnery was desperate to see Israel complete its supposed peace agreement with the Palestinian leader Yasser Arafat. As he often argued, he believed that Arafat alone could unify the Palestinians and persuade them to settle for the only two-state solution on the table: a big Israel, alongside a small Palestine.[5] In truth, Avnery's position was not so far from that of the distinctly unradical Oslo crowd of Rabin, Peres and Yossi Beilin. All four of them regarded Arafat as the Palestinian strongman who could secure Israel's future: Rabin hoped Arafat would police the Palestinians on Israel's behalf in their ghettoes; while Avnery hoped Arafat would forge a nation, democratic or otherwise, that would contain the Palestinians' ambitions for territory and a just solution to the refugee problem. Now with Arafat gone, Avnery and Gush Shalom have lost their ready-made solution to the conflict. Today, they still back two states and support engagement with Hamas. They have also not deviated from their long-standing positions on the main issues – Jerusalem, borders, settlements and refugees – even if they no longer have the glue, Arafat, that was supposed to make it all stick together.

Without Arafat as their strongman, however, Gush Shalom have no idea about how to address the impending issues of factionalism and potential civil war that Israel's meddling in the Palestinian political process is unleashing. They will also have no response if the tide on the Palestinian street turns against the two-state mirage offered by Oslo. If Palestinians look for other ways out of the current impasse, as they are starting to do, Avnery will quickly become an obstacle to peace rather than its great defender. In fact, such a development is all but certain. Few knowledgeable observers of the conflict believe the two-state solution based on the 1967 lines is feasible any longer, given Israel's entrenchment of its settlers in East Jerusalem and the West Bank, now numbering nearly half a million. Even the Americans have publicly admitted that most of the settlements cannot be undone.[6] It is only a matter of time before Palestinians make the same calculation. What will Avnery, and the diehards of Gush Shalom, do in this event? How will they respond if Palestinians start to clamour for a single state embracing both Israelis and Palestinians, for example?

The answer is that the 'radical' peaceniks will quickly need to find another solution to protect their Jewish state. There are not too many available:

- there is the 'Carry on with the occupation regardless' of Binyamin Netanyahu and Likud;
- there is the 'Seal the Palestinians into ghettoes and hope eventually they will leave of their own accord', in its Kadima (hard) and Labor (soft) incarnations;
- there is the 'Expel them all' of Avigdor Lieberman, Olmert's Minister of Strategic Threats.

Paradoxically, a variation on the last option may be the most appealing to the disillusioned peaceniks of Gush Shalom. Lieberman has his own fanatical and moderate positions, depending on his audience and the current realities. To some he says he wants all Palestinians expelled from Greater Israel so that it is available only for Jews.[7] But to others, particularly in the diplomatic arena, he suggests a formula of territorial and population swaps between Israel and the Palestinians that would create a 'Separation of Nations'.[8] Israel would get the settlements back in return for handing over some small areas of Israel, like the Little Triangle, densely populated with Palestinians. A generous version of such an exchange – though a violation of international law – would achieve a similar outcome to Gush Shalom's attempts to create a viable Palestinian state alongside Israel. Even if Avnery is unlikely to be lured down this path himself, there is a real danger that others in the 'radical' peace camp will prefer this kind of solution over sacrificing their absolute commitment to the Jewish state.

But fortunately, whatever Avnery claims, his peace camp is not the only alternative to the sham agonizing of Peace Now. Avnery is no more standing at the very edge of the abyss than Grossman. The only abyss Avnery is looking into is the demise of his Jewish state.

Other Zionist Jews, in Israel and abroad, have been grappling with the same kinds of issues as Avnery but have begun to move in a different direction, away from the doomed two-state solution towards a single state. A few prominent intellectuals like Tony Judt, Meron Benvenisti and Jeff Halper have publicly begun to question their commitment to Zionism and consider whether it is not part of the problem rather than the solution. They are not doing this alone. Small groups of Israelis, smaller than Gush Shalom, are abandoning Zionism and coalescing around new ideas about how Israeli Jews and Palestinians might live peacefully together, including inside one state. They include Ta'ayush, Anarchists Against the Wall, Zochrot and elements within the Israeli Committee against House Demolitions and Gush Shalom itself. Avnery hopes that his peace camp may be the small wheel that can push the larger wheel of organizations like Peace Now in a new direction and thereby shift Israeli opinion towards a real two-state solution. Given the realities on the ground, that seems highly unlikely. But one day, wheels currently smaller than Gush Shalom may begin to push Israel in the direction needed for peace.

Bad Faith
(September 2006)

A mistake too often made by those examining Israel's behaviour in the occupied territories – or when analysing its treatment of Arabs in general – is to assume that Israel is acting in good faith. Even its most trenchant critics can fall into this trap. Such a reluctance to attribute bad faith was demonstrated this week by Israel's foremost human rights group, B'Tselem, when it published a report into the bombing by the Israeli air force of Gaza's power plant in late June. The horrifying consequences of this act of collective punishment – a war crime, as B'Tselem rightly notes – are clearly laid out in the report.[9] The group warns that electricity is available to most of Gaza's 1.4 million inhabitants for a few hours a day, and running water for a similar period. The sewerage system has all but collapsed, with the resulting risk of the spread of dangerous infectious disease. In their daily lives, Gazans can no longer rely on the basic features of modern existence. Their fridges are as good as useless, threatening outbreaks of food poisoning. The elderly and infirm living in apartments can no longer leave their homes because elevators do not work, or are unpredictable. Hospitals and doctors' clinics struggle to offer essential medical services. Small businesses, most of which rely on the power and water supplies, from food shops and laundry services to factories and workshops, are being forced to close. Rapidly approaching, says B'Tselem, is the moment when Gaza's economy – already under an internationally backed siege to penalize the Palestinians for democratically electing a Hamas government – will simply expire under the strain.

Unfortunately, however, B'Tselem loses the plot when it comes to explaining why Israel would choose to inflict such terrible punishment on the people of Gaza. Apparently, it was out of a thirst for revenge: the group's report is even entitled *Act of Vengeance*. Israel, it seems, wanted revenge for the capture a few days earlier of an Israeli soldier, Gilad Shalit, from a border tank position used to fire artillery into Gaza. The problem with the 'revenge' theory is that, however much a rebuke it is, it presupposes a degree of good faith on the part of the vengeance-seeker. You steal my toy in the playground, and I lash out and hit you. I have acted badly – even 'disproportionately', to use a vogue word B'Tselem also adopts[10] – but no one would deny that my emotions were honest. There was no subterfuge or deception in my anger. I incur blame only because I failed to control my impulses. There is even the implication that, though my action was unwarranted, my fury was justified.

But why should we think Israel is acting in good faith, even if in bad temper, in destroying Gaza's power station? Why should we assume it was a hot-headed overreaction rather than a coldly calculated deed? In other words, why believe Israel is simply lashing out when it commits a war crime rather than committing it after careful advance planning? Is it not possible that such war crimes, rather than being spontaneous and random, are actually all pushing in the same direction? More especially, why should we give Israel the benefit of the doubt when its war crimes contribute, as the bombing of the power station in Gaza surely does, to easily deciphered objectives? Why not think of the bombing instead as one instalment in a long-running and slowly unfolding plan?

The occupation of Gaza did not begin this year, after Hamas was elected, nor did it end with the disengagement a year ago. The occupation is four decades old and still going strong in both the West Bank and Gaza. In that time Israel has followed a consistent policy of subjugating the Palestinian population, imprisoning it inside ever-shrinking ghettos, sealing it off from contact with the outside world, and destroying its chances of ever developing an independent economy.

Since the outbreak of the second intifada – the Palestinians' uprising against the occupation – Israel has tightened its system of controls. It has sought to do so through two parallel, reinforcing approaches. First, it has imposed forms of collective punishment to weaken Palestinian resolve to resist the occupation, and encourage factionalism and civil war. Second, it has 'domesticated' suffering inside the ghettos, ensuring each Palestinian finds himself isolated from his neighbours, his concerns reduced to the domestic level: how to receive a house permit, or get past the wall to school or university, or visit a relative illegally imprisoned in Israel, or stop yet more family land being stolen, or reach his olive groves. The goals of both sets of policies, however, are the same: the erosion of Palestinian society's cohesiveness, the disruption of efforts at solidarity and resistance, and ultimately the slow drift of Palestinians away from vulnerable rural areas into the relative safety of urban centres – and eventually, as the pressure continues to mount, on into neighbouring Arab states, such as Jordan and Egypt. Seen in this light, the bombing of the Gaza power station fits neatly into Israel's long-standing plans for the Palestinians. Vengeance has nothing to do with it.

Another recent, more predictable, example was an email exchange published on the Media Lens website involving the BBC's Middle East editor, Jeremy Bowen, who was questioned about why the BBC had failed to report on an important joint peace initiative begun this summer by a small group of Israeli rabbis and Hamas politicians.[11] A public meeting where the two sides would have unveiled their initiative was foiled when Israel's Shin Bet secret service, presumably with the approval of the Israeli government, blocked the Hamas MPs from entering Jerusalem.[12] Bowen, though implicitly critical of Israel's behaviour, believes the initiative was of only marginal significance. He doubts that the Shin Bet or the government were overly worried by the meeting – in his words, it was seen as no more than a 'minor irritant' – because the Israeli peace camp has shown a great reluctance to get involved with the Palestinians since the outbreak of the intifada in 2000. The Israeli government would not want Hamas looking 'more respectable', he admits, but adds that that is because 'they believe that it is a terrorist organization out to kill Jews and to destroy their country'. In short, the Israeli government cracked down on the initiative because they believed Hamas was not a genuine partner for peace. Again, at least apparently in Bowen's view, Israel was acting in good faith: when it warns that it cannot talk with Hamas because it is a terrorist organization, it means what it says.

But what if, for a second, we abandon the assumption of good faith? Hamas comprises a paramilitary wing, a political wing and a network of welfare charities. Israel chooses to characterize all these activities as terrorist in nature, refusing to discriminate between the group's different wings. It denies that Hamas could have multiple identities in the same way the Irish Republican Army, which included a political wing called Sinn Fein, clearly did. Some of Israel's recent actions might fit with such a simplistic view of Hamas. Israel tried to prevent Hamas from standing in the Palestinian elections, only backing down after the Americans insisted on the group's participation.[13] Israel now appears to be destroying the Palestinians' governing institutions, claiming that once in Hamas's hands they will be used to promote terror. The Israeli government, it could be argued, acts in these ways because it is genuinely persuaded that even the political wing of Hamas is cover for terrorist activity.

But most other measures suggest that in reality Israel has a different agenda. Since the Palestinian elections six months ago, Israel's policies towards Hamas have succeeded in achieving one end: the weakening of the group's moderates, especially the newly elected politicians, and the strengthening of the militants. In the debate inside Hamas about whether to move towards politics, diplomacy and dialogue, or concentrate on military resistance, we can guess which side is currently winning. The moderates, not the militants, have been damaged by the isolation of the elected Hamas government, imposed by the international community at Israel's instigation. The moderates, not the militants, have been weakened by Israel rounding up and imprisoning the group's MPs. The moderates, not the militants, have been harmed by the obstacles put in the way of Fatah and Hamas politicians by Israel to prevent a national unity government. And the approach of the moderates, not the militants, has been discredited by Israel's success in blocking the summer peace initiative between the Hamas MPs and the rabbis.

In other words, Israeli policies are encouraging the extremist and militant elements inside Hamas rather the political and moderate ones. So why not assume that is their aim? Why not assume that rather than wanting a dialogue, a real peace process and an eventual agreement with the Palestinians that might lead to Palestinian statehood, Israel wants an excuse to carry on with its four-decade occupation – even if it has to reinvent it through sleights of hand like the disengagement and convergence plans? Why not assume that Israel blocked the meeting between the rabbis and the Hamas MPs because it fears that such a dialogue might suggest to Israeli voters and the world that there are strong voices in Hamas prepared to consider an agreement with Israel, and that given a chance their strength and influence might grow? Why not assume that the Israeli government wanted to disrupt the contacts between Hamas and the rabbis for exactly the same reasons that it has repeatedly used violence to break up joint demonstrations in Palestinian villages like Bilin staged by Israeli and Palestinian peace activists opposed to the wall that is annexing Palestinian farmland to Israel?[14]

And why, unlike Bowen, not take seriously opinion polls like the one published this week that show 67 per cent of Israelis support negotiations with a Palestinian national unity government (that is, one including Hamas), and that 56 per cent favour talks with a Palestinian government whoever is leading it?[15] Could it be that faced with these kinds of statistics Israel's leaders are terrified that, if Hamas were given the chance to engage in a peace process, Israeli voters might start putting more pressure on their own government to make meaningful concessions? In other words, why not consider for a moment that Israel's stated view of Hamas may be a self-serving charade, that the Israeli government has invested its energies in discrediting Hamas, and before it secular Palestinian leaders, because it has no interest in peace and never has done? Its goal is the maintenance of the occupation on the best terms it can find for itself.

On much the same grounds, we should treat equally sceptically another recent Israeli policy: the refusal by the Israeli Interior Ministry to renew the tourist visas of Palestinians with foreign passports, thereby forcing them to leave their homes and families inside the occupied territories. Many of these Palestinians, who were originally stripped by Israel of their residency rights in violation of international law, often when they left to work or study abroad, have been living on renewable three-month visas for years, even decades.[16] Amazingly, this compounding of the original violation of these Palestinian families' rights has received almost no media coverage and so far provoked not a peep of outrage from the big international human rights organizations, such as Human Rights Watch and Amnesty International. I can hazard a guess why. Unusually Israel has made no serious attempt to justify this measure. Furthermore, unlike the two examples cited above, it is difficult to put forward even a superficially plausible reason why Israel needs to pursue this policy, except for the obvious motive: that Israel believes it has found another bureaucratic wheeze to deny a few more thousand Palestinians their birthright. It is another small measure designed to ethnically cleanse these Palestinians from what might have been their state, were Israel interested in peace.

Unlike the other two examples, it is impossible to assume any good faith on Israel's part in this story: the measure has no security value, not even of the improbable variety, nor can it be sold as an overreaction – vengeance – to a provocation by the group affected. Palestinians with foreign passports are among the richest, best educated and possibly among the most willing to engage in dialogue with Israel. Many have large business investments in the occupied territories they wish to protect from further military confrontation, and most speak fluently the language of the international community – English. In other words, they might have been a bridgehead to a peace process were Israel genuinely interested in one. But as we have seen, Israel isn't. If only our media and human rights organizations could bring themselves to admit as much. But because they cannot, the transparently bad faith underpinning Israel's latest administrative attempt at ethnic cleansing may be allowed to pass without censure.

No Right to Non-violent Resistance
(November 2006)

If one thing offered a terrifying glimpse of where the experiment in human despair that is Gaza under Israeli siege is leading, it was the news that a Palestinian woman in her sixties – a grandmother – chose to strap on a suicide belt and explode herself next to a group of Israeli soldiers invading her refugee camp. Despite the 'Man bites dog' news value of the story, most of the Israeli media played down the incident. Not surprisingly: it is difficult to portray Fatma al-Najar as a crazed fanatic bent on the destruction of Israel.[17] It is equally difficult not to pause and wonder at the reasons for her suicide mission: according to her family, one of her grandsons was killed by the Israeli army, another is in a wheelchair after his leg had to be amputated, and her house had been demolished. Or not to think of the years of trauma she and her family have suffered living in an open-air prison under brutal occupation, and now, since the 'disengagement', the agonizing months of grinding poverty, slow starvation, repeated aerial bombardments, and the loss of essentials like water and electricity. Or not to ponder at what it must have been like for her to spend every day under a cloud of fear, to be powerless against a largely unseen and malign force, and to never know when death and mutilation might strike her or her loved ones.

Yet Western observers, and the organizations that should represent the very best of their Enlightenment values, seem incapable of understanding what might drive a grandmother to become a suicide bomber. Their empathy fails them, and so does their humanity.[18] Just at the moment Fatma was choosing death and resistance over powerlessness and victimhood – and at a time when Gaza is struggling through one of the most oppressive and ugly periods of Israeli occupation in nearly four decades – Human Rights Watch (HRW) published its latest statement on the conflict. It is a document that shames the organization, complacent Western societies and Fatma's memory.

In its press release 'Civilians Must Not Be Used to Shield Homes Against Military Attacks', which was widely reported by the international media, HRW lambasts armed Palestinian groups for calling on civilians to surround homes that have been targeted for air strikes by the Israeli military.[19] Noting almost as an afterthought that more than 1,500 Palestinians have been made homeless from house demolitions in the past few months, and that 105 houses have been destroyed from the air, the press release denounces Palestinian attempts at non-violent and collective action to halt the Israeli attacks. HRW refers in particular to three incidents. On 3 November, Hamas appealed to women to surround a mosque in Beit Hanoun where Palestinian men had sought shelter from the Israeli army. Israeli soldiers opened fire on the women, killing two and injuring at least ten.[20] And last week on two separate occasions, crowds of supporters gathered around the houses of men accused of being militants by Israel who had received phone messages from the Israeli security forces warning that their families' homes were about to be bombed.[21]

In language that would have made George Orwell shudder, one of the world's leading organizations for the protection of human rights ignored the continuing violation of the Palestinians' right to security and a roof over their heads, arguing instead: 'There is no excuse for calling [Palestinian] civilians to the scene of a planned [Israeli] attack. Whether or not the home is a legitimate military target, knowingly asking civilians to stand in harm's way is unlawful.' There is good reason to believe that this reading of international law is wrong, if not Kafkaesque. Popular and peaceful resistance to the oppressive policies of occupying powers and autocratic rulers, in India and South Africa for example, has always been, by its very nature, a risky venture in which civilians are liable to be killed or injured. Responsibility for those deaths must fall on those doing the oppressing, not those resisting, particularly when they are employing non-violent means. On HRW's interpretation, Mahatma Gandhi and Nelson Mandela would be war criminals.

HRW also applies a series of terrible double standards in its press release. First, while it refuses Palestinians the right to protect their homes from attack, labelling these civilians 'human shields' even though most of the homes are not legitimate military targets, it has not said a word about the common practice in Israel of building weapons factories and army bases inside or next to Israeli communities. In this way Israel has forced many civilians to become permanent human shields for the army, as was all too obvious during the month-long war against Hizbullah in summer 2006. And second, HRW prefers to highlight a supposed violation of international law by the Palestinians – their choice to act as 'human shields' – and demand the practice end immediately, while ignoring the very real and continuing violation of international law committed by Israel in undertaking punitive house demolitions against Palestinian families.

But let us ignore even these important issues and assume that HRW is technically correct that such Palestinian actions do violate international law. Nonetheless, HRW is still failing us and mocking its mandate, because it has lost sight of the three principles that must guide the vision of a human rights organization: a sense of priorities, proper context and common sense.

Priorities   Every day HRW has to choose which of the many abuses of international law taking place around the world it highlights. It manages to record only a tiny fraction of them. The assumption of many outsiders may be that it focuses on only the most egregious examples. That would be wrong. The simple truth is that the worse a state's track record on human rights, the easier ride it gets, relatively speaking, from human rights organizations. That is both because, if abuses are repeated often enough, they become so commonplace as to go unremarked, and because, if the abuses are wide-ranging and systematic, only a small number of the offences will be noted. Israel, unlike the Palestinians, benefits in both these respects. After four decades of reporting on Israel's occupation of the Palestinians, HRW has covered all of Israel's many human-rights-abusing practices at least once before. The result is that after a while most violations get ignored. Why issue another report on house demolitions or 'targeted assassinations', even though they are occurring all the time? And how should HRW record the individual violations of tens of thousands of Palestinians' rights every day at checkpoints? One report on the checkpoints every few years has to suffice instead.

In Israel's case, there is an added reluctance on the part of organizations like HRW to tackle the extent and nature of Israel's trampling of Palestinian rights. Constant press releases denouncing Israel would provoke accusations, as they do already, that Israel is being singled out – and with it, the implication that anti-Semitism lies behind the special treatment. So HRW chooses instead to equivocate. It ignores most Israeli violations and highlights every Palestinian infraction, however minor. This way it makes a pact with the devil: it achieves the balance that protects it from criticism but only by sacrificing the principles of equity and justice.

In its press release, for example, HRW treats the recent appeal to Palestinians to exercise their right to protect their neighbours, and to act in solidarity with non-violent resistance to occupation, as no different from the dozens of known violations committed by the Israeli army of abducting Palestinian civilians as human shields to protect its troops. Women volunteering to surround a mosque become the equivalent of notorious incidents such as that in August 2002 when Nidal Abu Mohsen, aged 19, was killed while standing in front of Israeli soldiers and knocking on the door of a wanted man near Nablus, or another in April 2004 when 13-year-old Mohammed Badwan was tied to an Israeli army Jeep being driven towards children throwing stones.[22]

Context   The actions of ordinary Palestinians occur within a framework in which all of their rights are already under the control of their occupier, Israel, and can be violated at its whim. This means that it is problematic, from a human rights perspective, to hold the Palestinians culpable for actions related to the occupation without laying far greater weight at the same time on the situation to which the Palestinians are reacting. Here is an example: HRW and other human rights organizations have taken the Palestinians to task for the extrajudicial killings of those suspected of collaborating with the Israeli security forces.[23] Although it is blindingly obvious that the lynching of an alleged collaborator is a violation of that person's fundamental right to life, HRW's position of simply blaming the Palestinians for this practice raises two critical problems.

First, it fudges the issue of accountability. In the case of a 'targeted assassination', Israel's version of extrajudicial killing, we have an address to hold accountable: the apparatus of a state in the form of the

Israeli army which carries out the murder and the Israeli politicians who approve it. (These officials are also responsible for the bystanders who are invariably killed along with the target.) But unless it can be shown that Palestinian lynchings are planned and coordinated at a high level, a human rights organization should not be applying the same legal standards to a crowd of Palestinians gripped by anger and the thirst for revenge as it does to a state. The two are not equivalent and cannot be held to account in the same way. Palestinians carrying out a lynching are committing a crime punishable under ordinary domestic law, while the Israeli army carrying out a 'targeted assassination' is committing state terrorism, which must be tried in the court of world opinion.

Second, HRW's position ignores the context in which the lynching takes place: under occupation. The Palestinian resistance to occupation has failed to realize its chief goal – national liberation – mainly because of Israel's extensive network of collaborators, individuals who have usually been terrorized by threats to themselves or their family and/or by torture into 'cooperating' with Israel's occupation forces. The great majority of planned Palestinian attacks are foiled because one member of the team is collaborating with Israel. He or she not only sabotages the attack but often also gives Israel the information it needs to kill the leaders of the resistance (as well as bystanders). Collaborators, though common in the West Bank and Gaza, are much despised – and for good reason. They make the goal of national liberation impossible. Paradoxically, their activities also encourage Palestinian fighters to pick easier targets, civilians rather than soldiers, in the hope that these attacks will not be foiled.

Palestinians have been struggling to find ways to make collaboration less appealing. When the Israeli army is threatening to jail your son, or refusing a permit for your wife to receive the hospital treatment she needs, you may agree to help the occupier in spite of yourself. Armed groups and many ordinary Palestinians countenance the lynchings because they are seen as a counterweight to Israel's own powerful techniques of intimidation – a deterrence, even if a largely unsuccessful one. In issuing a report on the extrajudicial killing of

Palestinian collaborators, therefore, groups like HRW have a duty to highlight first and with much greater emphasis the responsibility of Israel and its decades-long occupation for the lynchings, as the context in which Palestinians are forced to mimic the barbarity of those oppressing them to stand any chance of defeating them. The latest press release, denouncing the Palestinians for choosing collectively and peacefully to resist house demolitions while not concentrating on the violations committed by Israel in destroying the houses and using military forms of intimidation and punishment against civilians, is a travesty for this very same reason.

Common sense   And finally human rights organizations must never abandon common sense, the connecting thread of our humanity, when making judgements about where their priorities lie.

In the past few months Gaza has sunk into a humanitarian disaster engineered by Israel and the international community. What has been HRW's response? It is worth examining its most recent reports, those on the front page of the Middle East section of its website. Four stories relate to Israel and Palestine. Three criticize Palestinian militants and the wider society in various ways: for encouraging the use of 'human shields', for firing home-made rockets into Israel, and for failing to protect women from domestic violence. One report mildly rebukes Israel, urging the government to ensure that the army properly investigates the reasons for the shelling that killed nineteen Palestinian inhabitants of Beit Hanoun.[24] This shameful imbalance, both in the number of reports being issued against each party and in terms of the failure to hold accountable the side committing the far greater abuses of human rights, has become the HRW's standard procedure in Israel–Palestine.[25] But in its latest release, on human shields, HRW plumbs new depths, stripping Palestinians of the right to organize non-violent forms of resistance and seek new ways of showing solidarity in the face of illegal occupation. In short, HRW treats the people of Gaza as mere rats in a laboratory – the Israeli army's view of them – to be experimented on at will.

8

Our Embedded Media

Our eyes and ears in conflict zones around the world are the media. We rely on journalists to explain to us what is happening in distant places, and most of us trust their reports as accurate and their judgements as balanced. But what if this is not the case? What if the media have an agenda largely unrelated to truth-seeking and truth-telling in the Israeli–Palestinian conflict? In these two essays I explore the reasons why the Western media fail to report fairly, let alone even-handedly, on what is happening to the Palestinians in the occupied territories, preferring instead to mirror closely the Israeli media's own interpretations of events.

In 'Kidnapped Correspondents' I take as an example British reporters' use of language in covering two contemporaneous incidents in summer 2006: the capture of an Israeli soldier by Palestinian fighters, and the Israeli army's seizure of Palestinian legislators. British journalists are often assumed to be more balanced in their coverage of Israel – or more hostile, depending on your point of view – than their American counterparts. My analysis, however, reveals that in this fairly typical example of coverage of the conflict the reporters consistently and uniformly distorted the accepted meaning of common words in order to conform with the Israeli media coverage. Thus, the Israeli soldier was considered 'kidnapped' rather than 'captured', and the Palestinian legislators were 'arrested' rather than 'seized'. The constant misrepresentation of such events creates the mistaken impression both that Israel is enforcing the rule of law inside the occupied territories when in fact it is running an illegal occupation of more than four decades, and that the Palestinians are criminals and rogues when in fact they have a right in international law to resist the occupation and select military targets, including soldiers, as part of that resistance.

In 'Covering up Gaza' I examine another problem in the coverage of the conflict: Israel's increasingly successful policy of exploiting the separation wall and its elaborate network of checkpoints to exclude independent journalists from Gaza and the West Bank. Instead, in an extension of the system of 'embedding' refined by the US army in Iraq, Israel is favouring 'reliable' journalists belonging to the large media organizations by giving them access to the occupied territories and denying it to others who have greater freedom to report things as they see them. As a result, coverage of the conflict is being ever more keenly skewed to Israel's benefit.

Kidnapped Correspondents
(*June 2006*)

Few readers of a British newspaper would have noticed the story. In the *Observer* of 25 June, it merited a mere paragraph hidden in the 'World in brief' section, revealing that the previous day a team of Israeli commandos had entered the Gaza Strip to 'detain' two Palestinians Israel claimed were members of Hamas. The significance of the mission was alluded to in a final phrase describing this as 'the first arrest raid in the territory since Israel pulled out of the area a year ago'.[1] More precisely, it was the first time the Israeli army had re-entered the Gaza Strip, directly violating Palestinian control of the territory, since it supposedly left in the 'disengagement' of August last year. As the *Observer* landed on doorsteps around the UK, however, another daring mission was being launched in Gaza that would attract far more attention from the British media – and prompt far more concern. Shortly before dawn, armed Palestinians slipped past Israeli military defences to launch an attack on an army post close by Gaza called Kerem Shalom. They sneaked through a half-mile underground tunnel dug under an Israeli-built electronic fence that surrounds the Strip and threw grenades at a tank, killing two soldiers inside. Seizing another, wounded soldier, Corporal Gilad Shalit, the gunmen disappeared back into Gaza.

Whereas the Israeli 'arrest raid' had passed with barely a murmur, the Palestinian attack a day later received very different coverage. The BBC's correspondent in Gaza, Alan Johnston, started the ball rolling later the same day in broadcasts in which he referred to the Palestinian attack as 'a major escalation in cross-border tensions'.[2] Johnston did not explain why the Palestinian attack on an Israeli army post was an escalation, while the Israeli raid into Gaza the previous day was not. Both were similar actions: violations of a neighbour's territory.

The Palestinians could justify attacking the military post because the Israeli army has been using it and other fortified positions to fire hundreds of shells into Gaza that have contributed to some thirty civilian deaths over the preceding weeks. Israel could justify launching its mission into Gaza because it blames the two men it seized for being behind some of the hundreds of home-made Qassam rockets that have been fired out of Gaza, mostly ineffectually, but occasionally harming Israeli civilians in the border town of Sderot.[3] Why was the Palestinian attack, and not the earlier Israeli raid, an escalation? The clue came in the same report from Johnston, in which he warned that Israel would feel compelled to launch 'retaliations' for the attack, implying that a reinvasion of the Gaza Strip was all but inevitable. So, in fact, the 'escalation' and 'retaliation' were one and the same thing. Although Johnston kept repeating that the Palestinian attack had created an escalation, what he actually meant was that Israel was choosing to escalate its response. Both sides could continue exchanging rocket fire, but only Israel was in a position to reinvade with tanks and ground forces.

There was another intriguing aspect to Johnston's framing of these fast-moving events, one that would be adopted by all the British media. He noted that the coming Israeli 'retaliation' – the reinvasion – had a specific cause: the brief Palestinian attack that left two Israeli soldiers dead and a third captured. But what about the Palestinian attack: did it not have a cause too? According to the British media, apparently not. Apart from making vague references to the Israeli artillery bombardment of the Gaza Strip over the previous weeks, Johnston and other reporters offered no context for the Palestinian attack. It had no obvious cause or explanation. It appeared to come out of nowhere, born presumably only of Palestinian malice. Or as a *Guardian* editorial phrased it: 'Confusion surrounds the precise motives of the gunmen from the Islamist group Hamas and two other armed organizations who captured the Israeli corporal and killed two other soldiers on Sunday. But it was clearly intended to provoke a reaction, as is the firing of rockets from Gaza into Israel.'[4]

It was not as though Johnston or the *Guardian* had far to look for the reasons for the Palestinian attack, explanations that might frame it as a retaliation no different from the Israeli one. In addition to the shelling that had caused some thirty civilian deaths and inflicted yet more trauma on a generation of Palestinian children, Israel has been blockading Gaza's borders to prevent food and medicines from reaching the population and it has successfully pressured international donors to cut off desperately needed funds to the Palestinian government. Then, of course, there was also the matter of the Israeli army's violation of Palestinian-controlled territory in Gaza the day before. None of this context surfaced to help audiences distinguish cause and effect, and assess for themselves who was doing the escalating and who the retaliating. That may have been because all of these explanations make sense only in the context of Israel's continuing occupation of Gaza. But that context conflicts with a guiding assumption in the

British media: that the occupation finished with Israel's disengagement from Gaza in August last year. With the occupation over, all grounds for Palestinian 'retaliation' become redundant.

The *Guardian*'s diplomatic editor, Ewen MacAskill, certainly took the view that Israel should be able to expect quiet after its disengagement. 'Having pulled out of Gaza last year, the Israelis would have been justified in thinking they might enjoy a bit of peace on their southern border.'[5] Never mind that Gaza's borders, airspace, electromagnetic frequencies, electricity and water are all under continuing Israeli control, or that the Palestinians are not allowed an army, or that Israel is still preventing Gazans from having any contact with Palestinians in the West Bank and East Jerusalem. Meetings of the Palestinian parliament have to be conducted over video links because Israel will not allow MPs in Gaza to travel to Ramallah in the West Bank.[6] These factors might have helped to explain continuing Palestinian anger, but in British coverage of the conflict they appear to be unmentionables.

There was another notable asymmetry in the media's use of language and their treatment of the weekend of raids by the Palestinians and Israelis. In the *Observer*, we learnt that Israel had 'detained' the two Palestinians in an 'arrest raid'. These were presented as the legitimate actions of a state that is enforcing the law within the sphere of its sovereignty (notably, in stark contrast to the other media assumption that the occupation of Gaza is over). So how did the media describe the Palestinians' seizure of the Israeli soldier the next day? According to Donald MacIntyre of the *Independent*, Gilad Shalit was 'kidnapped'.[7] His colleague Eric Silver considered the soldier 'abducted'.[8] Conal Urquhart of the *Guardian* referred to him as a 'hostage'.[9] And BBC Online believed him 'abducted' and 'kidnapped'.[10] It was a revealing choice of terminology. Soldiers who are seized by an enemy are usually considered to have been captured; along with being killed, it's an occupational hazard for a soldier. But Britain's liberal media preferred to use words that misleadingly suggested Shalit was a victim, an innocent whose status as a soldier was not relevant to his fate. The Palestinians, as kidnappers and hostage-takers, were clearly not behaving in a legitimate manner.

That this was a deviation from normal usage is suggested by the following report from the BBC in 2003, when Israel seized Hamas political leader Sheikh Mohammed Taha: 'Israeli troops have captured a founder member of the Islamic militant group Hamas during an incursion into the Gaza Strip.' This brief 'incursion' led to the deaths of eight Palestinians, including a pregnant woman and a child, according to the same report.[11] But one does not need to look back three years to spot the double standard being applied by the British media. A few days after the Palestinian attack on Kerem Shalom, the Israeli army invaded Gaza and the West Bank to grab dozens of Palestinian leaders, including cabinet ministers. Were they being kidnapped or taken hostage by the Israeli army? This is what a breaking news report from the *Guardian* had to say: 'Israeli troops today arrested dozens of Hamas ministers and MPs as they stepped up attempts to free a soldier kidnapped by militants in Gaza at the weekend. The Israeli army said 64 Hamas officials, including seven ministers and 20 other MPs, had been detained in a series of early morning arrests.'[12] BBC World took the same view. In its late morning report, Lyse Doucet told viewers that in response to the attack in which an Israeli soldier had been 'kidnapped', the Israeli army 'have been detaining Palestinian cabinet ministers'. In the same broadcast, another reporter, Wyre Davies, referred to 'Thirty Hamas politicians, including eight ministers, detained in the West Bank', calling this an attempt by Israel at 'keeping up the pressure'.[13]

'Arrested' and 'detained'? What exactly was the crime committed by these Palestinian politicians from the West Bank? Were they somehow accomplices to Shalit's 'kidnap' by Palestinian militants in the separate territory of Gaza? And, if so, was Israel intending to prove it in a court of law? In any case, what was the jurisdiction of the Israeli army in 'arresting' Palestinians in Palestinian-controlled territory? None of these questions needed addressing because in truth none of the media had any doubts about the answer. It was clear to all the reporters that the purpose of seizing the Palestinian politicians was to hold them as bargaining chips for the return for Shalit. In the *Guardian*, Conal Urquhart wrote: 'Israeli forces today arrested more than 60

Hamas politicians in the West Bank and bombed targets in the Gaza Strip. The moves were designed to increase pressure on Palestinian militants to release an Israeli soldier held captive since Sunday.'[14] The BBC's Lyse Doucet in Jerusalem referred to the 'arrests' as 'keeping up the pressure on the Palestinians on all fronts', and Middle East editor Jeremy Bowen argued that the detention of the Hamas MPs and ministers 'sends out a very strong message about who's boss around here. The message is: If Israel wants you, it can get you.'[15]

So why have the British media adopted such differing terminology for the two sides, language in which the Palestinians are consistently portrayed as criminals while the Israelis are seen as law-enforcers? Interestingly, the language used by the British media mirrors almost exactly that used by the Israeli media. The words 'retaliation', 'escalation', 'pressure', 'kidnap' and 'hostage' are all drawn from the lexicon of the Israeli press when talking about the Palestinians. The only Israeli term avoided in British coverage is the label 'terrorists' for the Palestinian militants who attacked the army post near Gaza on 25 June. In other words, the British media have adopted the terminology of the Israeli media, even though the latter proudly declare their role as cheerleading for their army against the Palestinian enemy.

The replication by British reporters of Israeli language in covering the conflict is mostly unconscious. It happens because of several factors in the way foreign correspondents operate in conflict zones, factors that almost always favour the stronger side over the weaker, independently of (and often in opposition to) other important contexts, such as international law and common sense. The causes of this bias can be divided into four pressures on foreign correspondents: identification with, and assimilation into, the stronger side's culture; overreliance on the stronger side's sources of information; peer pressure and competition; and, most importantly, the pressure to satisfy the expectations of editors back home in the media organization.

The first pressure derives from the fact that British correspondents, as well as the news agencies they frequently rely on, are almost exclusively based in Israeli locations, such as West Jerusalem and Tel Aviv, where they share the daily rituals of the host population. Correspondents have Israeli neighbours, not Palestinian ones; they drink and eat in Israeli, not Palestinian, bars and restaurants; they watch Israeli, not Palestinian, television; and they fear Palestinian suicide attacks, not Israeli army 'incursions'. Another aspect of this assimilation – this one unmentionable in newsrooms – is the long-standing tendency, though admittedly one now finally waning, by British media organizations to prefer Jewish reporters for the 'Jerusalem beat'.[16] The media justify this to themselves on several grounds: often a senior Jewish reporter on the staff wants to be based in Jerusalem, in some cases as a prelude to receiving Israeli citizenship; he or she may already speak some Hebrew; and, as a Jew living in a self-declared Jewish state, he or she is likely to find it easier to gain access to officials. The obvious danger that Jewish reporters who already feel an affinity with Israel before their posting may quickly start to identify with Israel and its goals is not considered an acceptable line of inquiry. Anyone raising it is certain to be dismissed as an anti-Semite.

The second pressure involves the wide range of sources of information foreign correspondents come to rely on in their daily reporting, from the Israeli media to the Israeli army and government press offices. Most of the big Israeli newspapers now have daily editions in English that arrive at reporters' doors before breakfast and update all day on the Internet.[17] The Palestinians do not have the resources to produce competing information.[18] Israeli officials, again unlike their Palestinian counterparts, are usually fluent in English (and other European languages) and ready with a statement on any subject. This asymmetry between Israeli and Palestinian sources of information is compounded by the fact that foreign correspondents usually consider Israeli spokespeople to be more 'useful'. It is, after all, Israeli decision-makers who are shaping and determining the course of events. The army's spokesperson can speak with authority about the timing of the next Gaza invasion, and the government press office knows by heart the themes of the prime minister's latest unilateral plans. Palestinian spokespeople, by contrast, are far less effective: they usually know nothing more about Israeli decisions than what they have read in the Israeli papers; they are rarely at the scene of Israeli military 'retaliations', and are often unreliable in the ensuing confusion; and internal political disputes, and a lack of clear hierarchies, often leave spokespeople unsure of what the official Palestinian line is. Given these differences, the Israeli 'version' is usually the first one to hit the headlines, both in the Israeli media and on the international television channels. Which brings us to the third pressure.

News is not an independent category of information journalists search for; it is the information that journalists collectively decide is worth seeking out. So correspondents look to each other to determine what is the 'big story'. This is why reporters tend to hunt in packs. The problem for British journalists is that they are playing second fiddle to the largest contingent of English-language correspondents: those from America. What makes the headlines in the US papers is the main story, and as a result British journalists tend to follow the same leads, trying to beat the American majors to the best lines of inquiry. The effect is not hard to predict: British coverage largely mirrors American coverage. And given the close identification of US politicians, business and media with Israel, American coverage is skewed very keenly towards a pro-Israel agenda. That has direct repercussions for British reporting. (It does, however, allow for occasional innovation in the British media too: for example, whereas American reporters were concerned to promote the largely discredited account by the Israeli army of how seven members of a Palestinian family were killed during artillery bombardment of a beach in Gaza on 9 June, their British colleagues had a freer hand to investigate the same events.[19])

Closely related to this sympathy of coverage between the British and American media is the fourth pressure. No reporter who cares about his or her career is entirely immune from the cumulative pressure of expectations from the news desk in London. The editors back home read the American dailies closely; they imbibe as authoritative the views of the major American columnists, like Thomas Friedman, who promote Israel's and Washington's agenda while sitting thousands of miles away from the events they analyse; and they watch the wire services, which are equally slanted towards the American and Israeli interpretation of events. The reporter who rings the news desk each day to offer the best 'pitch' quickly learns which angles and subjects 'fly' and which don't. 'Professional' journalists of the type that get high-profile jobs like Jerusalem correspondent have learnt long ago the predilections of the desk editors. If our correspondent really believes in a story, he or she will fight the desk vigorously to have it included. But there are only so many battles correspondents who value their jobs are prepared to engage in.

With this model for understanding the work of British correspondents, we can explain the confused sense of events that informs the recent reporting of the *Independent*'s Donald MacIntyre. He points out an obvious fact that seems to have eluded many of his colleagues: Israel's reinvasion of Gaza, its bombing of the only electricity station, and disruption to the water supply, its bombing of the main bridges linking north and south Gaza, and its terrifying sonic bombs over Gaza City are all forms of collective punishment of the civilian Palestinian population that are illegal under international law. Derar Abu Sisi, who runs the power station in Gaza, tells MacIntyre it will take a 'minimum of three to six months' to restore electricity supplies.[20] The same piece includes a warning that the petrol needed to run generators will soon run out, shutting off the power to hospitals and other vital services. This is more than the *Guardian*'s coverage managed on the same day. Conal Urquhart writes simply: 'Israel reoccupied areas of southern Gaza yesterday and bombed bridges and an electricity plant to force Palestinian militants to free the abducted soldier.' Blithely, Urquhart continues: 'In Gaza there was an uneasy calm as Israeli aircraft and forces operated without harming anyone. Missiles were fired at buildings, roads and open fields, but ground forces made no attempt to enter built-up areas.'[21]

In MacIntyre's article, despite his acknowledgement of Israel's 'collective punishment' of Gaza (note even this statement of the obvious needs quotation marks in the *Independent*'s piece to remove any suggestion that it can be attributed directly to the paper), he also refers to a Hamas call for a prisoner swap to end the stand-off as an 'escalation' of the 'crisis', and he describes the seizure of a Hamas politician by Israel as an 'arrest' and a 'retaliation'. In a similarly indulgent tone, the *Guardian*'s Ewen MacAskill calls Israel's reinvasion of Gaza 'an understandable over-reaction'. Understandable because 'Israel has good cause for taking tough action against the Palestinians in Gaza' – presumably a reference to the Palestinian 'escalation' by firing Qassam rockets. MacAskill does, however, pause to criticize the invasion, pointing out that 'Israel has to allow the Palestinians a degree of sovereignty.'[22] Not full sovereignty, note, just a degree of it. In MacAskill's view, invasions are out, but by implication 'targeted assassinations', air strikes and artillery fire, all of which have claimed dozens of Palestinian civilian lives over the past weeks, are allowed as they only partially violate Palestinian sovereignty.

But MacAskill finds a small sliver of hope for the future from what has come to be known as the 'Prisoners' Document', an agreement between the various Palestinian factions that implicitly limits Palestinian territorial ambitions to the West Bank, Gaza and East Jerusalem. 'The ambiguous document agreed between Hamas and Fatah yesterday does not recognize Israel's right to exist but it is a step in the right direction', writes MacAskill. A step in which direction? Answer: Israel's direction. Israel has been demanding three concessions from the Palestinians before it says it will negotiate with them: a recognition of Israel's right to exist; a renunciation of violence; and a decision to abide by previous agreements. A *Guardian* editorial shares MacAskill's assessment: 'Implicit recognition [of Israel] coupled with an end to violence [by the Palestinians] would be a solid basis on which to proceed.'[23]

If the Palestinians are being faulted for their half-hearted commitment to these three yardsticks by which progress can be judged, how does Israel's own commitment compare? First, whereas the long-dominant Palestinian faction Fatah recognized Israel nearly twenty years ago, and Hamas appears ready to agree a similar recognition,[24] Israel has made no comparable concession. It has never recognized the Palestinians' right to exist as a people or as a state, from Golda Meir's infamous dictum that there are 'no such thing as Palestinians' to Ehud Olmert's plans for stealing yet more Palestinian land in the West Bank to create a series of Palestinian ghettos there. Second, whereas the Palestinians have a right under international law to use violence to liberate themselves from Israel's continuing occupation, the various factions are now agreeing in the Prisoners' Document to limit that right to actions within the occupied territories. Israel, meanwhile, is employing violence on a daily basis against the general population of Gaza, harming civilians and militants alike, even though under international law it has a responsibility to look after the occupied population no different from its duties towards its own citizens. And third, whereas the Palestinians have been keen since the signing of the Oslo Accords to have their agreements with Israel honoured – most assume that they are their only hope of winning statehood – Israel has flagrantly and consistently ignored its commitments. During Oslo it missed all its deadlines for withdrawing from Palestinian territory, and during the Oslo and current Road Map peace negotiations it has continued to build and extend its illegal settlements on Palestinian land.

In other words, Israel has not recognized the Palestinians, it has refused to renounce its illegitimate use of violence against the population it occupies, and it has abrogated its recent international agreements. Will the media ever demand of Israel that it satisfies these three conditions before the Palestinians be expected to give up their right to resist the occupation?

Covering up Gaza
(*July 2006*)

One early and easy victory for Israel in Gaza has been in its battle to manage the news. Israel's invasion is a very private war against Gaza's population, to which only invited guests – the representatives of our major media outlets – are being given access. Just as in the Iraq war, where America required Western reporters to 'embed' with its forces before they were let near the battlefield, Israel is adopting similar measures to control the flow of bad news out of Gaza. The restrictions on who can report and what they can tell explain in part why, more than a fortnight after an Israeli soldier was captured, almost every Western reporter is still referring to him as 'kidnapped'; why the destruction of vital civilian infrastructure such as Gaza's only power plant is described as 'pressure' rather than what it is – collective punishment, a violation of international law and a war crime;[25] and why the deaths of large numbers of Palestinians, civilians and militants, in the current 'Operation Summer Rain' are receiving far less coverage than the killing of two soldiers and the capture of a third who were enforcing the occupation.[26]

Gaza – a giant open-air prison – could not be a more ideal environment for an occupier wanting to manage the news. Israel controls the borders and can decide who is allowed in and who is refused access. Freedom of the press is meaningless on such terms.

Israel has been working on its own 'embedding' strategy for some time. During the early stages of the second intifada, the head of Israel's Government Press Office, Daniel Seaman, developed a strategy of intimidating journalists and their employers as a way to get the coverage he wanted. Famously he 'boycotted' three senior journalists over what he considered to be their 'partisan' coverage: ABC's reporter Gillian Findlay, the *Guardian*'s Suzanne Goldenberg and the *Washington Post*'s bureau chief Lee Hockstader. Later he boasted to the Israeli media that he had ousted all three from their jobs, though the *Guardian* did at least seek to deny his claims, arguing that Goldenberg had simply been promoted.[27] But Israel began tightening its controls during the disengagement from Gaza last year and has not looked back since.[28] Only journalists from the big news organizations were allowed into the Strip, on special army buses that drove straight to the settlements. Those without accreditation from the main media organizations, and those who had upset Israel with their previous reports, had little hope of gaining entry. Journalists in disfavour were doubtless supposed to take note for next time, and change the tone of their coverage. The big media organizations have no interest in pointing out why they have special access to Gaza and at what price such privileges were bought. An admission from them would hint at some of the subtle pressures already influencing their reporting and might expose the cosy arrangement that offers them a monopoly on the flow of information at a time when they are already feeling the heat from the rise of an Internet journalism not subject to the agendas of wealthy owners and corporate advertisers.

Israel's system of embedding, like that operated by the US in Iraq, operates at two levels: it ensures that many potential journalists are not in a position to report first-hand from the 'war zone'; and then it imposes a range of pressures on those journalists who are there.

When Israel withdrew its settlers and soldiers from Gaza last August, the windfall was that it gained absolute control over who was allowed in and out of the tiny sliver of land on the Mediterranean coast. The result: just as Palestinians find it all but impossible to get out of Gaza, foreigners find it nearly as difficult to get in. The hermetic sealing off of Gaza follows a series of steps taken by Israel in the past few years to discourage foreigners from venturing into places where its soldiers prefer to go about their business unobserved. In late 2002 and early 2003 the Israeli army killed two peace activists with the International Solidarity Movement, Tom Hurndall and Rachel Corrie.[29] It was a very effective warning to other activists – as well as freelance journalists who might be mistaken for activists – not to consider living in the occupied territories. Foreigners stopped 'embedding' themselves in Palestinian areas, and in consequence there was a rapid loss of the Internet diaries of life under occupation and eyewitness accounts that were creating a fledgling but useful 'alternative journalism'.[30] Since then Israel has been on the lookout for anyone at its borders whom it suspects of belonging to peace groups or being recruited to work in Palestinian organizations. Non-Israelis are held for lengthy questioning and usually deported if Israel suspects them of planning to enter the occupied territories, whether their purposes are legitimate or not.[31] As a consequence, the West Bank and Gaza are now sorely deprived of the young idealists and hopeful journalists who once travelled around the occupied territories.

Israel has claimed that such measures are designed to protect these individuals and its own soldiers from unnecessary and dangerous confrontations. But in practice, Israel has ensured that independent witnesses – including those who were once able to describe at first hand and in their many native tongues the horrors being inflicted on the Palestinians – are now largely absent from the occupied territories. Instead 'professional' reporters, based in Israel, venture into these areas only to report after the event, when the best they can hope to achieve is to present two conflicting narratives: the Israeli official version against Palestinian eyewitness accounts. In practice, since the disengagement the only voices being heard are those of big-hitting journalists who have the sensitivities of their news desks back home and their careers to worry about. With an electronic fence surrounding Gaza on three sides, and the sea on the fourth, the only way into the Strip is through one of several crossing points controlled by the army. Where once journalists could freely roam around the occupied territories, reporting things as they saw them, they are now required to jump through several hoops before they are allowed to cross into Gaza.

So how does Israel's version of embedding work? First, to get into Gaza a journalist must be in possession of a press card issued by the Israeli Government Press Office (GPO). All other journalist cards – even international ones – are worthless in the eyes of the Israeli government. To be eligible for a GPO card, applicants must have accreditation with a recognized media organization. Freelance reporters and photographers are considered to be impostors unless they can prove that they have an assignment from just such an accredited organization. On the other hand, assignments on behalf of any 'alternative' media that have been critical of Israel in the past are invariably not going to qualify a journalist for a GPO card.[32] As a result, Israel makes it impossible for freelancers to do in Gaza what they would do in any other conflict zone: head off with an open mind to see what is happening on the ground. Now, the freelance journalist must have a specific assignment in mind, and have an agreement in advance with a large media organization to cover that assignment in its name. These conditions severely limit the freedom of freelance reporters and photographers to find stories that the main media organizations have overlooked. In practice, if a freelance journalist can get such an assignment (in itself a difficult task), it is likely to be for one of the stories the news desk thousands of miles away considers to be important: that is, the same stories the rest of the media pack are already pursuing. Innovation and difference of perspective are excluded from the outset.

Those journalists who do manage to gain a GPO card then have to jump through a second hoop: they must sign a 'waiver' form, exonerating Israel of all responsibility if they are injured while in the Gaza Strip, including from the actions of the Israeli army. The effect of the waiver is to impose a large financial burden on freelance journalists. While media organizations provide their staff with war insurance, an armoured car, and a flak jacket and helmet, they do not feel the same obligation towards freelancers, even those on assignment for them. This leaves freelance reporters and photographers in Gaza in an unenviable position: either they protect themselves in the Strip at a huge personal cost they are unlikely ever to recoup from their reporting, or they risk injury for which no one can be held accountable and made to pay. Even if it can be proven that an Israeli soldier took a malicious shot of the kind that in the past killed filmmaker James Miller and UN official Iain Hook and destroyed most of the face of activist Brian Avery, freelance journalists and their families will not be entitled to a penny of compensation. It can be assumed that this measure alone has seriously deterred many freelance journalists who might otherwise have considered making a name for themselves by reporting from the Gazan front line.

And then there is the third and most problematic hoop of all. Reporters who receive a GPO card must agree to submit any reports that touch on 'defence and security' matters to Israel's military censor.[33] Although in practice few Western reporters refer to the censor, the knowledge that they are breaking the terms of their agreement – and could have their privileges withdrawn – is intended to encourage 'self-restraint' on their part.[34] As long as the journalists' reports do not attract the attention of the Israeli authorities, this term of their contract with the army is unlikely to be enforced. If they keep their heads down, and stay within the pack, there is no danger they will be 'picked off'. Equally, if they go no further in their reporting than the largely loyal Israeli media, reproducing the same leads and angles, then they can be confident of not incurring the wrath of the GPO. By contrast, distinctiveness and daring from journalists is a recipe for upsetting the Government Press Office and complaints to the reporters' editors.

The most shocking aspect to this media embedding with the Israeli army is the silence from the journalists themselves, from their employers and from their professional federations. None has tried to challenge the restrictions imposed by Israel on those wishing to report from the occupied territories. The generally dismal standard of reporting during the recent invasion of Gaza has proven just how much a cosy club of well-paid journalists are being protected by these arrangements and what little incentive they have to rock the boat with either Israel or their news editors. As a result, Israel's language and agenda have come to dominate the coverage. Israel's invasion of Gaza, however, is not the end of this story of media complicity. As the West Bank wall nears completion, Israel's reach in managing the news will soon extend there too. And with it, doubtless, we will have yet more craven reporting from our embedded media.

9

Anti-Semitism and Its Abuses

Anti-Semitism has a long and sordid history, culminating in the horrors of the Nazi death camps of Europe. Paradoxically, Israel and its supporters today welcome the support of fanatical Christian evangelicals in the US and far-right politicians in Europe who might once have been expected to back the persecution of Jews rather than come to their aid. Instead, Israel prefers to play down historical anti-Semitism and concentrate on something it calls the 'new anti-Semitism'. Unlike the traditional variety espoused by the far right, 'new anti-Semitism' supposedly infects other groups: the Arab and Muslim populations of the Middle East, and left-wingers in the West. It also just so happens that these groups are at the forefront of criticism of Israel and its oppression of the Palestinians. In the following two essays, I look first at the uses to which the 'new anti-Semitism' is being put, and then examine the part played in this drama by a community positioned at the heart of the conflict, the Palestinian Christians.

In 'Hatred and Holocaust' I argue that Israel has exploited the 'new anti-Semitism' not only to stifle criticism of its policies but also to suggest that Muslim immigration to Europe is poisoning intellectual life there, reawakening latent anti-Semitism and bringing nearer a 'clash of civilizations', against which Israel is the sole bulwark in the Middle East. According to the new anti-Semitism thesis, Europeans must choose between joining Israel and the US in the war on terror or succumbing to the barbarism of an Islam that will soon dominate their continent.

Embarrassingly for Israel, the presence in the region of one community, the Palestinian Christians, confuses this comforting picture of a clash of civilizations, as I discuss in 'The Purging of Palestinian Christians'. These indigenous Christians, unlike modern Evangelicals, do not support Israel and have taken a notable lead in shaping Palestinian nationalism. Israel has therefore oppressed them, just as much as it has Palestinian Muslims, in an effort to persuade them to emigrate. While Israel seeks to blame the growing exodus of Palestinian Christians on the hostile climate being fomented in the Holy Land by its Muslims, it is in truth Israel and the ideology of Zionism that are creating a 'clash of civilizations' that forces local Christians onto the wrong side of the divide.

Hatred and Holocaust
(*September 2006*)

The trajectory of a long-running campaign that gave birth this month to the preposterous all-party British parliamentary report into anti-Semitism can be traced back to intensive lobbying by the Israeli government that began more than four years ago, in early 2002.[1] At that time, as Ariel Sharon was shredding the tattered remains of the Oslo Accords by reinvading West Bank towns handed over to the Palestinian Authority in his destructive rampage known as Operation Defensive Shield, he drafted the Israeli media into the fray. Local newspapers began endlessly highlighting concerns about the rise of a 'new anti-Semitism', a theme that was rapidly and enthusiastically taken up by the Zionist lobby in the US.

It was not the first time, of course, that Israel had called on American loyalists to help it out of trouble. In *Beyond Chutzpah*, Norman Finkelstein documents the advent of claims about a new anti-Semitism to Israel's lacklustre performance in the 1973 Yom Kippur War. On that occasion, it was hoped, the charge of anti-Semitism could be deployed against critics to reduce pressure on Israel to return Sinai to Egypt and negotiate with the Palestinians.[2] Israel alerted the world to another wave of anti-Semitism in the early 1980s, just as it came under unprecedented criticism for its invasion and occupation of Lebanon. What distinguished the new anti-Semitism from traditional anti-Jewish racism of the kind that led to Germany's death camps, said its promoters, was that this time it embraced the progressive left rather than the far right.[3]

The fresh claims about a new anti-Semitism began life in the spring of 2002, with the English-language website of Israel's respected liberal daily newspaper *Ha'aretz* flagging for many months a special online supplement of articles on the 'New anti-Semitism', warning that the 'age-old hatred' was being revived in Europe and America.[4] The refrain was soon taken up the *Jerusalem Post*, a right-wing English-language newspaper regularly used by the Israeli establishment to shore up support for its policies among Diaspora Jews.[5] Like its precursors, argued Israel's apologists, the latest wave of the 'new anti-Semitism' was the responsibility of Western progressive movements – though, on this occasion, with a fresh twist. An ever-present but largely latent Western anti-Semitism was being stoked into frenzy by the growing political and intellectual influence of extremist Muslim immigrants. The implication was that an unholy alliance had been spawned between the left and militant Islam. Such views were first aired by senior members of Sharon's cabinet. In an interview in the *Jerusalem Post* in November 2002, for example, Binyamin Netanyahu warned that latent anti-Semitism was again becoming active:

> In my view, there are many in Europe who oppose anti-Semitism, and many governments and leaders who oppose anti-Semitism, but the strain exists there. It is ignoring reality to say that it is not present. It has now been wedded to and stimulated by the more potent and more

overt force of anti-Semitism, which is Islamic anti-Semitism coming from some of the Islamic minorities in European countries. This is often disguised as anti-Zionism.[6]

Netanyahu proposed 'lancing the boil' by beginning an aggressive public relations campaign of 'self-defence'. A month later Israel's president, Moshe Katsav, picked on the softest target of all, warning during a state visit that the fight against anti-Semitism must begin in Germany, where 'voices of anti-Semitism can be heard'.[7] But, as ever, the main target of the new anti-Semitism campaign were audiences in the US, Israel's generous patron. There, members of the Israel lobby turned into a chorus of doom, resulting in surveys that showed American Jews – like Israeli Jews – put the threat of anti-Semitism among their top fears.[8]

In the early stages of the campaign, the lobby's true motivation was not concealed: it wanted to smother a fledgling debate by American civil society, particularly the churches and universities, to divest – withdraw their substantial investments – from Israel in response to Operation Defensive Shield. In October 2002, after Israel had effectively reoccupied the West Bank, the ever-reliable Abraham Foxman, director of the Anti-Defamation League, lumped in critics who were calling for divestment from Israel with the new anti-Semites. He urged a new body established by the Israeli government called the Coordination Forum for Countering Anti-Semitism to articulate clearly 'what we know in our hearts and guts: when that line [to anti-Semitism] is crossed'.[9] Foxman quickly got into his stride, warning that Jews were more vulnerable than at any time since the Second World War. 'I did not believe in my lifetime that I or we would be preoccupied on the level that we are, or [face] the intensity of anti-Semitism that we are experiencing,' he told the *Jerusalem Post*.[10] Echoing Netanyahu's warning, Foxman added that the rapid spread of the new anti-Semitism had been made possible by the communications revolution, mainly the Internet, which was allowing Muslims to relay their hate messages across the world within seconds, infecting people around the globe.

It is now clear that Israel and its loyalists had three main goals in mind as they began their campaign. Two were familiar motives from previous attempts at highlighting a 'new anti-Semitism'. The third was new.

The first aim, and possibly the best understood, was to stifle all criticism of Israel, particularly in the US. During the course of 2003 it became increasingly apparent to journalists like myself that the American media, and soon much of the European media, were growing shy of printing even the mild criticism of Israel they usually allowed. By the time Israel began stepping up the pace of construction of its monstrous wall across the West Bank in spring 2003, editors were reluctant to touch the story. As the fourth estate fell silent, so did many of the progressive voices in our universities and churches. Divestment was entirely removed from the agenda. McCarthyite organizations like CampusWatch helped enforce the reign of intimidation. Academics who stood their ground, like Columbia University's Joseph Massad, attracted the vindictive attention of new activist groups like the David Project.[11]

A second, less noticed, goal was an urgent desire to prevent any slippage in the numbers of Jews living inside Israel that might benefit the Palestinians as the two ethnic groups approached demographic parity in the area known to Israelis as Greater Israel and to Palestinians as historic Palestine. Demography had been a long-standing obsession of the Zionist movement: during the 1948 war, the Israeli army terrorized away or forcibly removed some 80 per cent of the Palestinians living inside the borders of what became Israel to guarantee its new status as a Jewish state. But by the turn of the millennium, following Israel's occupation of the West Bank and Gaza in 1967, and the rapid growth of the oppressed Palestinian populations both in the occupied territories and inside Israel, demography had been pushed to the top of Israel's policy agenda again.[12]

During the second intifada, as the Palestinians fought back against the Israeli war machine with a wave of suicide bombs on buses in major Israeli cities, Sharon's government feared that well-off Israeli Jews might start to regard Europe and America as a safer bet than

Jerusalem or Tel Aviv. The danger was that the demographic battle might be lost as Israeli Jews emigrated. By suggesting that Europe in particular had become a hotbed of Islamic fundamentalism, it was hoped that Israeli Jews, many of whom have more than one passport, would be afraid to leave. A survey by the Jewish Agency taken as early as May 2002 showed, for example, that 84 per cent of Israelis believed anti-Semitism had again become a serious threat to world Jewry.[13] At the same time Israeli politicians concentrated their attention on the two European countries with the largest Jewish populations, Britain and France, both of which also have significant numbers of immigrant Muslims. A supposed rise in anti-Semitism in these two countries was highlighted in the hope of attracting their Jewish populations to Israel.[14] In France, for example, peculiar anti-Semitic attacks were given plenty of media coverage: from a senior rabbi who was stabbed (by himself, as it later turned out) to a young woman attacked on a train by anti-Semitic thugs (except, as it later emerged, she was not Jewish and she had imagined the attack).[15] Sharon took advantage of the manufactured climate of fear in July 2004 to claim that France was in the grip of 'the wildest anti-Semitism', urging French Jews to come to Israel.[16]

The third goal, however, had not been seen before. It tied the rise of a new anti-Semitism to the increase of Islamic fundamentalism in the West, implying that Muslim extremists were asserting an ideological control over Western thinking. It chimed well with the post-9/11 atmosphere. In this spirit, American Jewish academics like Daniel J. Goldhagen characterized anti-Semitism as constantly 'evolving'. In a piece entitled 'The Globalization of Anti-Semitism' published in the American Jewish weekly *Forward* in May 2003, Goldhagen argued that Europe had exported its classical racist anti-Semitism to the Arab world, which in turn was reinfecting the West.

> Essentially, Europe has exported its classical racist and Nazi anti-Semitism to Arab countries, which they then applied to Israel and Jews in general. Then the Arab countries re-exported the new hybrid demonology back to Europe and, using the United Nations and other international institutions, to other countries around the world. In

Germany, France, Great Britain and elsewhere, today's intensive anti-Semitic expression and agitation uses old tropes once applied to local Jews – charges of sowing disorder, wanting to subjugate others – with new content overwhelmingly directed at Jews outside their countries.[17]

His theory of a 'free-floating' contagion of hatred towards Jews, being spread by Arabs and their sympathizers through the Internet, media and international bodies, found many admirers. The British neo-conservative journalist Melanie Phillips claimed popularly, if ludicrously, that British identity was being subverted and pushed out by an Islamic identity that was turning her country into the capital of terror, 'Londonistan'.[18]

This final goal of the proponents of 'the new anti-Semitism' was so successful because it could be easily conflated with other ideas associated with America's war on terror, such as the clash of civilizations. If it was 'us' versus 'them', then the new anti-Semitism posited from the outset that the Jews were on the side of the angels. It fell to the Christian West to decide whether to make a pact with good (Judaism, Israel, civilization) or evil (Islam, Osama bin Laden, Londonistan).

We are far from reaching the end of this treacherous road, both because the White House is bankrupt of policy initiatives apart from its war on terror, and because Israel's place is for the moment assured at the heart of the US administration's neoconservative agenda. That was made clear last week when Netanyahu, currently the most popular politician in Israel, added yet another layer of lethal mischief to the neoconservative spin machine as it gears up to confront Iran over its nuclear ambitions. Netanyahu compared Iran and its president, Mahmoud Ahmadinejad, to Adolf Hitler. 'Hitler went out on a world campaign first, and then tried to get nuclear weapons', he told a meeting of Israel's anti-terrorism policymakers. 'Iran is trying to get nuclear arms first. Therefore from that perspective, it is much more dangerous.'[19] Netanyahu's implication was transparent: Iran is looking for another Final Solution, this one targeting Israel as well as world Jewry. Netanyahu is far from alone. Tzipi Livni, Israel's foreign minister, claimed recently against all the evidence that Iran is only months away from possessing nuclear weapons.[20]

International terrorism is a mistaken term not because it doesn't exist, but because the problem is international militant Islam. That is the movement that operates terror on the international level, and that is the movement that is preparing the ultimate terror, nuclear terrorism.

Faced with the evil designs of the 'Islamic fascists', such as supposedly those in Iran, Israel's nuclear arsenal – and the nuclear holocaust Israel can and appears prepared to unleash – may yet be presented as the civilized world's salvation.

The Purging of Palestinian Christians
(*January 2007*)

There is an absurd though revealing scene in Palestinian writer Suad Amiry's recent book *Sharon and My Mother-in-Law* about Israeli Jews' attitude to the two other monotheistic religions. In 1992, long before Israel turned Amiry's home city of Ramallah into a permanent ghetto behind checkpoints and walls, it was still possible for West Bank Palestinians to drive to Jerusalem and even into Israel – at least if they had the right permit. On one occasion Amiry ventures out in her car to East Jerusalem, the half of the city that was Palestinian before the 1967 war and has since been engulfed by relentless illegal and state-organized Jewish settlement-building. There she sees an elderly Jew collapsing out of his car and on to the side of the road. She pulls over, realizes he is having a heart attack and bundles him into the back of her own car. Not able to speak Hebrew, she reassures him in English that she is taking him to the nearest hospital. But as it starts to dawn on him that she is Palestinian, Amiry realizes the terrible problem her charitable act has created: his fear may prompt him to have another heart attack. 'What if he had a fatal heart attack in the back seat of my car? Would the Israeli police ever believe I was just trying to help?' she wonders.[21] The Jewish man seeks to calm himself by asking Amiry if she is from Bethlehem, a Palestinian city known for being Christian. Unable to lie, she tells him she is from

Ramallah. 'You're Christian?' he asks more directly. 'Muslim', she admits, to his utter horror. Only when they finally make it to the hospital does he relax enough to mumble in thanks: 'There are good Palestinians after all.'

I was reminded of that story as I made the journey to Bethlehem on Christmas Day. The small city that Amiry's Jewish heart-attack victim so hoped she hailed from is today as much of an isolated enclave in the West Bank as other Palestinian cities – or at least it is for its Palestinian inhabitants. For tourists and pilgrims, getting in or out of Bethlehem has been made reasonably straightforward, presumably to conceal from international visitors the realities of Palestinian life. Seemingly oblivious to the distressing historical parallels, however, Israel forces foreigners to pass through a 'border crossing' – a gap in the menacing grey concrete wall – that recalls the stark black-and-white images of the entrance to Auschwitz. The gates of Auschwitz offered a duplicitous motto, 'Arbeit macht frei' (Work makes you free), and so does Israel's gateway to Bethlehem. 'Peace be with you' is written in English, Hebrew and Arabic on a colourful large notice covering part of the grey concrete. The people of Bethlehem have scrawled their own, more realistic assessments of the wall across much of its length.

Foreign visitors can leave, of course, while Bethlehem's Palestinians are now sealed into their ghetto. As long as these Palestinian cities are not turned into death camps, the West appears ready to turn a blind eye. Mere concentration camps, it seems, are acceptable.

In July 2004 the West briefly indulged in a bout of soul-searching about the wall following the publication of the International Court of Justice's advisory opinion condemning its construction.[22] Today the only rebukes, mild at best, come from Christian leaders around Christmas time. Britain's Archbishop of Canterbury, Dr Rowan Williams, was foremost among them this year.[23] Even those concerns, however, relate mainly to fears that the Holy Land's native Christians, once a significant proportion of the Palestinian population, are rapidly dwindling. There are no precise figures, but the Israeli media suggest that Christians, who once constituted as much as 15 per cent of the occupied territories' Palestinians, are now just 2 or 3 per cent.[24] Most are to be found in the West Bank close to Jerusalem, in Bethlehem, Ramallah and neighbouring villages. A similar pattern can be discerned inside Israel too, where Christians have come to comprise an ever smaller proportion of Palestinians with Israeli citizenship. In 1948 they were nearly a quarter of that minority (itself 20 per cent of the total Israeli population), and today they are a mere 10 per cent.[25] Most are located in Nazareth and nearby villages in the Galilee.

Certainly, the continuing fall in the number of Christians in the Holy Land concerns Israel's leadership almost as keenly as it does the patriarchs and bishops who visit Bethlehem at Christmas – but for quite the opposite reason. Israel is happy to see Christians leave, at least of the indigenous Palestinian variety. (More welcome are the crazed fundamentalist Christian Zionists from the United States who have been arriving to help engineer the departure of Palestinians, Muslims and Christians alike, in the belief that, once the Jews have dominion over the whole of the Holy Land, Armageddon and the 'End Times' will draw closer.[26]) Of course, that is not Israel's official story. Its leaders have been quick to blame the exodus of Christians on the wider Palestinian society from which they are drawn, arguing that a growing Islamic extremism, and the election of Hamas to lead the Palestinian Authority, have put Christians under physical threat. This explanation neatly avoids mentioning that the proportion of Christians has been falling for decades. According to Israel's argument, the decision by many Christians to leave the land where generations of their ancestors have been rooted is a reflection of the 'clash of civilizations', in which a fanatical Islam is facing down the Judeo-Christian West. Palestinian Christians, like Jews, have found themselves caught on the wrong side of the Middle East's confrontation lines.

Here, for example, is how the *Jerusalem Post* portrayed the fate of the Holy Land's non-Muslims in a Christmas editorial: 'Muslim intolerance toward Christians and Jews is cut from exactly the same cloth. It is the same jihad.' The *Post* concluded that only by confronting the jihadis would 'the plight of persecuted Christians – and of the persecuted Jewish state – be ameliorated'.[27]

Similar sentiments were recently aired in an article by Aaron Klein of WorldNetDaily republished on *Ynet*, Israel's most popular website, that preposterously characterized a procession of families through Nazareth on Eid al-Adha, the most important Muslim festival, as a show of strength by militant Islam designed to intimidate local Christians. Islam's green flags were 'brandished', according to Klein, whose reporting transformed a local troupe of Scouts and their marching band into 'Young Muslim men in battle gear ... beating drums'. Nazareth's youngsters, meanwhile, were apparently the next generation of Qassam rocket engineers: 'Muslim children launched firecrackers into the sky, occasionally misfiring, with the small explosives landing dangerously close to the crowds.'[28] Such sensationalist misrepresentations of Palestinian life are now a staple of the local and American media. Support for Hamas, for example, is presented as proof of jihadism run amok in Palestinian society rather than as evidence of either despair at Fatah's corruption and collaboration with Israel or a determination to find leaders prepared to counter Israel's terminal cynicism with proper resistance.

The 'clash of civilizations' thesis is usually ascribed to a clutch of American intellectuals, most notably Samuel Huntington, the title of whose book gave the idea popular currency, and the Orientalist academic Bernard Lewis.[29] But alongside them are the guiding lights of the neocon movement, a group of hawkish thinkers deeply embedded in the centres of American power who were recently described by *Ynet* as mainly comprising 'Jews who share a love for Israel'.[30] In fact, the idea of a clash of civilizations grew out of a world-view that was shaped by Israel's own interpretation of its experiences in the Middle East. An alliance between the neocons and Israeli leaders was cemented in the mid-1990s with the publication of a document titled *A Clean Break: A New Strategy for Securing the Realm*. Authored by leading neocons, it presented to the Israeli prime minister of the day, Binyamin Netanyahu, a vision of a regional policy designed to suit Israeli and American interests in the Middle East.[31]

When the neocons rose to power with George Bush's election to the White House, the birth of the bastard offspring of the clash of civilizations – the war on terror – was all but inevitable. Paradoxically, this vision of our future, set out by American and Israeli Jews, is steeped in fundamentalist Christian religious symbolism, from the promotion of a civilized West's crusade against the Muslim hordes to the implication that the final confrontation between these civilizations (a nuclear attack on Iran?) may be the End Times itself – and thereby lead to the return of the Messiah. If this clash is to be realized, it must be convincing at its most necessary confrontation point: the Middle East and more specifically the Holy Land. The clash of civilizations must be embodied in Israel's experience as a civilized, democratic state fighting for its very survival against its barbarian Muslim neighbours.

There is only one problem in selling this image to the West: the minority of Christian Palestinians who by and large have lived contentedly under Muslim rule in the Holy Land for centuries. Today, in a way quite infuriating to Israel, these Christians confuse the picture by continuing to take a leading role in defining Palestinian nationalism and resistance to Israel's occupation. They prefer to side with the Muslim 'fanatics' than with Israel, the Middle East's only supposed outpost of Judeo-Christian 'civilization'. The presence of Palestinian Christians reminds us that the supposed 'clash of civilizations' in the Holy Land is not really a war of religions but a clash of nationalisms, between the natives and European colonial settlers.

Inside Israel, for example, Christians have been the backbone of the Communist Party, the only non-Zionist party Israel allowed for several decades.[32] Many of the Palestinian artists and intellectuals who are most critical of Israel are Christians, including the late novelist Emile Habibi; the writer Anton Shammas and film-makers Elia Suleiman and Hany Abu Assad (all now living in exile); and the journalist Antoine Shalhat (who, for reasons unknown, has been placed under a loose house arrest, unable to leave Israel for more than a year).[33] The most notorious Palestinian nationalist politician inside Israel is Azmi Bishara, yet another Christian, who has been relentlessly hounded by the domestic security services.[34] Similarly, Christians have been at the core of the wider secular Palestinian national movement, helping to define its struggle. They range from exiled professors such as the late Edward Said to human rights activists in the occupied territories such as Raja Shehadeh.[35] The founders of the most militant wings of the national movement, the Democratic and Popular Fronts for the Liberation of Palestine, were Nayif Hawatmeh and George Habash, both Christians.

This intimate involvement of Palestinian Christians in the Palestinian national struggle is one of the reasons why Israel has been so keen to find ways to encourage their departure – and then blame it on intimidation by, and violence from, Muslims. In truth, however, the fall in the number of Christians can be explained by two factors, neither of which is related to a clash of civilizations.

Mundanely, the first is a lower rate of growth among the Christian population. According to the latest figures from Israel's Bureau of Census Statistics, the average Christian household in Israel contains 3.5 people compared to 5.2 in a Muslim household. Looked at another way, in 2005, 33 per cent of Christians were under the age of 19, compared to 55 per cent of Muslims.[36] In other words, the proportion of Christians in the Holy Land has been eroded over time by higher Muslim birth rates. But a second factor is equally, if not more, important. Israel has established an oppressive rule for Palestinians both inside Israel and in the occupied territories that has been designed to encourage the most privileged Palestinians, which has meant disproportionately Christians, to leave. This policy has been implemented with stealth for decades, but has been greatly accelerated in recent years with the erection of the wall and numerous checkpoints. The purpose has been to encourage the Palestinian elite and middle class to seek a better life in the West, turning their backs on the Holy Land.

Palestinian Christians have had the means to escape for two reasons. First, they have traditionally enjoyed a higher standard of living, as city-based shopkeepers and business owners, rather than poor subsistence farmers in the countryside. And second, their connection to the global Churches has made it simpler for them to find sanctuary abroad, often beginning as trips for their children to study overseas. Israel has turned Christian parents' financial ability and their children's increased opportunities to its own advantage, by making access to higher education difficult for Palestinians both inside Israel and in the occupied territories.

Inside Israel, for example, Palestinian citizens still find it much harder to attend university than Jewish citizens, and even more so to win places on the most coveted courses, such as medicine and engineering.[37] Instead, for many decades Israel's Christians and Muslims became members of the Communist Party in the hope of receiving scholarships to attend universities in Eastern Europe. Christians were also able to exploit their ties to the Churches to help them head off to the West. Many of these overseas graduates, of course, never returned, especially knowing that they would be faced with an Israeli economy much of which is closed to non-Jews. Something similar occurred in the occupied territories, where Palestinian universities have struggled under the occupation to offer a proper standard of education, particularly faced with severe restrictions on the movement of staff and students. Still today, it is not possible to study for a Ph.D. in either the West Bank or Gaza, and Israel has blocked Palestinian students from attending its own universities.[38] The only recourse for most who can afford it has been to head abroad. Again, many have chosen never to return.

But in the case of the Palestinians of Gaza and the West Bank, Israel found it even easier to close the door behind them. It established rules, in violation of international law, that stripped these Palestinians of their right to residency in the occupied territories during their absence. When they tried to return to their towns and villages, many found that they were allowed to stay only on temporary visas, including tourist visas, that they had to renew with the Israeli authorities every few months. Nearly a year ago, Israel quietly took a decision to begin kicking these Palestinians out by refusing to issue new visas.[39] Many of them are academics and business people who have been trying to rebuild Palestinian society after decades of damage inflicted by the occupying regime. A recent report by the most respected Palestinian university, Bir Zeit, near Ramallah, revealed that one department had lost 70 per cent of its staff because of Israel's refusal to renew visas.[40]

Although there are no figures available, it can probably be safely assumed that a disproportionate number of Palestinians losing their residency rights are Christian. Certainly the effect of further damaging the education system in the occupied territories will be to increase the exodus of Palestine's next generation of leaders, including its Christians. In addition, the economic strangulation of the Palestinians by the wall, the restrictions on movement and the international economic blockade of the Palestinian Authority are damaging the lives of all Palestinians with increasing severity. Privileged Palestinians, and that doubtless includes many Christians, are being encouraged to seek a rapid exit from the territories.

From Israel's point of view, the loss of Palestinian Christians is all to the good. It will be happier still if all of them leave, and Bethlehem and Nazareth pass into the effective custodianship of the international Churches. Without Palestinian Christians confusing the picture, it will be much easier for Israel to persuade the West that the Jewish state is facing a monolithic enemy, fanatical Islam, and that the Palestinian national struggle is really both a cover for jihad and a distraction from the clash of civilizations against which Israel is the ultimate bulwark. Israel's hands will be freed.

Israelis, like Amiry's heart-attack victim, may believe that Palestinian Christians are not really a threat to their or their state's existence, but be sure that Israel has every reason to continue persecuting and excluding Palestinian Christians as much as it does Palestinian Muslims.

AFTERWORD

Two-state Dreamers

If the Israeli–Palestinian conflict is one of the world's most intractable, much the same can be said of the parallel debate about whether its resolution can best be achieved by a single state embracing the two peoples living there or by a division of the land into two separate states, one for Jews and the other for Palestinians. The central argument of the two-staters is that the one-state idea is impractical and therefore worthless of consideration. Their rallying cry is that it is at least possible to imagine a consensus emerging behind two states, whereas Israelis will never accept a single state. The one-state crowd are painted as inveterate dreamers and time-wasters.

That is the argument advanced by Israel's only serious peace group, Gush Shalom. Here is the view of the group's indefatigable leader, Uri Avnery: 'After 120 years of conflict, after a fifth generation was born into this conflict on both sides, to move from total war to total peace in a Single Joint State, with a total renunciation of national independence? This is total illusion.'[1] Given Avnery's high-profile opposition to a single state, many in the international solidarity groups adopt the same position. They have been joined by an influential American intellectual, the philosopher Michael Neumann, who wrote the no-holds-barred book *The Case against Israel*. He appears to be waging a campaign to discredit the one-state idea too. Recently in defence of two states, he wrote: 'That Israel would concede a single state is laughable. … There is no chance at all [Israelis] will accept a single state that gives the Palestinians anything remotely like their rights.'[2]

Unlike the one-state solution, according to Neumann and Avnery, the means to realizing two states are within our grasp: the removal of the half a million Jewish settlers living in the occupied Palestinian territories. Both believe that, were Israel to withdraw to the pre-1967 borders, it would be possible to create two real states. 'A two-state solution will, indeed, leave Palestinians with a sovereign state, because that's what a two-state solution means', argues Neumann. 'It doesn't mean one state and another non-state, and no Palestinian proponent of a two-state solution will settle for less than sovereignty.'

There is something surprisingly naive about arguing that, just because something is called a two-state solution, it will necessarily result in two sovereign states. What are the minimum requirements for a state to qualify as sovereign, and who decides? True, the various two-state solutions proposed by Ariel Sharon, Ehud Olmert and George Bush, and supported by most of the international community, would fail according to the two-staters' chief criterion: these divisions are not premised on the removal of all the settlers. But an alternative two-state solution requiring Israel's withdrawal to the pre-1967 borders might still not concede, for example, a Palestinian army – equipped and trained by Iran? – to guard the borders of the West Bank and Gaza. Would that count? And how likely do the campaigners for two real states think it that Israel and the US would grant that kind of sovereignty to a Palestinian state? Importantly, Neumann and Avnery remind us that those with power are the ones who dictate solutions. In which case we can be sure that, when the time is right, Israel and its sponsor, the United States, will impose their own version of the two-state solution and that it will be far from the genuine article advocated by the two-state camp.

But let us return to the main argument: that the creation of two states is inherently more achievable and practical than the establishment of a single state. Strangely, however, from all the available evidence, this is not how it looks to Israel's current leaders.

Prime Minister Ehud Olmert, for example, has expressed in several speeches the fear that, should the Palestinian population under Israeli rule – both in the occupied territories and inside Israel proper – reach the point where it outnumbers the Jewish population, as demographers expect in the next few years, Israel will be compared to apartheid South Africa. In his words, Israel is facing an imminent and powerful 'struggle for one-man-one-vote' along the lines of the anti-apartheid movement.[3] According to Olmert, without evasive action, political logic is drifting inexorably towards the creation of one state in Israel and Palestine. This was his sentiment as he addressed delegates to the recent Herzliya conference:

> Once we were afraid of the possibility that the reality in Israel would force a bi-national state on us. In 1948, the obstinate policy of all the Arabs, the anti-Israel fanaticism and our strength and the leadership of David Ben-Gurion saved us from such a state. For 60 years, we fought with unparalleled courage in order to avoid living in a reality of bi-nationalism, and in order to ensure that Israel exists as a Jewish and democratic state with a solid Jewish majority. We must act to this end and understand that such a [bi-national] reality is being created, and in a very short while it will be beyond our control.[4]

Olmert's energies are, therefore, consumed with finding an alternative political programme that can be sold to the rest of the world. That is the reason he, and Sharon before him, began talking about a Palestinian state. Strangely, however, neither took up the offer of the ideal two-state solution – the kind Avnery and Neumann want – made in 2002. Then Saudi Arabia and the rest of the Arab world promised Israel peace in return for its withdrawal to the pre-1967 borders. They repeated their offer last year. Israel has steadfastly ignored them.[5] Instead an alternative version of two states – the bogus two-state solution – has become the default position of Israeli politics. It requires only that Israel and the Palestinians appear to divide the land, while in truth the occupation continues and Jewish sovereignty over all of historic Palestine is not only maintained but rubber-stamped by the international community. In other words, the Gazafication of the West Bank.

When Olmert warns that without two states 'Israel is finished',[6] he is thinking primarily about how to stop the emergence of a single state. So, if the real two-state camp is to be believed, Olmert is a dreamer too, because he fears that a one-state solution is not only achievable but dangerously close at hand. Sharon, it seems, suffered from the same delusion, given that demography was the main impulse for his disengaging from Gaza. Or maybe both of them understood rather better than Neumann and Avnery what is meant by a Jewish state, and what political conditions are incompatible with it.

In fact, the division of the land demanded by the real two-staters, however equitable, would be the very moment when the struggle for Israel to remain a Jewish state would enter its most critical and difficult phase. Which is precisely why Israel has blocked any meaningful division of the land so far and will continue to do so. In the unimaginable event that Israel were to divide the land, a Jewish state would not be able to live with the consequences of such a division for long. Eventually, the maintenance of an ethnic Israeli state would (and will) prove unsustainable: environmentally, demographically and ultimately physically. Division of the land simply 'fast-forwards' the self-destructiveness inherent in a Jewish state.

Let us examine just a few of the consequences for the Jewish state of a genuine two-state solution.

First, Israel inside its recognized, shrunken borders would face an immediate and very serious water shortage. That is because, in returning the West Bank to the Palestinians, Israel would lose control of the large mountain aquifers that currently supply most of its water, not only to Israel proper but also to the Jewish settlers living illegally in the occupied territories. Israel would no longer be able to steal the water, but would be expected to negotiate for it on the open market. Given the politics of water in the Middle East that would be no simple matter. However impoverished the new sovereign Palestinian state was, it would lose all legitimacy in the eyes of its own population were it to sell more than a trickle of water to the Israelis.

We can understand why by examining the current water situation. At the moment Israel drains off almost all of the water provided by the rivers and aquifers inside Israel and in the occupied territories for use by its own population, allowing each Palestinian far less than the minimum amount he or she requires each day, according to the World Health Organization.[7] In a stark warning last month, Israel's Water Authority reported that overdrilling has polluted with sea water most of the supply from the coastal aquifer – the main fresh water source inside Israel's recognized borders.[8] Were Palestinians to be allowed a proper water ration from their own mountain aquifer, as well as to build a modern economy, there would not be enough left over to satisfy Israel's first-world thirst. And that is before we consider the extra demand on water resources from all those Palestinians who choose to realize their right to return, not to their homes in Israel, but to the new sovereign Palestinian state.

In addition, for reasons that we will come to, the sovereign Jewish state would have every reason to continue its Judaization policies, trying to attract as many Jews from the rest of the world as possible, thereby further straining the region's water resources. The environmental unsustainability of both states seeking to absorb large populations would inevitably result in a regional water crisis. In addition, should Israeli Jews, sensing water shortages, start to leave in significant numbers, Israel would have an even more pressing reason to locate water, by fair means or foul. It can be expected that in a short time Israel, with the fourth most powerful army in the world, would seek to manufacture reasons for war against its weaker neighbours, particularly the Palestinians but possibly also Lebanon, in a bid to steal their water.

Water shortages would, of course, be a problem facing a single state too. But, at least in one state there would be mechanisms in place to reduce such tensions, to manage population growth and economic development, and to divide water resources equitably.

Second, with the labour-intensive occupation at an end, much of the Jewish state's huge citizen army would become surplus to defence requirements. In addition to the massive social and economic disruptions, the dismantling of the country's military complex would fundamentally change Israel's role in the region, damage its relationship with the only global superpower and sever its financial ties to Diaspora Jews. Israel would no longer have the laboratories of the occupied territories for testing its military hardware, its battlefield strategies and its booming surveillance and crowd-control industries. If Israel chose to fight the Palestinians, it would have to do so in a proper war, even if one between very unequal sides. Doubtless the Palestinians, like Hezbollah, would quickly find regional sponsors to arm and train their army or militias.

The experience and the reputation Israel has acquired – at least among the US military – in running an occupation and devising new and supposedly sophisticated ways to control the 'Arab mind' would rapidly be lost, and with it Israel's usefulness to the US in managing its own long-term occupation of Iraq and assisting the booming 'homeland security' industry. Also, Israel's vital strategic alliance with the US in dividing the Arab world, over the issue of the occupation and by signing peace treaties with some states and living in a state of permanent war with others, would start to unravel. With the waning of Israel's special relationship with Washington and the influence of its lobby groups, as well as the loss of billions of dollars in annual subsidies, the Jewish Diaspora would begin to lose interest in Israel. Its money and power ebbing away, Israel might eventually slip into Middle Eastern anonymity, another Jordan. In such circumstances it would rapidly see a large exodus of privileged Ashkenazi Jews, many of whom hold second passports.

Third, the Jewish state would not be as Jewish as some might think: currently one in five Israelis is not Jewish but Palestinian. Although in order to realize a real two-state vision all the Jewish settlers would probably need to leave the occupied territories and return to Israel, what would be done with the Palestinians with Israeli citizenship? These Palestinians have been citizens for six decades and live legally on land that has belonged to their families for many generations. They are also growing in number at a rate faster than the Jewish population, the reason they are popularly referred to in Israel as a 'demographic timebomb'.[9] Were these 1.3 million citizens to be removed from Israel by force under a two-state arrangement, it would be a violation of international law by a democratic state on a scale unprecedented in the modern era, and an act of ethnic cleansing even larger than the 1948 war that established Israel. The question would be: why even bother advocating two states if it has to be achieved on such appalling terms?

Assuming instead that the new Jewish state is supposed to maintain, as Israel currently does, the pretence of being a liberal democracy, these citizens would be entitled to continue living on their land and exercising their rights. Inside a Jewish state that had officially ended its conflict with the Palestinians, demands would grow from Palestinian citizens for equal rights and an end to their second-class status. Most significantly, they would insist on two rights that challenge the very basis of a Jewish state. They would expect the right, backed by international law, to be able to marry Palestinians from outside Israel and bring them to live with them; and they would want a Right of Return for their exiled relatives on a similar basis to the Law of Return for Jews. Israel's Jewishness would be at stake, even more so than it is today from its Palestinian minority. It can be assumed that Israel's leaders would react with great ferocity to protect the state's Jewishness. Eventually Israel's democratic pretensions would have to be jettisoned and the full-scale ethnic cleansing of Palestinian citizens implemented.

Still, do these arguments against the genuine two-state arrangement win the day for the one-state solution? Would Israel's leaders not put up an equally vicious fight to protect their ethnic privileges by preventing, as they are doing now, the emergence of a single state? Yes, they would and they will. But that misses my larger point. As long as Israel is an ethnic state, it will be forced to deepen the occupation and intensify its ethnic cleansing policies to prevent the emergence of genuine Palestinian political influence – for the reasons

I cite above and for many others I don't. In truth, both a one-state and a genuine two-state arrangement are impossible given Israel's determination to remain a Jewish state.

The obstacle to a solution, then, is not the division of the land but Zionism itself, the ideology of ethnic supremacism that is the current orthodoxy in Israel. As long as Israel is a Zionist state, its leaders will allow neither one state nor two real states. There can be no hope of a solution until the question of how to defeat Zionism is addressed. It just so happens that the best way this can be achieved is by confronting the illusions of the two-state dreamers and explaining why Israel is in permanent bad faith about seeking peace.

In other words, if we stopped distracting ourselves with the Holy Grail of the two-state solution, we might channel our energies into something more useful: discrediting Israel as a Jewish state, and the ideology of Zionism that upholds it. Eventually the respectable facade of Zionism might crumble. And without Zionism, the obstacle to creating either one or two states will finally be removed. If that is the case, then why not also campaign for the solution that will best bring justice to both Israelis and Palestinians?

Notes

Introduction

1. Bush's criticism of the wall peaked in summer 2003 as he tried to shore up the position of the newly created Palestinian prime minister, filled by Mahmoud Abbas, and pressure Sharon to abide by the Road Map: Reuters, 'Israel makes peace pledges, Abbas meets Bush', 26 July 2003.
2. See my 'A 1,000-kilometer fence preempts the road map', *International Herald Tribune*, 27 May 2003.
3. A photograph of the letters page, 'Defining a land', published by the *International Herald Tribune* on 30 May 2003, can be viewed at http://electronicintifada.net/ v2/article1865.shtml.
4. A notable exception was the minor storm that greeted the publication of an article in the *London Review of Books* by two leading American academics, Stephen Walt and John Mearsheimer – later adapted into a book entitled *The Israel Lobby* – criticizing the lobby's power. Not that the pair's argument was treated with sympathy, but the fact that it was noted by the media was a breakthrough of sorts.
5. Camera has been described as 'a McCarthyist group that persecutes journalists' by Israeli journalist Gideon Levy: 'Let's be done with all the Talanskys', *Ha'aretz*, 11 May 2008.
6. Edward Said, 'America's last taboo', in Carey 2001, p. 260.
7. An edited version of the letter of complaint was published under the headline 'Cooked up charges against Israel' on the Camera website at www.camera.org/ index.asp?x_context=2&x_outlet=139&x_article=511.

8. 'CAMERA's half-baked attack on Cook', *Electronic Intifada*, 30 August 2003, available at http://electronicintifada.net/v2/article1865.shtml.

9. A sympathetic editor offered me another chance to write for the paper a year later. When that article, 'Nonviolent protest offers little hope for Palestinians', *International Herald Tribune*, 31 August 2004, was greeted with even greater outrage from the Israel lobby, the newspaper severed contact with me.

10. Lemche 1991, p. 162, cited in Masalha 2007, p. 254.

11. Quoted in the brochure produced by the Tel Amal 'tower and stockade' museum.

12. Masalha 2000, pp. 6–7.

13. 'Sabra' – 'Tzabar' in Hebrew – is the indigenous 'prickly pear' cactus. Identifying with it confers an instant 'nativeness' to the Israeli Jew, as well as a justification for his (and the characterization usually refers to a man) contrasting qualities of external prickliness and inner sweetness.

Chapter 1

1. Massad 2006, pp. 86 and 131.

2. Ibid., p. 15.

3. Masalha 2007, p. 6.

4. Beit-Hallahmi 1992, p. 119.

5. 'The lion and the gazelle', *Counterpunch*, 21 April 2008.

6. Elon 2000, pp. 307–8.

7. Halper 2008, p. 71.

8. 'Deconstructing the walls of Jericho: Who are the Jews?', *Ha'aretz*, 29 October 1999.

9. 'Israel digs into the past', BBC Online, 23 December 1999.

10. Lemche 1991, p. 162, cited in Masalha 2007, p. 254.

11. 'An invention called "the Jewish people"', *Ha'aretz*, 29 February 2008.

12. Masalha 2007, p. 36.

13. 'The lion and the gazelle'.

14. 'Shattering a "national mythology"', *Ha'aretz*, 21 March 2008.

15. Interview in the *Sunday Times*, 15 June 1969.

16. In his book *Imagined Communities*, Benedict Anderson highlights the role of the capitalist print media in creating the conditions necessary for nationalism by forging common ideas of national belonging.

17. See Cook 2008, particularly chapter 3.

18. Khalidi 2007, p. 106.

19. Ibid., pp. 107–8.

20. Ibid., p. 36.

21. Silberstein 1999, p. 51, cited in Mearsheimer and Walt 2007, p. 92.

22. 'Hard talk', *Ha'aretz*, 15 February 2008.

23. 'It's not racism, it's colonialism', *Guardian*, 8 August 2001.

24. Quoted in Masalha 2007, p. 17.

25. Quoted in Rodinson 1973, p. 40.

26. Quoted in Masalha 1997, pp. 61–2.

27. What constituted the Promised Land was unclear too. Even the secular Ben-Gurion believed the Jewish birthright was to include more than Palestine. He

included the East Bank of Jordan, south Lebanon up to the Litani River, areas of Syria, and much of the Sinai: Morris 2001, p. 75.

28. Khalidi 2007, p. 32–3. The only Jew in the British cabinet, Edwin Montagu, responded to the Declaration with a memo that 'the policy of His Majesty's Government is anti-Semitic' and would 'prove a rallying ground for anti-Semites in every country in the world': 'Saddam, Arafat and the Saudis hate the Jews and want to see them destroyed', *New Statesman*, 2 December 2002. Other ministers appeared to harbour a hope that the Second Coming might be hastened were Jews encouraged to return to the Promised Land – a view shared by millions of evangelicals in the US today: Rose 2004, chapter 7. A more important reason, however, as Rose notes, was a strong concern among Western European powers about the possible spread of Bolshevism and the role of East European Jews in its promotion. Rodinson (1973, p. 45) points out that the Balfour Declaration was issued only five days before the Bolsheviks took power in Russia.

29. In an attempt to raise money, the Ottoman Empire sold off swathes of common land farmed by Palestinian peasants to rich absentee owners, making the Palestinian farmers tenants. When the JNF bought this land, it usually sought to evict the Palestinians: Uri Avnery, 'Dunam after dunam', *Znet*, 7 February 2005.

30. The JNF had purchased only about half of this land, or some 900,000 dunams (225,000 acres), with the rest bought privately by wealthy Jews and institutions: Benvenisti 2000, p. 177.

31. Pappe 2006, p. 19; Benvenisti 2000, pp. 70–78.

32. The traditional Zionist narrative of the Partition Plan ignores important aspects of the unfolding events. The eleven officials of the UN Special Committee on Palestine (UNSCOP) who drafted the plan had no experience of the Middle East, made their decision after a brief visit to Palestine, and appear to have been most influenced by their visit to the Nazi death camps and by strong lobbying by Russia and the US, both of which had their own interests in promoting a Jewish state. The Plan's first draft assigned 62 per cent of Palestine to the Jewish state and 38 per cent to the Arab one: Segev 1998, p. 21n. The final plan was a majority report and only adopted by the General Assembly after much arm-twisting by the US and Russia. In May 1948 the UN reassessed its policy and appointed a mediator, Count Folke Bernadotte, to devise a new solution. Bernadotte was later assassinated by the Jewish underground: Pappe 2004, pp. 123–33.

33. Pappe 2006, p. 35. The UN was apparently concerned by how the Jewish state would maintain control of its large Palestinian population. According to recently declassified documents, the UN planned to create a Jewish militia and supply it 'with combat aircraft, using British military techniques': 'UN archives reveal plan to arm Jewish militia', *Ha'aretz*, 29 November 2007.

34. Benny Morris, 'A personal assessment of the Zionist experience', *Tikkun*, March/April 1998.

35. 'The 29th of November, then and now', *Ha'aretz*, 29 November 2007.

36. 'The watchman', *Time*, 16 August 1948.

37. Pappe 2006, p. xii.

38. Quoted in Morris, 'A personal assessment'.

39. Quoted in Fischbach 2003, p. 6.

40. Pappe 2006, p. 155.

41. Ibid., pp. xv and 104.

42. In the early 1990s Aryeh Kitzhaki, a former director of the Israeli army's archives,

admitted he had seen confidential records of ten large massacres (of more than fifty Palestinians) committed by the army and another hundred smaller massacres. Benny Morris says the archivists refused to show him such documents: 'Not only Deir Yassin', *Ha'ir*, 6 May 1992, trans. Elias Davidsson. Pappe (2006, p. 258) notes that thirty-seven massacres have been identified.

43. From an Israeli government protocol quoted by Benny Morris in an interview with *Yediot Abaronot* in December 1994, cited in Charley Reese, 'What Israeli historians say about 1948 ethnic cleansing', *Washington Report on Middle East Affairs*, September 1999.

44. Ben-Ami 2006, pp. 35–6.

45. Morris 1994, p. 15, cited in Mearsheimer and Walt 2007, p. 82.

46. Ben-Ami 2006, p. 36.

47. Estimates of the number of villages cleansed varies from 360 to more than 500, depending on the definitions used: Fischbach 2003, p. 4. Today, most Palestinians living in what Israel calls 'mixed cities' are internal refugees later relocated to the cities to build apartments for new Jewish immigrants.

48. Khalidi 1992, p. xxxi.

49. Fouzi el-Asmar provides an eyewitness account of these events in *To be an Arab in Israel*. His family was allowed to remain in Lydd, along with a few other railway employees' families, because they knew how to operate the track.

50. These lines were censored from Rabin's memoirs but later published in the *New York Times*, on 29 October 1979. Quoted in Pappe 2006, p. 169.

51. For a detailed overview of what was lost, consult Salman Abu-Sitta's large reference work, *Atlas of Palestine 1948*.

52. This pact, endorsed by Britain, was first brought to public attention by the Israeli historian Avi Shlaim in his book *Collusion across the Jordan* (1988). See also Morris 2003.

53. From 1950 the refugees were cared for by the specially created United Nations Relief and Works Agency (UNRWA). Pappe (2006, p. 236) points out that Israel was determined the International Refugee Organization, dealing with Jewish refugees in Europe, not be involved in case a comparison between the two groups was made.

54. Segev 1998, p. 28.

55. Pappe 2006, p. 175.

56. Segev 1998, p. 69.

57. Fischbach 2003, p. 9; Jiryis 1976, pp. 80–81.

58. The definition of an absentee included any Palestinian who, subsequent to 29 November 1947, the date of the UN Partition Plan resolution, was away from his or her place of residence for any length of time and for any reason: Fischbach 2003, pp. 21–4. Often an individual was assigned such status based only on the testimony of a collaborator or village leader. The original law allowed any property later acquired by an absentee to be seized too, though this provision was later revoked: Jiryis 1976, pp. 83–8.

59. *The Times*, 24 December 1980, cited in Davis 2003, p. 33.

60. The holdings of the *waqf*, an Islamic trust overseeing religious buildings as well as farmland and property bequeathed for charitable purposes, amounted to a tenth of the land in Palestine in 1946: Lustick 1980, p. 189. The Custodian sold most *waqf* property to the Development Agency in 1953, though it appears he never received payment. Control of religious buildings, mainly mosques and cemeteries,

was passed to trustees handpicked by the state: Jiryis 1976, pp. 119–21. On the other hand, the Custodian did return most land belonging to the Christian churches, for fear of the international repercussions: Fischbach 2003, p. 39. In 2007 Palestinians petitioned the courts to regain *waqf* property in the city of Jaffa. In response, the state refused to list confiscated *waqf* properties, claiming 'the requested information would seriously harm Israel's foreign relations': 'State refuses to release list of Waqf properties in Tel Aviv, Jaffa', *Ha'aretz*, 14 November 2007.

61. Segev 1998, pp. 72–3.

62. Ibid., p. 73.

63. A dunam corresponds to a quarter of an acre, or a tenth of a hectare.

64. The figures produced by the UN Conciliation Committee for Palestine (UNCCP) in 1964 excluded the vast Bersheeva district in the Negev, thereby greatly under-estimating the true total: Fischbach, 'Records of Palestinian dispossession are gathering dust', *Daily Star*, 23 June 2003. The Israeli Ministry of Agriculture believed the true total was 16.5 million dunams, close to the 70 per cent figure cited by the Custodian in 1980: Fischbach 2003, pp. 50–52.

65. Dealing with a related but separate matter, a team of Israeli, Palestinian and inter-national negotiators known as the Aix-en-Provence Group assessed the money needed to 'resolve' the issue of the Palestinian right of return at between $55 billion and $85 billion: 'Refugees and Jerusalem: A question of money', *Ha'aretz*, 23 November 2007.

66. Fischbach 2003, p. 32.

67. Ori Nir, *Ha'aretz*, 29 January 2002 (Hebrew).

68. Amnon Kapeliouk, 'Camp David dialogues', *Le Monde diplomatique*, September 2000.

69. Pappe 2006, p. 188.

70. Fischbach (2003, pp. 10–11) says official figures show that more than 100,00 immigrants were living in Palestinian refugees' buildings by spring 1949.

71. According to Walid Khalidi, of some 400 abandoned Palestinian villages 70 per cent were totally destroyed and 22 per cent partially destroyed. Seven villages remained untouched and were inhabited by Jews: cited in Masalha 2007, p. 66.

72. Benvenisti 2000, pp. 18–23.

73. Tom Segev, 'Where are all the villages? Where are they?' *Between the Lines*, October 2002, translated from the original Hebrew article in *Ha'aretz*, 6 September 2002; Benvenisti 2000, p. 168; Jiryis 1976, p. 80.

74. The first, unreliable Israeli census in November 1948 counted 69,000 Palestinians inside the new borders. The figure had reached 150,000 a year later: Lustick 1980, pp. 48–9.

75. Davis 2003, p. 33. The 1965 Building and Planning Law recognized 124 Palestin-ian communities but 'unrecognized' dozens more. Most belonged to the Bedouin, the weakest Palestinian community.

76. The figures of the Central Bureau of Statistics refer indiscriminately to the 1.2 million Palestinians with citizenship and the 250,000 Palestinians of East Jerusalem as 'Israeli Arabs', even though the latter are residents of Israel rather than citizens.

77. A more accurate translation from Hebrew would be 'Israel's Arabs', perhaps explaining the minority's general antipathy towards its official title.

78. Al-Haj 1995, p. 121. Similarly, Segev (1998, p. 65) notes a secret memo from the ruling Mapai party in 1959: 'The government's policy … has sought to divide the Arab population into diverse communities and regions'.

79. Quoted in Lustick 1980, p. 146.

80. Jiryis 1976, p. 179.

81. Benvenisti 2000, p. 7. Israel blocked the development of Palestinian urban spaces inside Israel to prevent a Palestinian intellectual and cultural elite from emerging.

82. On seeing so many Palestinians left in Nazareth after its capture, Ben-Gurion angrily asked the local commander: 'Why are there so many Arabs? Why didn't you expel them?' Quoted in Masalha 2007, p. 61.

83. Israel threatened to seize the strategic ridges of the Wadi Ara (also known as the Little Triangle) by force if Jordan's King Abdullah did not cede them as part of the agreement in 1949: Avi Shlaim 2000, p. 44. The Israeli cabinet simply assumed the area's Palestinian inhabitants would be expelled. Foreign Minister Moshe Sharett observed: 'The interests of security demand that we get rid of them': Segev 1998, p. 28. The failure to do so is a decision much lamented by later politicians because of the Wadi Ara's large number of Muslims.

84. For more on this system of 'branding' the 'inside Palestinians' to distinguish them from those outside, see Robinson 2005, especially chapters 1 and 2.

85. Benvenisti 2000, p. 157. More precisely, Israeli leaders feared that should the treatment of these Palestinian citizens come to the attention of the international community, the pressure might grow for them to be given self-determination in their own, overwhelmingly Palestinian areas. For similar reasons, Israel lobbied successfully to end the United Nations' oversight of the Palestinian internal refugees: Lustick 1980, p. 62.

86. Though not all. More than 30,000 internal refugees had to wait until the Nationality Law was amended in 1980 before receiving citizenship: Davis 2003, pp. 104–5.

87. Jiryis 1976, p. 4. By 1950, a handful of Palestinian refugees outside Israel had devised a strategy to convert to Judaism in the hope of claiming citizenship under the newly passed Law of Return. Israel acted quickly to block their path: Robinson 2005, p. 89.

88. Masalha 1997, pp. 15–21.

89. Ibid., p. 11.

90. Ibid., p. 9.

91. Ibid., p. 11.

92. Ibid., p. 13. See also Jiryis 1976, pp. 81–2.

93. Masalha 1997, p. 33.

94. Ibid., pp. 21–35. It would be more than fifty years before the state formally apologized for the deaths: 'President Peres apologizes for Kafr Qasem massacre of 1956', *Ha'aretz*, 21 December 2007.

95. Masalha 1997, p. 34.

96. Ibid., pp. xviii–xix.

97. Quoted in Jiryis 1976, pp. 105–6.

98. Ibid., pp. 83–4. A right-wing Knesset member pointed out an additional discriminatory quality to the legislation, though not one enforced: 'According to this law, the Israeli army is full of absentees … Every man who went to war on or after November 29 [the date of the proposed UN Partition Plan], that is to say, left

his city – is an absentee': Segev 1998, p. 81.

99. Benvenisti 2000, p. 201; Jiryis 1976, p. 128.
100. The category of present absentee was added to the law after Foreign Minister Moshe Sharett pointed out that, were it not, thousands of internal refugees might claim the right to return to their original villages. Presciently, he also noted that if Israel later conquered the refugee camps of the West Bank, a development he thought likely, those refugees would be able to claim a right to return too: Segev 1998, p. 80.
101. Jiryis 1976, pp. 78–9.
102. The JNF paid between $4 and $18 per dunam, when the market value stood at hundreds of dollars per dunam: 'The land of Zion', *The Economist*, 29 September 2007.
103. 'Erasures', *New Left Review*, July–August 2001.
104. After these transactions, the JNF tripled its land holdings to 2.7 million dunams: Benvenisti 2000, p. 177. Lustick (1980, p. 308n) notes, however, that, if state land over which the JNF has exclusive administrative control is included, the figure rises to 4.5 million dunams, or approximately 22 per cent of Israel.
105. For accounts of the military government, see Jiryis 1976, particularly chapters 1 and 2; and El-Asmar 1975.
106. Jiryis 1976, p. 53.
107. There was widespread opposition to these regulations, which had been used against Jewish militias in the pre-state period. Yaakov Shapira, who later became justice minister, said: 'The regime created by the Emergency Regulations is without precedent in a civilized country. Even Nazi Germany had no such laws': Segev 1998, p. 50.
108. Jiryis 1976, p. 19.
109. Segev 1998, p. 52.
110. Yehoshua Palmon, a later adviser on Arab affairs, justified the segregation in an interview in 1983: 'I preferred separate development. True, this prevented the Arabs from integrating into the Israeli democracy. Yet they had never had democracy before. Since they had never had it, they never missed it. The separation made it possible to maintain a democratic regime within the Jewish population alone': Ibid., p. 67.
111. In his diary Ben-Gurion referred to the Ministerial Committee for Abandoned Property, which oversaw the clearing of Palestinians from such areas, as the Committee 'for Removal and Expulsion': Ibid., p. 59.
112. Jiryis 1976, chapter 2. See also Lustick 1980, pp. 228–9. Teddy Kollek, an aide to Ben-Gurion and later the mayor of Jerusalem, observed: 'The Arab voters were secured through the military government': Segev 1998, pp. 66–7.
113. Jiryis 1998, p. 50. Benvenisti (2000, p. 218) points out that the word 'infiltration' was preferred because it suggested a threatening and malicious intent on the part of the refugees rather than the fact that most were simply trying to return home, tend their crops or visit relatives. This depiction of the refugees also justified the army's shoot-to-kill policy against them.
114. Lustick 1980, p. 196. In the 1970s, the government claimed 1.5 million of the 2 million dunams as state land: ibid., p. 312n.
115. The 'scattered' Bedouin communities were considered to be in need of 'concentrating'. Officials showed little self-consciousness about using such terminology,

despite the recent horrors faced by Jews in Europe. For an overview of the Bedouin's treatment, see Maddrell 1990.

116. See, for example, Ibrahim 2004.

117. See, for example, two articles in *Middle East Report*: Oren Yiftachel, 'The shrinking space of citizenship: Ethnocratic politics in Israel', 223, Summer 2002; and my 'Bedouin in the Negev face new "transfer"', published in the online version on 10 May 2003.

118. Jiryis 1976, pp. 89–90.

119. Benvenisti 2000, pp. 158–9; Jiryis 1976, pp. 94–5; Lustick 1980, p. 178. Jiryis makes the point that land confiscated under this law had to be returned once the state of emergency ended – one of the reasons presumably why it continues to this day.

120. Lustick 1980, p. 176. By 1948 only 5 million dunams, or a quarter of Israel's total territory, had been surveyed and registered: Jiryis 1976, pp. 112–13.

121. 'Public interest' in the case of the confiscation of land from Nazareth was the construction of a Jewish settlement, Upper Nazareth, to contain Nazareth's growth: Lustick 1980, p. 177.

122. Jiryis 1976, p. 117.

123. Pappe 2006, p. 223; Lustick 1980, pp. 276n and 296n. According to Lustick, more than 1 million dunams of land was taken from the Palestinian minority, leaving them with about 600,000 dunams.

124. Benvenisti 2000, p. 161.

125. Jiryis 1976, pp. 215–18; Lustick 1980, p. 167.

126. Quoted in Sultany 2005, p. 34.

127. Benvenisti 2000, pp. 227–8.

128. Abu Hussein and McKay 2003, pp. 216–20. For a case study of the Kafkaesque restrictions on land use facing Palestinian families, see my 'Apartheid targets Palestinian home-owners inside Israel', *Electronic Intifada*, 10 March 2005.

129. 'The first Arab city', *Ha'aretz*, 17 February 2008.

130. According to the American Jewish newspaper *Forward*, JNF land is 'home to 70% of the population' – presumably a reference to Israel's Jewish population: 'In watershed, Israel deems land-use rules of Zionist icon "discriminatory"', 4 February 2005.

131. Abu Hussein and McKay 2003, p. 153.

132. Benvenisti 2000, pp. 176–7.

133. Pappe 2006, pp. 222–3.

134. A description of how this works is provided in Nathan 2005, pp. 149–54.

135. In the UK, for instance, the JNF describes itself as 'humanitarian' and 'non-political' (www.jnf.co.uk). Its influence is such that Gordon Brown rushed to become a patron in 2007 on becoming prime minister. In doing so, he joined his predecessor, Tony Blair, and the Conservative Party leader David Cameron: 'Brown takes on JNF role', *Jewish Chronicle*, 27 July 2007.

136. 'Saved from the brink of oblivion', *Ha'aretz*, 4 February 2008.

137. See: www.jnf.org/site/PageServer?pagename=el_sustainAfforest.

138. Nathan 2005, pp. 129–31. See also my chapter on the unrecognized village of Ayn Hawd, in Masalha 2005.

139. 'Apartheid Israel: An interview with Uri Davis', 17 September 2004, available at www.fromoccupiedpalestine.org/node/1419.

140. For background on the JNF and the latest legal developments in its relationship with the state, see the Adalah website: www.adalah.org/eng/jnf.php.
141. Selection committees oversee admission to almost 700 such agricultural and cooperative associations, accounting for more than two-thirds of all communities in Israel. These communities are home to 5 per cent of the population but control 80 per cent of Israel's total territory: *Adalah's Newsletter* 42, November 2007.
142. 'In watershed, Israel deems land-use rules.'
143. 'Bill allocating JNF land to Jews only passes preliminary reading', *Ha'aretz*, 19 July 2007. Left-wing MKs who backed the discrimination embodied in the bill justified their support on the grounds that the land had been bought by the JNF with donations from Jews: 'Arab MK leads campaign against bill allocating state land to Jews only', *Ha'aretz*, 23 October 2007. This ignored two historical facts: first, that the state had transferred substantial absentee land to the JNF; and second, that the JNF and state had subsequently confiscated land from Palestinian citizens. Little of the land belonging to the JNF had been sold by Palestinians or paid for using such donations.
144. 'Poll: 81% of Israelis want JNF land for Jews only', *Ynet*, 10 November 2007. Among Labor Party supporters, 89 per cent backed this position.
145. The Qaadans were refused membership of the Katzir community by an admissions committee. The justices ruled that the Israel Lands Authority, a government body, had breached its duty not to discriminate in allocating the plots of land in Katzir by delegating the programme to the Jewish Agency. The court, however, avoided ruling on whether the discriminatory policies of the Jewish Agency and Jewish National Fund were unlawful in themselves: Abu Hussein and McKay 2003, pp. 192–4.
146. For the story of the land grab behind Karmiel's establishment, see Jiryis 1976, pp. 109–11.
147. 'In watershed, Israel deems land-use rules'.
148. *Adalah's Newsletter* 14, June 2005.
149. 'Deal would have state, JNF swap 60,000 dunams', *Ha'aretz*, 30 October 2007; 'Shackles law raises hackles', *Ha'aretz*, 28 January 2008.
150. See Kanaaneh 2002.
151. Cook 2006, chapter 3.
152. 'The democracy index: Major findings 2003', Israel Democracy Institute, available at www.idi.org.il/sites/english/PublicationsCatalog/Pages/The_2003_Israeli_Democracy_Index/Publications_Catalog_7735.aspx.
153. 'Poll: 62% want Arab emigration', *Ynet*, 9 May 2006.
154. 'Poll: Israeli Jews shun Arabs', *Ynet*, 22 March 2006.
155. See Cook 2006.
156. 'A new opening for Mideast peace', *Washington Post*, 3 December 2004.
157. 'Lieberman: The unfaithful cannot be citizens', *Ynet*, 10 December 2006.
158. 'Gov't to support bill on revoking citizenship for disloyalty to state', *Ha'aretz*, 7 January 2007.
159. 'FM Livni: Palestinian state should satisfy Israeli Arab national desires', *Israel Insider*, 18 November 2007.
160. 'Abbas opposes exchange of populated territory with Israel', *Ha'aretz*, 26 August 2007.

Chapter 2

1. Segev 1998, p. 6.
2. Convenient because it can be assumed that the large body of security personnel involved in the military government inside Israel until 1966, like all significant bureaucracies, lobbied hard on the need for their continuing employment in a similar roles in the occupied territories. This process reversed during the withdrawals from the occupied territories of the Oslo period, when the Shin Bet persuaded the government that Israel's Palestinian citizens posed a security threat that only they could deal with: Cook 2006, p. 79.
3. Segev 2007, p. 300, cited in Mearsheimer and Walt 2007, p. 85.
4. Quoted in Hirst 2003, p. 337.
5. Ben-Ami 2006, p. 103.
6. 'The seventh day', *New Yorker*, 28 May 2007.
7. Ben-Ami 2006, p. 104.
8. Ibid., pp. 106–7.
9. This is the impression Gorenberg (2006) attempts weakly to maintain, despite the information he unearths suggesting that most of the Israeli leadership shared an ambition to cleanse the territories of their native inhabitants and annex much or all of the land, even if they were hesitant about how best to do it.
10. Ben-Ami 2006, p. 115.
11. Ibid., p. 116.
12. 'Grab more hills, expand the territory', *London Review of Books*, 10 April 2008.
13. On 19 June the cabinet passed a resolution offering Egypt and Syria a return to the international borders, but did not include either Gaza or the West Bank in the pullback: Gorenberg 2006, pp. 52–3.
14. Morris 2001, p. 328.
15. Masalha 1997, pp. 84–7.
16. Morris 2001, pp. 328–9.
17. Hirst 2003, p. 355.
18. Zertal and Eldar 2007, p. 342.
19. Gorenberg 2002, pp. 99–100.
20. Gorenberg 2006, pp. 42–5.
21. 'A strange struggle for Jerusalem', *Ha'aretz*, 9 December 2007.
22. Gorenberg 2006, pp. 47 and 59.
23. In 1988 another 15 sq km were added to the city's western side, making the Jerusalem municipal area more than twice the size of Tel Aviv.
24. Stephen Langfur, 'Catch 67 in Jerusalem', *Challenge*, May–June 2005.
25. The interview, with *Ma'ariv* on 10 October 1990, is cited in the B'Tselem report *A Policy of Discrimination*, May 1995.
26. Gorenberg 2006, p. 46.
27. 'Crying wolf?', *Counterpunch*, 15 March 2003. Avnery observes that a large section of Qalqilya was wrecked and the inhabitants expelled to Nablus before the army relented, possibly after Avnery's intervention.
28. Cited in Masalha 1997, p. 83.
29. Mayhew and Adams 2006, pp. 92–3.
30. Nathan 2005, pp. 227–9.
31. Gorenberg 2006, p. 124. Golda Meir also observed: 'The borders are determined

by where Jews live, not where there is a line on a map': Noam Chomsky, 'Middle East diplomacy: Continuities and change', *Z Magazine*, December 1991.

32. The erasing of the Green Line briefly became a politically charged issue in 2006 when a dovish education minister, Yuli Tamir, demanded the line be reintroduced on maps in school textbooks: 'Meet the Green Line', *Ha'aretz*, 5 December 2006.

33. Zertal and Eldar 2007, p. 336. The army issued an order in December 1967 stating: 'The term Judea and Samaria area will be identical for all purposes ... to the term West Bank area.'

34. Elon 2000, p. 27.

35. Ibid., p. 30.

36. Ibid., p. 32.

37. Benvenisti 2000, p. 36.

38. Masalha 2007, p. 45.

39. Gorenberg 2006, pp. 50–51.

40. Ibid., p. 79.

41. For a while Allon, for example, thought it might be possible to create just such a Palestinian entity along the mountain ridge north of Jerusalem: ibid., p. 51.

42. Elon 2000, p. 26.

43. Gorenberg 2006, p. 81.

44. Zertal and Eldar 2007, p. 278.

45. Gorenberg 2006, p. 81.

46. Ibid., p. 82.

47. Ibid., pp. 172–3. Notably, Dayan's political apprentice, Shimon Peres, has argued to this day for Israel to continue constructing 'industrial parks' for Palestinian workers to create what he has called 'economic democracy' for them.

48. 'Crying wolf?'

49. Benvenisti 2000, p. 168.

50. 'Yet another June story', *Ha'aretz*, 7 June 2004.

51. Yitzhak Laor, 'Orchestrated panic', *London Review of Books*, 1 November 2007.

52. Masalha 1997, p. 93.

53. Ibid., pp. 92 and 97.

54. Ibid., p. 92.

55. Gorenberg 2006, pp. 141–2.

56. Ibid., p. 152.

57. Masalha 1997, pp. 111–19.

58. Quoted in Masalha 2007, p. 41.

59. Kretzmer 2002, pp. 32–4. Kretzmer points out that Israel's reading of the Convention is taken from the second paragraph of Article 2, even though this applies to occupations that are not the result of armed conflict. The occupation of the West Bank and Gaza is covered by the first paragraph of Article 2. In this paragraph, territory is considered occupied whatever its legal status before the occupation.

60. Al-Haq was originally called Law in the Service of Man.

61. Shehadeh 1993, pp. 97–102.

62. Ibid., Part VI.

63. Hajjar 2005, p. 51.

64. Ibid., pp. 55–6.

65. Zertal and Eldar 2007, p. 344.

66. See ICAHD's website at www.icahd.org/eng/.

67. See, for example: www.ipc.gov.ps/ipc_new/english/prisoners/details.asp?name
=15358.
68. Cited in Mearsheimer and Walt 2007, p. 100.
69. See Yesh Din, *Backyard Proceedings: The implementation of due process rights in the military courts in the occupied territories*, December 2007.
70. Kretzmer 2002, pp. 2–3.
71. 'Legality is in the eye of the beholder', *Ha'aretz*, 29 September 2003.
72. Until 1979 the settlements were administered as 'religious councils': Shehadeh 1993, p. 36.
73. 'But he loves me the most', *Ha'aretz*, 18 January 2008; 'High Court closes off use of major highway to Palestinians', *Ha'aretz*, 19 March 2008.
74. 'Tyranny in tar', *Ha'aretz*, 24 January 2008.
75. 'Israel's new road plans condemned as "apartheid"', *Guardian*, 5 December 2004.
76. 'Israel accused of "road apartheid" in West Bank', *Guardian*, 20 October 2005.
77. Hajjar 2005, p. 58.
78. Zertal and Eldar 2007, p. 386.
79. Ibid., pp. 371–96.
80. Ibid., p. 385.
81. See, for example, my two accounts in *al-Ahram Weekly*: 'Olives and lives', 31 October 2002, and 'Alone with the settlers', 21 November 2002.
82. From *Occupier's Law: Israel and the West Bank*, cited in Hajjar 2005, p. 63.
83. 'A shame for the government', *Ha'aretz*, 3 February 2002.
84. Shehadeh 1993, p. 110.
85. For a description of life for Palestinian workers in Israel during the first intifada, see Grossman 2002, chapter 15.
86. Roy 2007, p. 33.
87. Kimmerling 2003, pp. 3–4.

Chapter 3

1. Quoted in Morris 2001, p. 91.
2. Shehadeh 2007, pp. 13–14.
3. 'The optimist from East Jerusalem', *Ha'aretz*, 4 September 2007.
4. 'Legality is in the eye of the beholder', *Ha'aretz*, 29 September 2003.
5. 'Israel bars Palestinian Americans for first time since 1967', *Ha'aretz*, 10 July 2006. After months of bad publicity, Israel temporarily halted implementation of the rule in December 2006: 'Expected rule change could re-unite thousands in West Bank', *Ha'aretz*, 26 December 2006. When new regulations were announced in March 2007, they left wide scope for abuse by Israeli officials. It was reported that one or two Palestinians were being refused visas each day: 'Foreign Ministry informs embassies of new West Bank entry visa policy', *Jerusalem Post*, 12 March 2007.
6. Shehadeh 1993, p. 57. I use the metaphor of a 'glass wall' to describe the mechanism used by Israel to exclude its Palestinian citizens from all influence while protecting its image as a democratic state inside its own recognized borders in my book *Blood and Religion*.
7. Shehadeh 2007, pp. 73–4.

8. Ibid., chapter 2.

9. In 1968 the then attorney general Meir Shamgar announced that the effective annexation of East Jerusalem did not justify 'taking a person's property' and recommended the 1950 law not be applied: '"Absentee" land slated for E. Jerusalem homes', *Ha'aretz*, 6 January 2008.

10. 'AG reverses gov't decision to seize East Jerusalem land', *Ha'aretz*, 1 February 2005.

11. '"Absentee" land slated for E. Jerusalem homes'.

12. Shehadeh 1993, p. 63.

13. Ibid., p. 64.

14. 'JNF-owned company bought land in the territories', *Ha'aretz*, 17 February 2005. Himanuta, established in 1938, is formally an independent company but, according to one Israeli analyst, 'is the JNF by another name'. The JNF holds 99 per cent of Himanuta's shares and the two share offices. Its main purchases are near Jerusalem, including land at Beit Jala, Beit Safafa and the Etzion Bloc.

15. One of the earliest military orders declared the whole of the West Bank a closed military area, allowing the army to control entry into and exit from the territory.

16. Gorenberg 2006, p. 101.

17. Ibid., pp. 116 and 120. Settling the Etzion area was considered the correction of a historic injustice, because an earlier Jewish settlement had been abandoned following the massacre of its residents during the 1948 war.

18. Ibid., pp. 138–40.

19. Zertal and Eldar 2007, p. 346.

20. During the second intifada, the security line around the settlements was extended from 50 metres to 400 metres: ibid., p. 300.

21. Ibid., chapter 6.

22. 'Time of reckoning', *Ha'aretz*, 26 September 2005.

23. Zertal and Eldar 2007, p. 363.

24. Yoav Peled, 'Zionist Realities', *New Left Review*, March–April 2006.

25. In the Beit El case, Justice Alfred Witkon wrote that a civilian settlement would 'make it easier for the army to fulfill its role' because terrorists would be less active in an area where 'there are also people who are likely to keep them under surveillance and inform the authorities of any suspicious movement': Zertal and Eldar 2007, p. 351.

26. Ibid., p. 358.

27. They were settled at another site close by, one that was supposedly on state land, also named Elon Moreh.

28. 'Legality is in the eye of the beholder'.

29. Ibid.

30. Zertal and Eldar 2007, p. 99.

31. Under the Order in Council of 1922, the British did introduce the concept of 'state land' to Palestine but only to a very limited extent, in the case of land on which state offices were actually built: Shehadeh 1993, pp. 24–5.

32. Ibid., p. 11.

33. Ibid., p. 125.

34. Ibid., pp. 80–82.

35. Ibid., pp. 87–8.

36. 'Israel has seized 42% of West Bank, report says', *Guardian*, 15 May 2002. The full report, *Land Grab*, is available at www.btselem.org/English/Publications/Summaries/200205_Land_Grab.asp.
37. 'Report: Settlers use just 9% of state-allocated West Bank land', *Ha'aretz*, 7 July 2007.
38. 'Papers detail settlers' West Bank land grab', *Ha'aretz*, 17 March 2008.
39. Shehadeh 2007, pp. 167–8.
40. Ibid., p. 112.
41. 'Words won't stop the construction', *Ha'aretz*, 1 January 2008.
42. 'Israel redraws the roadmap, building quietly and quickly', *Guardian*, 18 October 2005.
43. 'Promised settlement freeze raises more questions than answers', *Ha'aretz*, 15 November 2007.
44. Amos Elon, 'Olmert & Israel: The change', *New York Review of Books*, 14 February 2008.
45. Hirst 2003, pp. 502–3.
46. Zertal and Eldar 2007, p. 99.
47. Hirst 2003, pp. 504–5.
48. Roy 2007, p. 324.
49. 'The lights of Netzarim', *Ha'aretz*, 7 November 2003.
50. 'The enemy within', *Ha'aretz*, 30 August 2002.
51. 'The extra civilian price tag: at least NIS 2.5 billion a year', *Ha'aretz*, 26 September 2003. The investigation was carried in a supplement that can be accessed at www.haaretz.com/hasen/pages/ShArt.jhtml?itemNo=344415&contrassID=2&subContrassID=1&sbSubContrassID=0&listSrc=.
52. Shehadeh 2007, p. 103.
53. 'Legality is in the eye of the beholder'.
54. 'Citing security, state refuses to release data on settlements', *Ha'aretz*, 7 January 2008.
55. 'A third of settlements on land taken for "security purposes"', *Ha'aretz*, 17 February 2008.
56. 'If the land isn't private?', *Ha'aretz*, 21 February 2008.
57. Shehadeh 2007, p. 80.
58. Available at www.mfa.gov.il/MFA/Peace+Process/Reference+Documents/Exchange+of+letters+Sharon-Bush+14–Apr-2004.htm.
59. 'Homes in illegal Israeli settlements for sale at London expo', *Guardian*, 17 November 2007.
60. 'Israel to build in East Jerusalem', *Guardian*, 5 December 2007.
61. 'Ministry pushes new neighborhood for Jews in E. J'lem', *Ha'aretz*, 19 December 2007.
62. 'The battle over settling Silwan simmers', *Ha'aretz*, 12 June 2007.
63. Yigal Bronner and Neve Gordon, 'The politics of archaeology in East Jerusalem', *Counterpunch*, 11 April 2008.
64. 'Jerusalem municipality delays demolition of Silwan homes', *Ha'aretz*, 22 June 2005.
65. 'ILA leasing Arab-owned land in Jerusalem to Ateret Cohanim', *Ha'aretz*, 20 August 2007.
66. 'Peace Now says West Bank settlements are still growing', *Ha'aretz*, 7 November 2007.

67. 'Olmert approves construction of 750 new homes in Givat Ze'ev', *Ha'aretz*, 10 March 2008.
68. 'Israelis Claim Secret Agreement With U.S.', *Washington Post*, 24 April 2008.
69. 'Settlers on Israel's eastern frontier', *Le Monde diplomatique*, August 2006.
70. 'The price is right', *Ha'aretz*, 29 September 2003.
71. 'A moral witness to the "intricate machine"', *New York Review of Books*, 6 December 2007.
72. 'Documents reveal illegal West Bank settlement building', *Ha'aretz*, 3 January 2006.
73. 'There's a system for turning Palestinian property into Israel's state land', *Ha'aretz*, 27 December 2005.
74. 'Bush, accessory after the facts', *Ha'aretz*, 9 January 2008.
75. 'Provocative words raise Mideast tensions', *CNN Online*, 16 November 1998.
76. Zertal and Eldar 2007, pp. 308–12.
77. 'Peace Now asks Egged to halt bus lines to illegal W. Bank outposts', *Ha'aretz*, 12 December 2007.
78. 'Dressed like the pioneers', *Ha'aretz*, 8 January 2008.
79. 'Three years after Sasson, over 100 outposts remain', *Ha'aretz*, 7 January 2008.
80. 'The defense minister and the case of the disappearing outposts', *Ha'aretz*, 2 July 2002. A human rights group, Yesh Din, for example, found in 2008 that 10 of 11 outposts the government claimed to have dismantled had been of the same outpost, called Shvut Ami: 'Border Police let settlers retake illegal West Bank outpost', *Ha'aretz*, 6 April 2008.
81. 'Eitam claims Sharon knew of illegal outpost approvals', *Ha'aretz*, 9 March 2005.
82. 'Cabinet approves Sasson Report panel', *Jerusalem Post*, 13 March 2005.
83. 'Israel accused of assisting illegal outposts', *Guardian*, 10 March 2005.
84. 'Sasson – more than meets the eye', *Jerusalem Post*, 10 March 2005.
85. 'The game is up', *Ha'aretz*, 10 March 2005.
86. 'Peace Now says West Bank settlements are still growing'.
87. 'Israel strikes deal with settlers', *Alternative Information Centre*, 9 March 2008.
88. 'Civil Admin: Hundreds of homes okayed for West Bank', *Ha'aretz*, 12 December 2007.

Chapter 4

1. Shehadeh 2007, p. 189.
2. The details of the document were provided in three articles in *Ha'aretz* on 13 December 2007: 'Document shows progress on core issues at Camp David summit'; 'Gov't to Clinton in 2000: Special authority for J'lem's "holy basin"'; and 'Israel–PA talks resume under shadow of Camp David lessons'.
3. 'Bush should stay home', *Ha'aretz*, 12 May 2008.
4. 'It would bring about a terrible response', *Bitterlemons*, 4 February 2002.
5. 'End of a journey', *Ha'aretz*, 14 September 2001.
6. From an entry dated 12 June 1895, cited in Morris 2001, pp. 21–2.
7. 'Survival of the fittest', *Ha'aretz*, 9 January 2004.
8. Khalidi 2007, p. 188.

9. Colin Schindler, 'Ze'ev Jabotinsky vs Menachem Begin', *Jerusalem Post*, 4 February 2006.
10. Shlaim 2000, p. 14.
11. Quoted in Hirst 2003, p. 253.
12. 'Legitimising anti-Arab racism', *Ha'aretz*, 21 February 2002.
13. At the height of the Histadrut's influence in the 1970s, not a single Histadrut-owned firm or factory was located in an Arab community; nor were there any Palestinian managers in its 600 industries: Lustick 1980, pp. 96–7.
14. Ibid., p. 263.
15. See Cook 2006, chapter 3.
16. Chris McGreal, 'Brothers in arms', *Guardian*, 7 February 2006.
17. 'Sharon's South African strategy', *Ha'aretz*, 18 September 2002.
18. 'Sharon's dream', *Ha'aretz*, 18 June 2007.
19. 'Israeli army orders confiscation of Palestinian land in West Bank', *Guardian*, 10 October 2007.
20. 'The fence: Stakes in the heart of the settlers' dream', *Ha'aretz*, 18 June 2002.
21. Roy 2007, p. 331.
22. 'The fight of Sharon's life: His place in history', *Ha'aretz*, 28 May 2003.
23. Available at www.whitehouse.gov/news/releases/2005/04/20050414–4.html.
24. Quoted in Hirst 2003, p. 522.
25. Kimmerling 2003, p. 76.
26. 'The Gaza bombshell', *Vanity Fair*, April 2008.
27. The 53-page leaked report can be read at http://image.guardian.co.uk/sys-files/Guardian/documents/2007/06/12/DeSotoReport.pdf.
28. 'The Gaza Bombshell'.
29. 'Washington rallies behind Abbas with end to Palestinian boycott', *Guardian*, 19 June 2007.
30. 'Our debt to Jimmy Carter', 15 April 2008.
31. 'A short history of apartheid', *Al-Ahram Weekly*, 8 January 2004.
32. Teveth 1985, p. 140.
33. Published in *Yediot Aharonot* on 28 May 1993, cited in Halper 2008, p. 63.
34. 'A short history of apartheid'.
35. Gorenberg 2006, p. 173.
36. Ibid., p. 175.
37. 'The "Jordanian option," the plan that refuses to die', *Ha'aretz*, 25 July 2007.
38. Ibid.
39. Gorenberg 2006, pp. 153 and 163.
40. 'The new partition plan', *Ha'aretz*, 2 September 2005.
41. 'The "Jordanian option," the plan that refuses to die'.
42. 'Israel wants Saudis in on peace efforts', *Jerusalem Post*, 22 June 2007.
43. 'Netanyahu calls for deployment of Jordanian troops in West Bank', *Ha'aretz*, 21 June 2007.
44. 'Olmert may allow Jordanian Army to help PA in West Bank', *Jerusalem Post*, 30 July 2007.
45. 'Between Tehran and Jerusalem', *Ha'aretz*, 3 August 2007.
46. 'Keeping the Palestinians out of sight', *Ha'aretz*, 19 August 2007.
47. Quoted in Gorenberg 2006, p. 132.
48. 'Water, water everywhere', *Ha'aretz*, 7 March 2008.
49. Halper 2008, pp. 163–4.

50. 'Water Authority: Israel is rapidly losing its water sources', *Ha'aretz*, 7 February 2008.
51. 'Water Authority: Israel must act to avoid humanitarian crisis', *Ha'aretz*, 19 March 2008.
52. Kav La'Oved, *On the Verge of Slave Labour*, February 2002.
53. 'More like partners than enemies', *Ha'aretz*, 10 February 2008.
54. 'The Gaza Strip blockade could seriously harm Israel's economy', *Ha'aretz*, 10 February 2008.
55. 'As the Hamas team laughs', *Ha'aretz*, 19 February 2006.
56. 'Ending the stranglehold on Gaza', *Boston Globe*, 26 January 2008.
57. 'UN shocked by "grim" life in Gaza', BBC Online, 15 February 2008.
58. Halper 2008, p. 157.
59. 'Children in the Gaza Strip suffer malnutrition', *British Medical Journal*, 9 November 2002.
60. 'Ending the stranglehold on Gaza'.
61. 'Study: Gaza humanitarian situation worst since 1967', *Ha'aretz*, 6 March 2008.
62. 'The strangulation of Gaza', *The Nation*, 1 February 2008.
63. 'Humanitarian crisis? In Gaza?', *Ha'aretz*, 24 January 2008.
64. Klein 2007, p. 428.
65. Ibid., p. 436.
66. 'The new walls of Baghdad', *Foreign Policy in Focus*, 21 April 2008.
67. Klein 2007, p. 442.
68. Press release, 'Contrary to Israel's Chief of Staff, at least half of those killed in Gaza did not take part in the fighting', 3 March 2008.
69. 'Israeli minister warns of Holocaust for Gaza if violence continues', *Guardian*, 1 March 2008.
70. 'J'lem diplomats briefed on "hasbara"', *Jerusalem Post*, 1 March 2008.
71. 'I'll Shoah you mine, if you Shoah me yours', *Ha'aretz*, 7 March 2008.
72. Press release, 'Gaza Strip/Israel: Civilians bear brunt of attacks', HRW, 29 February 2008.
73. 'Israeli mayor of bombarded border town offers to break ranks and talk to Hamas', *Guardian*, 23 February 2008.
74. 'Poll: Most Israelis back direct talks with Hamas on Shalit', *Ha'aretz*, 27 February 2008.
75. 'Barak rethinking "Iron Dome" defense system in face of Gaza rockets', *Ha'aretz*, 16 March 2008.
76. For example, an Israeli youth who had just completed three years in the Israeli army, Gil Na'amati, was shot in the knee by an Israeli sniper at a similar non-violent protest at the village of Masha: Reinhart 2002, p. 195–6.
77. 'Hamas "spent months cutting through Gaza wall in secret operation"', *The Times*, 24 January 2008.
78. 'An explosive, dangerous balance', *Ha'aretz*, 29 February 2008.
79. 'Gaza protesters form human chain', BBC Online, 25 February 2008.
80. 'The breakthrough that did not happen', *Ha'aretz*, 27 February 2008.
81. 'Nothing to sell the Palestinians', *Ha'aretz*, 16 July 2007.
82. 'Maximum Jews, minimum Palestinians', *Ha'aretz*, 13 November 2003.
83. 'Olmert to Haaretz: Two-state solution, or Israel is done for', *Ha'aretz*, 29 November 2007.

84. 'Cabinet declares Gaza "hostile territory"', *Ha'aretz*, 20 September 2007.
85. 'IDF to impose aerial siege, step up killings after Qassam hurts 4', *Ha'aretz*, 23 December 2005.
86. 'Court upholds cuts to Gaza electricity', *Jerusalem Post*, 30 January 2008.
87. 'PA seeks int'l intervention as Gaza power cuts imminent', *Ha'aretz*, 26 October 2007.
88. 'Egypt rejects idea of Israel waiving responsibility for Gaza', *Ha'aretz*, 24 January 2008.
89. 'Official says Israel wants to sever Gaza connections', *International Herald Tribune*, 24 January 2008.
90. 'Egypt to take over supplying Gaza power in draft deal', *Ha'aretz*, 20 March 2008.
91. 'PM: Gazans can't expect normal lives while rockets hit Israel', *Ha'aretz*, 23 January 2008.
92. 'Darkness falls on Gaza as Israel takes revenge for rocket attacks', *The Times*, 21 January 2008.
93. 'Sheetrit: We should level Gaza neighborhoods', *Ynet*, 10 February 2008.
94. 'Barak mulls legality of artillery fire at population centers', *Ha'aretz*, 3 March 2008.
95. 'Barak seeks legal okay to move Gazan civilians from homes', *Ha'aretz*, 4 March 2008.
96. Lemkin's life, and his death in penury, are discussed in 'Genocide. So what?', *Ha'aretz*, 25 April 2008.
97. Available at http://en.wikipedia.org/wiki/Genocide.
98. Available at www.unhchr.ch/html/menu3/b/p_genoci.htm.
99. Kimmerling 2003, p. 211.
100. Quoted in Curtis (ed.) 1975, p. 185, cited in Eitan Felner, 'Creeping annexation of the West Bank', *Le Monde diplomatique*, November 1999.
101. 'Legality is in the eye of the beholder', *Ha'aretz*, 29 September 2003.
102. 'A "Palestinian state": Sharon's real purpose is to create foreigners', *International Herald Tribune*, 25 September 2002.
103. 'This exodus presents us Egyptians with a threat – and an opportunity', *Guardian*, 27 January 2008.

Chapter 5

'Finishing the job' originally published in *Al-Ahram Weekly* 612, 14–20 November 2002; 'Minister of strategic threats' originally published as 'Israel's minister of strategic threats', *Counterpunch*, 25 October 2006; 'The persecution of Azmi Bishara' originally published as 'The Shin Bet and the persecution of Azmi Bishara', *Counterpunch*, 5 June 2007.

1. Benny Morris, 'A New Exodus for the Middle East?', *Guardian*, 3 October 2002. Morris' views hardened further during the second intifada. In 2007 he observed: 'We are an outpost of the West, as they see it and as we also see ourselves, in a largely Islamic, backward and in some ways even barbaric area. ... There is a problem here with Islam': 'Israel revisited', *Washington Post*, 11 March 2007.

2. Polls have consistently shown that between 60 and 65 per cent of Israeli Jews favour the emigration of Israeli Arabs: Sultany 2005, pp. 65, 125–8.

3. These last three represented the most distinctive strands of pre-state Zionism, and have modern equivalents: Ben-Gurion's Labor Zionism informs the policies of the Labor party; Jabotinsky's Revisionism is the inspiration for the Greater Israel ambitions of the Likud Party; and Buber's discomfort with realizing Jewish nationalism through the establishment of an ethnic state prefigures many of the debates in the dovish Meretz Party.

4. See, for example, Morris 2004.

5. The Mizrahim were soon a majority of Israel's Jewish population and remained so until the immigration of more than 1 million 'Russians' during the 1990s, following the collapse of the Soviet Union. See Massad 2006, particularly chapter 3.

6. Ben-Gurion had been keen to conquer the West Bank during the 1948 war. 'We should not look at the West Bank as stony hills and enemy territory; it is Judea-Samaria. We are redeeming it, we are liberating it': 'Coming to terms with Israel: Conversations with Ian Lustick', 4 March 2002, on the University of California, Berkeley, website, http://globetrotter.berkeley.edu/people2/Lustick/lustick-con1.html. In 1955 Ben-Gurion also promoted a plan to capture the Gaza Strip: Shlaim 2000, pp. 129–30. After 1967, however, he called for withdrawal from the West Bank and Gaza, apparently appreciating the demographic consequences: Pappe 2006, p. 192.

7. See Finkelstein 2000, pp. 16–23.

8. The total amount of US aid is difficult to quantify as the money comes in many guises. In a typical year, Israel receives about $3 billion in direct foreign and military aid, more than a third of the total US foreign aid budget. Uniquely, Israel receives the money as a lump sum at the beginning of the fiscal year – thereby gaining substantial bank interest (typically about $250 million) – and does not account for how the money is spent. Other hidden aid arrives in the following forms: loans never repaid; the inclusion of defence programmes from Israeli contractors in the Pentagon budget; underpriced transfers of military technology, which Israel can sell on in its own weapons systems; and the use of Israeli contractors for USAID projects. Financial ties are tightened further by Washington's issuing of 'loan guarantees' on Israel's behalf and the investment by US pension funds in Israeli bonds. See Paul de Rooij, 'US aid to Israel', *Counterpunch*, 12 November 2002.

9. Pappe (2006, p. 238) characterises these two camps as the 'custodians' (sanctuary Zionists) and the 'redeemers' (expansionist Zionists).

10. For more on Israel's plans to become a regional superpower, see Cook 2008, especially chapter 3.

11. 'The ultimate entertainment', *Ha'aretz*, 18 May 2007.

12. Menachem Begin personifies the inadequacy of such simple characterizations, according to a new biography in Hebrew by Avi Shilon. Begin, a pre-state militia leader and later a far-right prime minister, prevented Ben-Gurion from arresting dissident journalist Uri Avnery; stopped attempts to ban Peace Now demonstrations during the 1982 invasion of Lebanon; and encouraged the passage of Israel's most liberal piece of legislation, the Basic Law on Human Dignity and Freedom: 'From rabble-rouser to recluse', *Ha'aretz*, 21 December 2007.

13. 'Every settler a king', *Ha'aretz*, 1 February 2002.

14. This was written before the Qassam rocket attacks from Gaza, which looked to some Palestinians like the most viable form of resistance, violent or non-violent, as Palestinians were sealed into their ghettoes.

15. Cook 2006, especially pp. 118–22.

16. Nahad Abu Kishaq and Kais Obeid had their citizenship revoked in late 2002. A *Ha'aretz* editorial noted that no Jew had ever lost their citizenship, not even Yigal Amir, Rabin's assassin: 'Who is a citizen?', 7 August 2002.

17. Amendments to Israel's election laws in 2002 allowed individual candidates and parties to be banned if their platform supported either the armed struggle of an enemy country or denied Israel's existence as a Jewish and democratic state. Two Arab Knesset candidates, Ahmed Tibi and Azmi Bishara, were barred from the 2003 election, as was Bishara's party. The decision was overturned on appeal to the Supreme Court: 'Court: MKs Tibi, Bishara and far-right activist Marzel can run', *Ha'aretz*, 11 January 2003.

18. Lieberman was feted by American political leaders, including Secretary of State Condoleezza Rice: Yossi Sarid, 'Let's air it out', *Ha'aretz*, 19 January 2007.

19. Lieberman and his party publicly opposed the appointment of an Arab MK, Raleb Majadele, to the cabinet: 'Cabinet okays appointment of Majadele as first Arab minister', *Ha'aretz*, 28 January 2007.

20. 'A "lite" plan for the enlightened voter', *Ha'aretz*, 21 March 2006.

21. 'Poll: Majority wants Olmert out', *Ynet*, 25 August 2006. According to the results, Netanyahu was favourite with 22 per cent of votes, followed by Lieberman with 18 per cent and Shimon Peres with 12 per cent.

22. 'A mere 5 Laborites openly reject Lieberman as gov't partner', *Ha'aretz*, 25 November 2006.

23. Ibid.

24. For details of the 4 billion shekel plan, see Shuli Dichter and As'ad Ghanem (eds), *The Sikkuy Report 2001–2002*, July 2002.

25. 'Netanyahu: Israel's Arabs are the real demographic threat', *Ha'aretz*, 18 December 2003. He made the same point again in January 2007, when he explained the 'positive' benefits of the child allowance cuts he introduced in 2002 in producing 'a dramatic drop in the birth rate' of the 'non-Jewish public': 'Netanyahu: Pensions cut – Arabs' birth rate declined', *Ynet*, 3 January 2007.

26. 'Maximum Jews, minimum Palestinians', *Ha'aretz*, 13 November 2003.

27. See my 'Disturbing Israeli ideas from Herzliya', *Daily Star* (Beirut), 27 January 2006.

28. See Cook 2006, pp. 117–18, 161–2.

29. Sultany 2005, pp. 122–3.

30. Ben-Gurion's determination to ignore the existence of Arab citizens in Israel extended both to refusing his identity card because it was written in part in Arabic, and to refusing to visit any of the country's Arab communities. Quoted in Gilmour 1982, pp. 93–4, cited in Masalha 1997, pp. xi–xii.

31. One commentator observed: 'Too many of us see Israeli Arabs, as a group, as hypocrites, parasites, their dual-loyalty a thin disguise for support of terror in the service of Palestine. … It is, in many ways, a form of classical anti-Semitism in which the Semites in question happen to be Israeli Arabs': Bradley Burston, 'We like our Arabs to be traitors', *Ha'aretz*, 14 April 2007.

32. See Cook 2006, especially chapter 4.

33. Sofer 2001, p. 35.

34. Available at www.arabhra.org/HRaAdmin/UserImages/Files/SilencingDissent English.pdf.
35. 'It smells like discrimination', *Ha'aretz*, 10 May 2007.
36. There was a precedent for Bishara's treatment. Israel's first independent Arab party, the nationalist al-Ard movement, was banned by the Shin Bet from the 1965 elections. See Ghanem 2001.
37. The Shin Bet's role in the appointment of teachers was supposed to be phased out in early 2005: 'Shin Bet will no longer scrutinize Arab educators', *Ha'aretz*, 6 January 2005. However, its interference continued under different guises. See Ismael Abu-Saad, 'Palestinian education in Israel: The legacy of the military government', *Holy Land Studies*, vol. 5, no. 1, May 2006, pp. 21–56.
38. 'Poll: 75% of Israeli Arabs support Jewish, democratic constitution', *Ha'aretz*, 29 April 2007.
39. 'Azmi Bishara as an example', *Ha'aretz*, 11 April 2007.
40. Bishara submitted his resignation from the Knesset at the Israeli embassy in Cairo: 'In Cairo, Bishara quits the Knesset', *Ha'aretz*, 23 April 2007.
41. The head of the Shin Bet, Yuval Diskin, argued that his organization was entitled to bug the phone of anyone involved in subversive activities, even if such activities were legal. 'The service's view is that "subversion" could include seeking to change the state's basic values by abolishing its democratic character or its Jewish character': 'Shin Bet: Wiretaps can be used to guard state's Jewish nature', *Ha'aretz*, 21 May 2007.
42. 'MK A-Sana: AG's silence proves Arab MKs' phones are tapped', *Ha'aretz*, 13 May 2007.
43. 'Is Bishara another Fahima?', *Ha'aretz*, 27 April 2007.
44. 'Gag lifted, details of Bishara's alleged treason emerge', *Ha'aretz*, 3 May 2007.
45. 'Police forces search Azmi Bishara's Knesset office', *Ha'aretz*, 1 May 2007.
46. See my article 'The real target', *Al-Ahram Weekly*, 22–28 May 2003.
47. For more on the accusations against Salah, see a report by the Arab Association for Human Rights in Nazareth, available at www.arabhra.org/HRA/Secondary Articles/SecondaryArticlePage.aspx?SecondaryArticle=1461.
48. 'Plea deal secures Islamists' release', *Ha'aretz*, 12 January 2005. Veteran analyst Uzi Benziman compared Bishara's treatment to that of the Palestinian poet Mahmoud Darwish, who left Israel in the 1970s 'tired of the harassment of the authorities and opting to leave the country': 'Azmi Bishara as an example'.
49. *Journal of Palestine Studies*, vol. 36, no. 2, Winter 2007, p. 69.
50. See my article 'Targeting Haram Al-Sharif', *Al-Ahram Weekly*, 31 January 2003.
51. The quotation, translated from Hebrew, is from the National Democratic Assembly party's background document 'The Ongoing Attack Against MK Azmi Bishara and the NDA', April 2007.
52. Ayalon narrowly lost to his rival, Ehud Barak, a former Labor prime minister: 'Barak wins Labor primary, named new party chairman', *Ha'aretz*, 13 June 2007.
53. See my two articles in *Al-Ahram Weekly* on the trials: 'In the hot seat', 8 November 2001, and 'An ominous prelude', 28 February 2002. *Ha'aretz* has a collection of articles from the build-up to the trials available at www.haaretz.com/hasen/pages/ShArt.jhtml?itemNo=91740&contrassID=3&subContrassID=0&sbSubContrassID=0.

54. An amendment to the Prevention of Infiltration Law ended the diplomatic immunity enjoyed by Knesset members visiting 'enemy states'. Instead MKs had to apply to the Interior Ministry for authorization. Claiming the ministry always refused their requests, Bishara and other Arab MKs continued to visit states like Syria. In retaliation, the ministry sought the revocation of their passports: 'Bar-On wants passports of Arab MKs who visited Syria revoked', *Ha'aretz*, 11 September 2006.

55. The allegations came from a Shin Bet 'expert' known simply as Nadav: 'The ongoing attack against MK Azmi Bishara and the NDA'. State prosecutor Talia Sasson helped the Central Elections Committee interpret the Shin Bet evidence 'as saying that Bishara denies Israel's right to exist as a Jewish state. But beyond that, a picture takes shape that conflicts not only with Israel as a Jewish state, but as any kind of state.' *Jerusalem Post* reporters fleshed out the details: 'According to one piece of Shin Bet evidence, Bishara said that all Jews who arrived here after 1948 would have to leave after a Palestinian state is established. According to another, he called on members of the Balad youth movement to act like soldiers, since they would one day form the Palestinian army that would defeat the Zionists in battle': 'Elections panel bars second Arab lawmaker from seeking reelection', 1 January 2003.

56. 'Court: MKs Tibi, Bishara and far-right activist Marzel can run', *Ha'aretz*, 11 January 2003.

57. 'The ongoing attack against MK Azmi Bishara and the NDA'. *Ha'aretz*'s reporter Meron Rapoport refers to the *Ma'ariv* report in 'Will he come or will he go?', 13 April 2007.

58. Available at www.adalah.org/eng/democratic_constitution-e.pdf.

59. 'Israeli Arabs seek right to return to villages abandoned in 1948', *Ha'aretz*, 3 December 2006.

60. Available at www.adalah.org/newsletter/eng/dec06/tasawor-mostaqbali.pdf.

61. Available at www.mada-research.org/archive/haifaenglish.pdf.

62. 'PMO to Balad: We will thwart anti-Israel activity even if legal', *Ha'aretz*, 17 March 2003.

63. Yitzhak Laor, 'Democracy for Jews only', *Ha'aretz*, 30 May 2007. Laor pointed out: 'Israeli law defines the state as Jewish and democratic. The Shin Bet is now trying to turn the "and" into an "or".'

64. 'It smells like discrimination'.

65. 'Democracy for Jews only'.

Chapter 6

'Watching the checkpoints' originally published as 'Apartheid looks like this', *Al-Ahram Weekly* 833, 22–28 February 2007; 'Israel's latest bureaucratic obscenity' originally published in *Electronic Intifada*, 12 July 2006; 'An experiment in human despair' originally published in *Counterpunch*, 5 July 2006; 'The struggle for Palestine's soul' originally published in Anti-war.com, 7 October 2006.

1. www.machsomwatch.org/eng/homePageEng.asp?link=homePage&lang=eng.

2. See Amira Hass, 'An effective strategy of containment and repression', *Journal of Palestine Studies*, vol. 31 no. 2, Spring 2002.

3. 'PM calls for ease of Palestinian movement at W. Bank crossings', *Ha'aretz*, 16 January 2007.
4. 'Impossible travel', *Ha'aretz*, 19 January 2007.
5. Available at http://permanent.access.gpo.gov/lps35389/1996/268.htm.
6. See, for example, World Bank, 'West Bank and Gaza update', April 2006.
7. 'IDF source admits: 44 "removed" barriers didn't exist', *Ha'aretz*, 22 January 2007.
8. 'Israel shocked by image of soldiers forcing violinist to play at roadblock', *Guardian*, 29 November 2004. An army investigation concluded that the violinist chose to play. Available at www.mfa.gov.il/MFA/Government/Communiques/2004/ Investigation+of+incident+of+Palestinian+playing+violin+30-Nov-2004.htm.
9. See, for example, 'Challenging the NGO mythology', *Jerusalem Post*, 11 March 2006.
10. 'The checkpoint generation', *Ha'aretz*, 29 November 2006.
11. 'Israeli fence "will harm one in three Palestinians"', *Independent*, 12 November 2003.
12. 'Jabara residents struggle to deal with fence', *Ha'aretz*, 21 October 2003.
13. On the urinating episode, see 'Checkpoint comradeship', *Ha'aretz*, 24 January 2007.
14. 'The checkpoint generation'.
15. Ibid.
16. At this checkpoint, Nomi told me a story illustrating the future use such checkpoints might be put to in separating Palestinians in the occupied territories from Palestinians inside Israel and in finding a pretext for stripping the latter of citizenship. Palestinian citizens were being allowed to pass through checkpoints to enter Nablus to see relatives, but when they left were being detained and issued letters warning that they would be tried if again caught visiting 'enemy' areas. This echoed a discussion by the Israeli cabinet in April 2006 at which ministers argued over classifying the Palestinian Authority as an 'enemy entity'. The move was rejected because, as one official said: 'There are international legal implications in such a declaration, including closing off border crossings, that we don't want to do yet': 'More Hamas MPs may lose residency', *Jerusalem Post*, 20 April 2006. Will Israel, after it has completed the West Bank wall and its 'border' terminals, classify visits by Israeli Arabs to relatives as 'visiting an enemy state'? And will such visits be grounds for revoking citizenship under loyalty legislation Israel's Justice Ministry is drafting? For more, see my article 'We the Jewish state', *Al-Ahram Weekly*, 18 January 2007.
17. Rashid Khalidi, 'The Palestinians and 1948: The underlying causes of failure', in Rogan and Shlaim 2001, p. 14.
18. Olmert explained the purpose of the sonic booms: 'I want nobody to sleep at night in Gaza': 'Sharon's Shadow', *Newsweek*, 17 July 2006.
19. 'Israel bars Palestinian Americans for first time since 1967', *Ha'aretz*, 10 July 2006.
20. Amira Hass, 'No direction home', *Ha'aretz*, 13 October 2005.
21. Such cases were highlighted in articles, including 'Accidental emigrant', *Ha'aretz*, 28 August 2006, and 'The slippery slope of expulsion', *Ha'aretz*, 1 October 2006. Roy (2007, p. 331) has catalogued other restrictions on entry into the occupied territories – for foreigners, journalists and Jews – and movement between areas of the occupied territories for Palestinians. Among West Bankers, for example,

less than a third are eligible to apply for travel permits and less than 10 per cent actually try to apply, meaning 'at least 90 per cent of the population is totally confined to [its] territorial enclaves'.

22. 'Israel bars Palestinian Americans for first time since 1967'.

23. The video can be seen at www.metacafe.co.il/watch/188108/jon_snow_interviews_the_israeli_ambassador/.

24. 'Someone even managed to defecate into the photocopier', *Ha'aretz*, 6 May 2002.

25. In May 2006 the Interior Ministry gave four Hamas MPs – Muhammad Abu Tir, Ahmed Abu Atoun, Khaled Abu Arafa and Mahmoud Totach – 30 days to renounce Hamas membership. A month later the four were seized by the Israeli army, along with sixty other Hamas officials, and stripped of their Jerusalem residency: 'Hamas members' residency revoked', *Jerusalem Post*, 30 June, 2006.

26. 'West Bank crisis grows as Israelis arrest Hamas leaders in revenge', *Daily Telegraph*, 1 July 2006. Also see my essay 'Kidnapped correspondents' in this collection.

27. 'PM: We won't balk at "extreme action"', *Jerusalem Post*, 28 June 2006.

28. 'Report: Shalit to be freed if Mashaal enters Gaza', *Ynet*, 6 October 2006; 'Olmert tells Rice Israel interested in boosting Abbas', *Jerusalem Post*, 5 October 2006.

29. See, for example, 'Five soldiers killed in Gaza, Hebron. Hamas, Fatah, Islamic Jihad claim joint attack', *Jerusalem Post*, 9 June 2003.

30. 'Lessons of the Palestinian fighting', *Ha'aretz*, 7 October 2006. Israel and the US tried various ways to strengthen Fatah against Hamas, including training the Badr Brigade in Jordan and sending shipments of arms from Egypt: 'U.S. general says building up Abbas's guard', *Reuters*, 24 November 2006; 'PA official: Haniyeh, Abbas will meet in Jordan later this week', *Ha'aretz*, 25 December 2006; 'Israel confirms arms shipment sent to aid Abbas', *New York Times*, 28 December. In early 2007 Abbas was promised nearly $80 million funding to strengthen his security apparatus: 'U.S. offers to fund an additional 10,000 of Abbas' soldiers', *Ha'aretz*, 3 February 2007.

31. 'Expert: Hamas–Fatah friction delaying Shalit's release', *Ynet*, 3 October 2006.

32. In December 1988 Arafat accepted UN Resolution 242, which requires Israel to withdraw to the 1967 lines, and thereby implicitly recognized its existence within the Green Line. In his 1993 letter to Yitzhak Rabin, Arafat stated: 'The PLO recognizes the right of the State of Israel to exist in peace and security.' Rabin promised only 'to recognize the PLO as the representative of the Palestinian people'. Available at www.jewishvirtuallibrary.org/jsource/Peace/recogn.html.

33. Reinhart (2006, pp. 198–217) describes the Palestinian leadership's complicity with Israel's wall-building.

34. In line with US wishes, Mahmoud Abbas kept up the pressure on Hamas to agree to a cabinet of technocrats: 'Hamas: Call for vote is coup attempt', *Ha'aretz*, 17 December 2006. When Hamas refused, Abbas agreed to a meeting in Mecca, overseen by the Saudis, at which a national unity government was approved: 'Hamas and Fatah reach deal in Mecca', *International Herald Tribune*, 8 February 2007. Israel sought to undermine the arrangement: 'Olmert: New Palestinian gov't must abide by Quartet demands', *Ha'aretz*, 11 February 2007; 'Israel to tighten economic screws on PA', *Ha'aretz*, 19 March 2007. The US recruited Fatah strongman Mohammed Dahlan to topple Hamas in Gaza but were foiled when Hamas routed the coup plotters in summer 2007: 'The Gaza Bombshell',

Vanity Fair, April 2008. Immediately afterwards, Abbas created an alternative government – of technocrats – in the West Bank that was recognized by the US and Europe.

35. Israel had been seeking for some time to persuade the world that al-Qaeda had infiltrated the occupied territories. In 2002 Israel promoted stories, widely discredited, that al-Qaeda had set up a cell in Gaza. The Palestinian Authority accused the Shin Bet of trying to recruit impressionable youngsters into a front group: 'Ibrahim, the Shin Bet wants you to join Qaida', *Ha'aretz*, 15 December 2002; 'Palestinians: Israel faked Gaza Al Qaeda presence', Reuters, 7 December 2002.

Chapter 7

'Hollow visions of the future' originally published as 'Hollow visions of Palestine's future', Anti-war.com, 18 November 2006; 'Bad faith' originally published as 'Bad faith and the destruction of Palestine', *Counterpunch*, 29 September 2006; 'No right to non-violent resistance' originally published as 'Palestinians are being denied the right to non-violent resistance', *Znet*, 30 November 2006.

1. A translation of the speech, delivered on 4 November 2006, is available at www.guardian.co.uk/g2/story/0,,1941046,00.html.

2. This quote is usually attributed to Meir on meeting Anwar Sadat, before the peace talks with Egypt: http://en.wikiquote.org/wiki/Golda_Meir.

3. 'Grossman's dilemma', Gush Shalom website, 18 November 2006.

4. 'Israeli Jews fret over possibility of a binational state', *Ha'aretz*, 5 November 2003.

5. See, for example, 'Assassinating Arafat: A disaster foretold', *Counterpunch*, 15 September 2003.

6. 'Exchange of letters between PM Sharon and President Bush': www.mfa.gov.il/MFA/Peace+Process/Reference+Documents/Exchange+of+letters+Sharon-Bush+14–Apr-2004.htm.

7. 'A "lite" plan for the enlightened voter', *Ha'aretz*, 21 March 2006.

8. 'Lieberman presents to Russia plan to expel "disloyal Arabs"', *Ha'aretz*, 30 May 2004.

9. B'Tselem, *Act of Vengeance: Israel's Bombing of the Gaza Power Plant and its Effects*, September 2006, available at www.btselem.org/english/Publications/Summaries/200609_Act_of_Vengeance.asp.

10. 'Disproportionate' was the term favoured by the media to describe Israel's devastation of Lebanon in summer 2006 without referring to it as collective punishment or a war crime. See, for example, Editorial, 'Disproportionate, dangerous, destructive', *Guardian*, 14 July 2006.

11. http://medialens.org/forum/viewtopic.php?t=1729.

12. 'Shin Bet foils Hamas–Jewish meeting', *Jerusalem Post*, 26 June 2006. Months earlier, one of the rabbis leading the initiative, Menachem Froman, wrote about the need to talk to Hamas: 'Maybe, we do have someone to talk to', *Ha'aretz*, 27 January 2006.

13. Reinhart 2006, pp. 105–7.

14. Many reports can be found at www.bilin-village.org/temoignages_en.php#news.

15. 'Poll: 67% of Israelis want talks with PA gov't including Hamas', *Ha'aretz*, 27 September 2006.

16. 'Israel bars Palestinian Americans for first time since 1967', *Ha'aretz*, 10 July 2006.

17. Her age was disputed: Israeli newspapers preferred 57, while the international media settled on 64 or 70.

18. Right-wing media in the US, such as the *New York Post*, called her 'evil', overlooking the fact that under international law she had a right to take part in military action against an occupying army: 'Gran bomb', 24 November 2006.

19. The press release, dated 22 November 2006, was later retracted after a campaign of protest, of which this article was a part. Prominent attacks came from Norman Finkelstein ('Human Rights Watch must retract its shameful press release', *Counterpunch*, 29 November 2006) and the International Solidarity Movement ('Nonviolent resistance is not illegal: Human Rights Watch Should retract statement', 1 December 2006). The HRW retraction, on 16 December 2006, with the original press release, is available at http://hrw.org/english/docs/2006/11/22/isrlpa14652.htm.

20. 'Gaza women killed in mosque siege', BBC Online, 3 November 2006.

21. 'IDF calls off strike after hundreds shield Gaza militant's house', *Ha'aretz*, 19 November 2006; 'Gaza: Use of human shields continues', *Jerusalem Post*, 19 November 2006.

22. 'Refuse to be a human shield? No such thing', *Ha'aretz*, 7 July 2003; 'Israel faces human shield claim', BBC Online, 23 April 2004. Another incident, involving three Palestinians, was documented in my article 'Miriam as human shield', *Al-Ahram Weekly*, 28 November 2002. The Supreme Court finally outlawed the use of human shields by the Israeli army in October 2005. However, reports of such abuses continued to appear, including of an 11-year-old girl in Nablus: 'B'Tselem: IDF used Palestinian girl as human shield in Nablus', *Ha'aretz*, 9 March 2007. An HRW press release on this incident did not call it a 'war crime', the phrase it used when referring to incidents of Palestinians protecting homes: 'Israel: Stop forcing civilians to assist military operations', 16 March 2007. Palestinian testimonies of being used as human shields have been collected at www.btselem.org/English/Testimonies/Index.asp?TF=12.

23. Examples of such reports can be found at http://hrw.org/english/docs/2001/11/30/isrlpa3392.htm; http://web.amnesty.org/report2003/pse-summary -eng.

24. http://hrw.org/english/docs/2006/11/22/isrlpa14652.htm; http://hrw.org/english/docs/2006/11/18/isrlpa14639.htm;http://hrw.org/english/docs/ 2006/11/07/palab14496.htm;http://hrw.org/english/docs/2006/11/10/isrlpa14550.htm.

25. A typical example of the double standard was to be found in a press release issued on 29 June 2006, when HRW referred to Israel's destruction of Gaza's only power station – a war crime – as an act that 'needlessly punishes the civilian population and has created the potential for a serious humanitarian crisis'. In the next sentence HRW condemned the actions of armed Palestinian groups in capturing an Israeli soldier as 'a war crime', available at www.hrw.org/english/docs/2006/06/29/isrlpa13662.htm.

Chapter 8

'Kidnapped correspondents' originally published as 'Kidnapped by Israel: The British media and the invasion of Gaza', *Media Lens*, 30 June 2006; 'Covering up Gaza' originally published in *Al-Ahram Weekly* 803, 13–19 July 2006.

1. Available at http://observer.guardian.co.uk/world/story/0,,1805354,00.html. See also 'IDF commandos enter Gaza, capture two Hamas terrorists', *Jerusalem Post*, 25 June 2006.
2. On BBC World News, 10 a.m. GMT, 25 June 2006. The filmed report was shown throughout the day.
3. Brothers Osama and Mustafa Mu'amar, aged 31 and 20 and both students, were accused by Israel of being in the final stages of planning a Hamas attack. Hamas denied they were members.
4. 'Storm over Gaza', *Guardian*, 29 June 2006.
5. 'An understandable over-reaction', Comment is Free, *Guardian*, 28 June 2006.
6. See, for example, 'Hamas "seeks dialogue with West"', BBC Online, 26 March 2006.
7. 'Israel set for military raid over kidnapped soldier', *Independent*, 27 June 2006.
8. 'Israel hunts for abducted soldier after dawn raid by militants', *Independent*, 26 June 2006.
9. 'Palestinians hunt for Israeli hostage', *Guardian*, 26 June 2006.
10. 'Israel warns of "extreme action"', BBC Online, 28 June 2006.
11. 'Israel captures Hamas founder', BBC Online, 3 March 2003.
12. 'Israel detains Hamas ministers', *Guardian*, 29 June 2006.
13. BBC World News, 10 a.m. GMT, 29 June 2006.
14. 'Israel rounds up Hamas politicians', *Guardian*, 29 June 2006.
15. BBC World News, 6 p.m. GMT, 29 June 2006.
16. For more on this phenomenon in the 1960s and 1970s, see Mayhew and Adams 2006, chapter 5. Notably, Jewish publications excitedly reported the appointment of two Jews to the BBC's bureau in Jerusalem in late 2006: 'Jewish reporters join BBC's Israel team', totallyjewish.com, 2 November 2006.
17. Of Israel's four big daily newspapers, three – *Yediot Aharonot*, *Ha'aretz* and the *Jerusalem Post* – have English editions in print or on the Internet. The fourth, *Ma'ariv*, briefly had an English Internet edition.
18. A Palestinian daily newspaper in English, the *Palestine Times*, existed for a few months before folding: 'Palestinian news: Now in English', *Ha'aretz*, 18 January 2006. It depended on Israeli distributors to be viable.
19. See, for example, 'Death on the beach', *Guardian*, 10 June 2006.
20. 'Israeli missiles pound Gaza into a new Dark Age in "collective punishment"', *Independent*, 29 June 2006.
21. 'Israel rounds up Hamas politicians', 11.45 a.m. update, 29 June 2006.
22. 'An understandable over-reaction'.
23. 'Storm over Gaza'.
24. Such comments from Hamas leaders were rarely given coverage. See, for example, 'Hamas: We'll recognize Israel within '67 borders', *Ynet*, 11 May 2006.
25. 'Gaza Strip to remain without full electrical power for a year', *Ha'aretz*, 27 September 2006.
26. Operation Summer Rain claimed 240 Palestinian lives in two months, of which 197 were civilians, including 48 children: 'Palestinian children pay price of Israel's

Summer Rain offensive', *Guardian*, 7 September 2006.

27. 'Editors dismiss Israeli press chief's allegation of bias', *Guardian*, 17 October 2002. Another incident came to light in October 2006 when Jorg Bremer of the *Frankfurter Allgemeine* and other journalists discovered that a 2003 change in the law had made them illegal residents. Seaman reassured Bremer that he would get a work visa would from a special committee but others would not, and that was 'why I like the committee'. When *Ha'aretz* confronted Seaman, he responded: 'I told him not to make noise', 'I feel like screwing him over' and 'He's a piece of shit': 'Foreign reporter challenges GPO over visa policy', *Ha'aretz*, 15 October 2006. A statement from the Interior Ministry that it would 'be lenient where we are asked to be' in issuing visas restated the problem rather than solved it: 'Interior Ministry: Veteran foreign journalists will be given visas', *Ha'aretz*, 20 November 2006. In March 2007 Seaman was investigated over complaints he was denying press passes to 'hostile' foreign journalists: 'Civil Service investigating complaints against GPO head', *Ha'aretz*, 12 March 2007. And in early 2008, Israel announced it was denying visas to Al Jazeera staff because the channel was 'prioritising Palestinian suffering': 'Israel accuses al-Jazeera of bias', BBC Online, 12 March 2008.

28. See my 'How to cover disengagement?', *Electronic Intifada*, 8 August 2005.

29. The parents of Briton Tom Hurndall carried out an investigation showing major flaws in the Israeli army's account of their son's killing. A British jury later found that he had been 'intentionally killed': 'British peace activist was "intentionally killed"', *Guardian*, 10 April 2006. Rachel Corrie, an American, died under the blade of an Israeli army bulldozer destroying Palestinian homes in Rafah. Extracts from her diaries were adapted into a stage play.

30. Some Internet diaries are still published on the ISM and *Electronic Intifada* websites.

31. This policy was apparently formalized: 'ISM foreign protestors to be expelled', *Ma'ariv*, 22 June 2006, available in translation at http://electronicintifada.net/cgi-bin/artman/exec/view.cgi/12/4953.

32. One British journalist, 26-year-old Eva Jasiewicz, was arrested trying to enter Israel, and told she was not objective in her reporting. Jasiewicz, who had previously been involved with the International Solidarity Movement, had an assignment for a left-wing British magazine, *Red Pepper*. She eventually agreed to deportation rather than launch a legal battle that could create a precedent for banning other journalists. See 'IDF detains three BBC journalists in Nablus', *Ha'aretz*, 12 August 2004, and 'A personal bias', *Guardian*, 26 August 2004.

33. A little light was cast on the world of the censor in two articles: 'Sensing the censor', *Ha'aretz*, 27 May 2002, and 'The return of the censor', *Ha'aretz*, 18 January 2005.

34. The media try to conceal from their audiences this form of self-imposed restraint. An insight, however, was offered during Israel's 2006 war on Lebanon when a senior BBC editor's email to staff was leaked. He advised reporters: 'The more general we are, the free-er hand we have; more specific and it becomes increasingly tricky.' The editor said the channel would notify viewers of restrictions in 'the narrative of the story'. In practice, however, BBC correspondents, like other reporters, rarely if ever highlight the fact they are operating under censorship, or self-censorship. See my article 'Israel, not Hizbullah, is putting civilians in danger on both sides of the border', *Counterpunch*, 3 August 2006.

Chapter 9

'Hatred and holocaust' originally published as 'From the new anti-Semitism to nuclear holocaust', *Counterpunch*, 23–24 September 2006; 'The purging of Palestinian Christians' originally published as 'Israel's purging of Palestinian Christians', *Counterpunch*, 9 January 2007.

1. The report is available at www.thepcaa.org/.
2. Finkelstein 2005, p. 24.
3. Ibid., pp. 26–31.
4. An online collection of *Ha'aretz* articles about the 'New anti-Semitism' is available at www.haaretz.com/hasen/pages/ShArt.jhtml?itemNo=119115&contrassID=3&subContrassID=0&sbSubContrassID=0.
5. For example, the *Jerusalem Post* published an article by President Bush's favourite political philosopher, Natan Sharansky: 'Anti-Semitism in 3D', 23 February 2004.
6. 'Netanyahu: As prime minister I'd work for solutions', *Jerusalem Post*, 7 November 2002.
7. 'Katsav urges Germans to fight against anti-Semitism', *Jerusalem Post*, 9 December 2002.
8. The American Jewish Committee's 2002 'Survey of Jewish opinion' found 95 per cent of respondents thought anti-Semitism in the US was very serious or somewhat serious: 'US Jews continue to fear anti-Semitism above all', *Jerusalem Post*, 25 January 2003.
9. 'ADL head: Anti-Semitism is a real threat', *Jerusalem Post*, 21 October 2002.
10. 'ADL director: Today's anti-Semitism worst since World War II', *Jerusalem Post*, 21 October 2002.
11. The CampusWatch site is at www.campus-watch.org/. David Horowitz, who runs a related pro-Israel website called FrontPage Magazine, wrote a book on the same theme: *The Professors: The 101 Most Dangerous Academics in America* (2006). The David Project made a film, *Columbia Unbecoming*, in 2004 about the Middle East department of Columbia University, which under Rashid Khalidi has remained one of the few not tainted by a pro-Israel agenda. The Project's main target was the non-tenured Joseph Massad. In response, the university established a committee which rejected all but one of the film's accusations – that Massad had spoken angrily to a pro-Israel student in a seminar – despite the fact that almost everyone in the class denied the incident had taken place. See two articles by Massad in *Al-Ahram Weekly*: 'Intimidating Columbia University', 4 November 2004, and 'Targeting the university', 2 June 2005.
12. See Cook 2006, especially chapter 3.
13. 'ADL director: Today's anti-Semitism worst since World War II'.
14. For example, Israel claimed a 2003 EU report, *Manifestations of anti-Semitism in the European Union,* had been suppressed because it revealed that Muslims were behind many anti-Semitic incidents. In fact, it was withheld because officials were unhappy with the sample size and there were doubts about whether criticism of Israel had been distinguished from anti-Semitism. According to one Israeli researcher, denying Israel's right to exist – by arguing, for example, that an ethnic state should be reformed – was defined as anti-Semitic in the study: 'Prodi suspends anti-Semitism talks', *IHT*, 6 January 2004; 'Norway up in arms after author asserts Israel has lost right to exist', *Ha'aretz*, 12 August 2006.

15. The rabbi, Gabriel Farhi, was stabbed twice in the stomach and later had his car torched: 'France tackles tide of anti-Semitism', *Guardian*, 9 January 2003. Almost no coverage was provided of later evidence suggesting he staged the attack: 'French Jews stunned by claims that rabbi faked own stabbing', *Ha'aretz*, 24 January 2003. The other attack, supposedly on a 23-year-old woman known as Marie L, was condemned as a 'shameful act' by President Jacques Chirac. Her story unravelled when CCTV footage of the platform showed the gang never disembarked from the train. She later admitted she had made up the story: 'Woman arrested for inventing racist attack', *Independent*, 14 July 2004.

16. 'French Jews "must move to Israel"', BBC Online, 18 July 2004. For more on Israel's interest in stoking fears of anti-Semitism among world Jewry, see my article 'Selling anti-Semitism', *Al-Ahram Weekly*, 10 October 2002.

17. *Forward*, 2 May 2003. For a critique of Goldhagen's argument, see my article 'The new anti-Semitism?', Electronic Intifada, 3 June 2003.

18. Phillips's progression from liberal journalist to neoconservative began in the 1980s, prefiguring that of many other British journalists following 9/11. In 2006 some signed up to a document called the Euston Manifesto, which, in the words of Phillips, 'repudiates anti-Americanism, resurgent Judeophobia and the proclivity of the left to line up with tyranny and against democracy'. See: www.melanie phillips.com/diary/archives/001681.html.

19. 'Bibi: Iran president more dangerous than Hitler', *Ynet*, 12 September 2006. For more such scaremongering, see my 'Israel's Jewish problem in Tehran', *Counterpunch*, 3 August 2007.

20. 'Livni: World may have only "few months" to avoid nuclear Iran', *Ha'aretz*, 17 September 2006.

21. Amiry 2005, pp. 113–16.

22. The court's advisory opinion is available at www.icj-cij.org/icjwww/ipresscom/ipress2004/ipresscom2004–28_mwp_20040709.htm.

23. In a cautiously worded statement, Williams observed: 'There are some disturbing signs of Muslim anti-Christian feeling, despite the consistent traditions of coexistence. But their plight is made still more intolerable by the tragic conditions created by the 'security fence' that almost chokes the shrinking town': 'Archbishop of Canterbury: Mideast Christians in jeopardy', *Jerusalem Post*, 23 December 2006.

24. Daphne Tsimhoni, 'Israel and the Territories – Disappearance', *Middle East Quarterly*, vol. 8, no. 1, Winter 2001. The figures for West Bank Christians supplied by Zionists, including the author above, should be treated with caution as they exclude the significant population of Christians in East Jerusalem – in line with Israel's official policy – since the area was illegally annexed by Israel.

25. Jiryis 1976, p. 291; '148,000 Christians living in Israel', *Ha'aretz*, 25 December 2006.

26. See Gorenberg 2002.

27. See, for example, 'Christians in crisis', *Jerusalem Post*, 24 December 2006.

28. 'Nazareth Muslims: Islam will dominate world', *Ynet*, 1 January 2007.

29. The first use of this phrase is attributed to Lewis in his article 'The roots of Muslim rage', *Atlantic Monthly*, September 1990. Huntingdon's *The Clash of Civilizations and the Remaking of World Order* was first published in 1996, although he had used the term before, in 1993, in the journal *Foreign Affairs*.

30. 'Neocons: We expected Israel to attack Syria', *Ynet*, 16 December 2006.

31. Available at www.iasps.org/strat1.htm.
32. In the state's early years, the Israeli Communist Party was dominated by Jews, their presence offering some protection to Arab citizens who joined. Christians were attracted because the party offered a non-sectarian outlet for joint political activity with Jews and Muslims. Today, most of the party's votes come from the Arab population, though few are Communists in more than a very loose ideological sense.
33. Habibi, from Haifa, is best known for his satirical novel about the constant and soul-destroying compromises implicit in being an Israeli Arab, *The Secret Life of Saeed the Pessoptimist*; Shammas, from Fassuta, the first Israeli Arab to write a successful novel in Hebrew (*Arabesques*), left to teach in the United States; Suleiman, from Nazareth, caused controversy with his movie *Divine Intervention*, particularly for a final scene in which the heroine is transformed into a Christ figure as armed Israelis try to execute her; Hany Abu Assad, also from Nazareth, gained awards – and notoriety – for his movie about two Palestinian suicide bombers, *Paradise Now*; Antoine Shalhat, from Acre, who has translated many famous Hebrew novels into Arabic, was issued with an order not to leave the country in January 2006 on undisclosed evidence.
34. See my essay 'The Persecution of Azmi Bishara' in this collection.
35. Shehadeh published a memoir, *Strangers in the House*, in 2002.
36. '148,000 Christians living in Israel'.
37. 'Today more Israeli Arabs in higher education, still far less than Jews', *Ha'aretz*, 4 December 2006. Israel continues to make entrance to higher education more difficult for Arab students by weighting matriculation scores in favour of those who excel in Hebrew rather than Arabic, by imposing special admission requirements (including age restrictions related to military service), by using culturally biased psychometric tests, and by conducting interviews in Hebrew. In 2003 changes agreed by the universities to reduce the reliance on psychometric tests were reversed when it was discovered that more Arab students were winning places as a result: 'Universities return to aptitude exams to keep Arabs out', *Ha'aretz*, 27 November 2003.
38. 'Palestinian battles to study in East Jerusalem', BBC Online, 27 October 2006; 'Outstanding student falls victim to Israel's ban on Palestinians', *Independent*, 14 October 2006.
39. 'Israel bars Palestinian Americans for first time since 1967', *Ha'aretz*, 10 July 2006.
40. 'Israel's policy of denying entry to foreign passport holders hits Palestinian higher education hard', a press release from Bir Zeit University's Right to Education Campaign, available at http://right2edu.birzeit.edu/news/article456.

Afterword

Originally published as 'Two-state dreamers: If one state is impossible, why is Olmert so afraid of it?', *Monthly Review*, 12 March 2008.

1. 'Two states or one state', the transcript of a debate between Avnery and the revisionist historian Ilan Pappe, is available at www.countercurrents.org/pappe110607.htm.

2. 'The one-state illusion: More is less', *Counterpunch*, 10 March 2008.
3. 'Maximum Jews, minimum Palestinians', *Ha'aretz*, 13 November 2003.
4. Available at www.israelnewsagency.com/herzliyaconferenceaddressehudolmert
   israelspeechlebanongazaterrorism48012308.html.
5. 'Sharon tells cabinet: Saudi plan threatens Israel's security', *Ha'aretz*, 4 March
   2002.
6. 'Olmert to Haaretz: Two-state solution, or Israel is done for', *Ha'aretz*, 29 November 2007.
7. For more on water issues in the conflict, see: www.palestine-pmc.com/pissue/
   water.asp.
8. 'Water Authority: Israel is rapidly losing its water sources', *Ha'aretz*, 7 February
   2008.
9. See Cook 2006.

Bibliography

Abu Hussein, Hussein, and Fiona McKay (2003) *Access Denied: Palestinian Land Rights in Israel*, Zed Books, London.

Abu-Sitta, Salman (2004) *Atlas of Palestine 1948*, Palestine Land Society, London.

Abunimah, Ali (2006) *One Country: A Bold Proposal to End the Israeli–Palestinian Impasse*, Metropolitan Books, New York.

Aburish, Said (1998) *Arafat: From Defender to Dictator*, Bloomsbury, London.

Al-Haj, Majid (1995) *Education, Empowerment and Control: The Case of the Arabs in Israel*, SUNY, New York.

Amiry, Suad (2005) *Sharon and My Mother-in-law*, Granta, London.

Bar-Zohar, Michael (2005) *Ben-Gurion*, Magal Books, Tel-Aviv.

Beinin, Joel, and Rebecca L. Stein (eds) (2006) *The Struggle for Sovereignty: Palestine and Israel 1993–2005*, Stanford University Press, Stanford.

Beit-Hallahmi, Benjamin (1992) *Original Sins: Reflections on the History of Zionism and Israel*, Pluto Press, London.

Ben-Ami, Shlomo (2006) *Scars of War, Wounds of Peace: The Israeli–Arab Tragedy*, Phoenix, London.

Ben Cramer, Richard (2004) *How Israel Lost: The Four Questions at the Heart of the Middle East Crisis*, Free Press, London.

Benvenisti, Meron (2000) *Sacred Landscape: The Buried History of the Holy Land since 1948*, University of California Press, Berkeley.

Bishara, Marwan (2002) *Palestine/Israel: Peace or Apartheid*, Zed Books, London.

Brecher, Daniel Cil (2007) *A Stranger in the Land: Jewish Identity Beyond Nationalism*, Other Press, New York.

Carey, Roane (ed.) (2001) *The New Intifada*, Verso, London.

Carey, Roane et al. (eds) (2002) *The Other Israel: Voices of Refusal and Dissent*, New Press, New York.

Carter, Jimmy (2007) *Palestine: Peace Not Apartheid*, Simon & Schuster, New York.

Bibliography

Chacour, Elias (2003) *Blood Brothers*, Chosen Books, Michigan.

Chomsky, Noam (1999) *Fateful Triangle: The United States, Israel and the Palestinians*, Pluto Press, London.

Cohen, Yoel (2005) *Whistleblowers and the Bomb: Vanunu, Israel and Nuclear Secrecy*, Pluto Press, London.

Cook, Catherine, Adam Hanieh and Adah Kay (2004) *Stolen Youth: The Politics of Israel's Detention of Palestinian Children*, Pluto Press, London.

Cook, Jonathan (2006) *Blood and Religion: The Unmasking of the Jewish and Democratic State*, Pluto Press, London.

———— (2008) *Israel and the Clash of Civilisations: Iraq, Iran and the Plan to Remake the Middle East*, Pluto Press, London.

Curtis, Michael (ed.) (1975) *The Palestinians*, Transaction Books, New Jersey.

Davis, Uri (2003) *Apartheid Israel: Possibilities for the Struggle Within*, Zed Books, London.

Edwards, David, and David Cromwell (2006) *Guardians of Power: The Myth of the Liberal Media*, Pluto Press, London.

El-Asmar, Fouzi (1975) *To Be an Arab in Israel*, Frances Pinter, London.

Ellis, Marc H. (2002) *Israel and Palestine Out of the Ashes: The Search for Jewish Identity in the Twenty-First Century*, Pluto Press, London.

Elon, Amos (2000) *A Blood-Dimmed Tide*, Allen Lane, London.

Evron, Boaz (1995) *Jewish State or Israeli Nation?* Indiana University Press, Bloomington.

Ezrahi, Yaron (1998) *Rubber Bullets: Power and Conscience in Modern Israel*, University of California Press, Berkeley.

Finkelstein, Norman (2000) *The Holocaust Industry*, Verso, London.

———— (2001) *Image and Reality of the Israel–Palestine Conflict*, Verso, London.

———— (2005) *Beyond Chutzpah: On the Misuse of Anti-Semitism and the Abuse of History*, University of California Press, Berkeley.

Fischbach, Michael R. (2003) *Records of Dispossession: Palestinian Refugee Property and the Arab–Israeli Conflict*, Columbia University Press, New York.

Fisk, Robert (2002) *Pity the Nation*, Nation Books, New York.

———— (2005) *The Great War for Civilisation: The Conquest of the Middle East*, Fourth Estate, London.

Friel, Howard, and Richard Falk (2007) *Israel–Palestine on Record: How the 'New York Times' Misreports Conflict in the Middle East*, Verso, London.

Ghanem, As'ad (2001) *The Palestinian–Arab Minority in Israel, 1948–2000: A Political Study*, SUNY Press, New York.

Gilmour, David (1982), *Dispossessed*, Sphere Books, London.

Golan-Agnon, Daphna (2005) *Next Year in Jerusalem*, New Press, New York.

Goldberg, J.J. (1996) *To the Promised Land*, Penguin Books, London.

Gorenberg, Gershom (2002) *The End of Days: Fundamentalism and the Struggle for the Temple Mount*, Oxford University Press, New York.

———— (2006) *The Accidental Empire: Israel and the Birth of the Settlements, 1967–1977*, Times Books, New York.

Grossman, David (1993) *Sleeping on a Wire: Conversations with Palestinians in Israel*, Farrar, Straus & Giroux, New York.

———— (2002) *The Yellow Wind*, Picador, New York.

———— (2003) *Death as a Way of Life*, Bloomsbury, London.

Habiby, Emile (2002) *The Secret Life of Saeed, the Pessoptimist*, Interlink, New York.

Hajjar, Lisa (2005) *Courting Conflict: The Israeli Military Court System in the West Bank and Gaza*, University of California Press, Berkeley.

Halevy, Efraim (2006) *Man in the Shadows: Inside the Middle East Crisis with a Man Who Led the Mossad*, Phoenix, London.

Halper, Jeff (2008) *An Israeli in Palestine: Resisting Dispossession, Redeeming Israel*, Pluto Press, London.

Harkaby, Yehoshafat (1998) *Israel's Fateful Hour*, Harper & Row, New York.

Hass, Amira (1999) *Drinking the Sea at Gaza*, Owl Books, New York.

Hazony, Yoram (2001) *The Jewish State: The Struggle for Israel's Soul*, Basic Books, New York.

Hilal, Jamil (ed.) (2007) *Where Now for Palestine? The Demise of the Two-State Solution*, Zed Books, London.

Hirst, David (2003) *The Gun and the Olive Branch*, Faber, London.

Horowitz, David (2006) *The Professors: The 101 Most Dangerous Academics in America*, Regnery Publishing, Washington DC.

Ibrahim, Tarek (2004) *By All Means Possible*, Arab Association for Human Rights, Nazareth.

Jiryis, Sabri (1976) *The Arabs in Israel*, Monthly Review Press, New York.

Kanaaneh, Rhoda (2002) *Birthing the Nation*, University of California Press, Berkeley.

Karmi, Ghada (2002) *In Search of Fatima*, Verso, London.

Kashua, Sayed (2004) *Dancing Arabs*, Grove Press, New York.

———— (2007) *Let It Be Morning*, Atlantic Books, London.

Khalidi, Rashid (2007) *The Iron Cage: The Story of the Palestinian Struggle for Statehood*, Beacon Press, Boston MA.

Khalidi, Walid (1992) *All That Remains: The Palestinian Villages Occupied and Depopulated by Israel in 1948*, Institute of Palestine Studies, Washington DC.

Kidron, Peretz (2004) *Refusenik! Israel's Soldiers of Conscience*, Zed Books, London.

Kimmerling, Baruch (2003) *Politicide: Ariel Sharon's War against the Palestinians*, Verso, London.

———— (2005) *The Invention and Decline of Israeliness: State, Society and the Military*, University of California Press, Berkeley.

Kimmerling, Baruch, and Joel Migdal (2003) *The Palestinian People: A History*, Harvard University Press, Cambridge MA.

Klein, Naomi (2007) *The Shock Doctrine: The Rise of Disaster Capitalism*, Allen Lane, London.

Kovel, Joel (2007) *Overcoming Zionism*, Pluto Press, London.

Kretzmer, David (2002) *The Occupation of Justice: The Supreme Court and the Occupied Territories*, SUNY, New York.

Landau, Jacob M. (1969) *The Arabs in Israel: A Political Study*, Oxford University Press, Oxford.

Laqueur, Walter, and Barry Rubin (eds) (2001) *The Israel–Arab Reader*, Penguin Books, New York.

Lemche, Niels Peter (1991) *The Canaanites and Their Land*, Academic Press, Sheffield.

Lustick, Ian (1980) *Arabs in the Jewish State: Israel's Control of a National Minority*, University of Texas Press, Austin.

Maddrell, Penny (1990) *The Beduin of the Negev*, Minority Rights Group Report No. 81, London.

Masalha, Nur (1997) *A Land without a People: Israel, Transfer and the Palestinians, 1949–96*, Faber, London.

Bibliography

————— (2000) *Imperial Israel and the Palestinians: The Politics of Expulsion*, Pluto Press, London.

————— (2003) *The Politics of Denial: Israel and the Palestinian Refugee Problem*, Pluto Press, London.

————— (ed.) (2005) *Catastrophe Remembered: Palestine, Israel and the Internal Refugees*, Zed Books, London.

————— (2007) *The Bible and Zionism: Invented Traditions, Archaeology and Post-Colonialism in Palestine–Israel*, Zed Books, London.

Massad, Joseph (2006) *The Persistence of the Palestinian Question: Essays on Zionism and the Palestinians*, Routledge, London.

Mayhew, Christopher, and Michael Adams (2006) *Publish It Not: The Middle East Cover-up*, Signal Books, Oxford.

Mearsheimer, John, and Stephen Walt (2007) *The Israel Lobby and U.S. Foreign Policy*, Farrar, Straus & Giroux, New York.

Morris, Benny (1994) *1948 and After: Israel and the Palestinians*, Oxford University Press , Oxford.

————— (2001) *Righteous Victims: A History of the Zionist–Arab Conflict, 1881–2001*, Vintage, New York.

————— (2003) *The Road to Jerusalem: Glubb Pasha, Palestine and the Jews*, I.B. Tauris, New York.

————— (2004) *The Birth of the Palestinian Refugee Problem Revisited*, Cambridge University Press, New York.

Nathan, Susan (2005) *The Other Side of Israel: My Journey Across the Jewish–Arab Divide*, HarperCollins, London.

Neslen, Arthur (2006) *Occupied Minds: A Journey Through the Israeli Psyche*, Pluto Press, London.

Neumann, Michael (2005) *The Case against Israel*, Counterpunch, California.

Nimni, Ephraim (ed.) (2003) *The Challenge of Post-Zionism: Alternatives to Israeli Fundamentalist Politics*, Zed Books, London.

Pappe, Ilan (2004) *A History of Modern Palestine: One Land, Two Peoples*, Cambridge University Press, Cambridge.

————— (2006) *The Ethnic Cleansing of Palestine*, One World, Oxford.

Pearlman, Wendy (2003) *Occupied Voices*, Nation Books, New York.

Prior, Michael (1999) *Zionism and the State of Israel*, Routledge, London.

Rabinowitz, Dan, and Khawla Abu-Baker (2005) *Coffins on Our Shoulders: The Experience of the Palestinian Citizens of Israel*, University of California Press, Berkeley.

Reinhart, Tanya (2002) *Israel/Palestine: How to End the War of 1948*, Seven Stories Press, New York.

————— (2006) *The Road Map to Nowhere: Israel/Palestine since 2003*, Verso, London.

Robinson, Shira (2005), 'Occupied Citizens in a Liberal State: Palestinians under Military Rule and the Colonial Formation of Israeli Society, 1948–1966', Ph.D. thesis, Stanford University, Stanford.

Rodinson, Maxime (1973) *Israel: A Colonial Settler State?*, Pathfinder, New York.

Rogan, Eugene, and Avi Shlaim (eds) (2001), *The War for Palestine: Rewriting the History of 1948*, Cambridge University Press, Cambridge.

Rose, Jacqueline (2005) *The Question of Zion*, Princeton University Press, Princeton.

Rose, John (2004) *The Myths of Zionism*, Pluto Press, London.

Rouhana, Nadim (1997) *Palestinian Citizens in an Ethnic Jewish State*, Yale University Press, New Haven.

Roy, Sara (2007) *Failing Peace: Gaza and the Palestinian–Israeli Conflict*, Pluto Press, London.

Said, Edward (1996) *Peace and its Discontents: Essays on Palestine in the Middle East Peace Process*, Vintage, New York.

———— (2001) *The End of the Peace Process: Oslo and After*, Granta, London.

Segev, Tom (1998) *1949: The First Israelis*, Owl Books, New York.

———— (2002) *Elvis in Jerusalem: Post-Zionism and the Americanization of Israel*, Metropolitan Books, New York.

———— (2007) *1967*, Metropolitan Books, New York.

Shahak, Israel (1994) *Jewish History, Jewish Religion: The Weight of Three Thousand Years*, Pluto Press, London.

———— (1997) *Open Secrets: Israeli Nuclear and Foreign Policies*, Pluto Press, London.

Shahak, Israel, and Norton Mezinsky (1999) *Jewish Fundamentalism in Israel*, Pluto Press, London.

Shammas, Anton (2001) *Arabesques*, University of California Press, Berkeley.

Shehadeh, Raja (1993) *The Law of the Land: Settlements and Land Issues under Israeli Military Occupation*, Passia, Jerusalem.

———— (2002) *Strangers in the House: Coming of Age in Occupied Palestine*, Profile, London.

———— (2007) *Palestinian Walks: Notes on a Vanishing Landscape*, Profile, London.

Shipler, David (1987) *Arab and Jew: Wounded Spirits in a Promised Land*, Penguin Books, New York.

Shlaim, Avi (1988) *Collusion across the Jordan*, Columbia University Press, New York.

———— (2000) *The Iron Wall: Israel and the Arab World*, Penguin Books, London.

Silberstein, Laurence J. (1999) *The Postzionism Debates*, Routledge , New York.

Slyomovics, Susan (1998) *The Object of Memory: Arab and Jew Narrate the Palestinian Village*, University of Pennsylvania Press, Philadelphia.

Sofer, Arnon (2001) *Israel, Demography 2000–2020: Dangers and Opportunities*, University of Haifa, Haifa.

Sternhell, Zeev (1999) *The Founding Myths of Israel*, Princeton University Press, New Jersey.

Sultany, Nimr (ed.) (2005) *Israel and the Palestinian Minority: 2004*, Mada, Haifa.

Swisher, Clayton E. (2004) *The Truth About Camp David*, Nation Books, New York.

Teveth, Shabtia (1985) *Ben-Gurion and the Palestinian Arabs: From Peace to War*, Oxford University Press, Oxford.

Thomas, Gideon (1999) *Gideon's Spies: Mossad's Secret Warriors*, Pan Books, New York.

Tilley, Virginia (2005) *The One-State Solution: A Breakthrough for Peace in the Israeli–Palestinian Deadlock*, University of Michigan Press, Michigan.

Usher, Graham (1999) *Dispatches from Palestine: The Rise and Fall of the Oslo Peace Process*, Pluto Press, London.

Van Creveld, Martin (2004) *Moshe Dayan*, Weidenfeld & Nicolson, London.

Wasserstein, Bernard (2002) *Divided Jerusalem: The Struggle for the Holy City*, Profile Books, London.

———— (2003) *Israel and Palestine: Why They Fight and Can They Stop?*, Profile Books, London.

Watzal, Ludwig (1999) *Peace Enemies: The Past and Present Conflict between Israel and Palestine*, Passia, Jerusalem.

Zertal, Idith, and Akiva Eldar (2007) *Lords of the Land: The War Over Israel's Settlements in the Occupied Territories 1967–2007*, Nation Books, New York.

Index

Basic Law on Freedom and Human Dignity,
161, 270n
BBC (British Broadcasting Corporation), 216,
217, 218, 278n, 279n
Beersheva (Bir Saba), 33, 180
Begin, Menachem, 48, 102–3, 270n
Beilin, Yossi, 148, 150, 197
Beit Alpha kibbutz, 4, 253n
Beit El settlement, 77–8, 264n
Beit Hanoun, 211; mosque, 207
Beit Iba checkpoint, 171
Beit Sahour, 74
Beit Shean (Bisan), 4, 180
Beit-Hallahmi, Benjamin, 15
Ben-Ami, Shlomo, 26, 48, 50, 101, 146
Ben Elyahu, Eitan, 134
Ben-Gurion, David: 1948 war, 24–7, 55, 116,
193, 246, 270n; 1967 war, 143, 270n;
Bible, 22; borders, 46, 253–4n;
Judaization, 34; refugees, 29, 258n;
transfer, 5, 25, 101–2, 115–16, 140–41,
158, 257n; view of Palestinians, 17, 270n
Ben Tzvi, Yitzhak, 15, 17
Ben-Porat, Miriam, 72
Benn, Aluf, 118–19, 121
Benvenisti, Meron, 32, 35, 129, 199
Benziman, Uzi, 34, 272n
Bernadotte, Folke, 254n
Bir Saba, *see* Beersheva
Bir Zeit University, 173, 242
Bisan, *see* Beit Shean
Bishara, Azmi, 115–16, 126, 140, 157, 159–64,
166, 240, 271n, 272n, 273n
Bowen, Jeremy, 202, 204, 218
Britain (UK), 19–20, 182, 184; Balfour
Declaration, 22, 24, 254n; defence
regulations, 62, 258n; Jordan pact, 255n;
journalists, 212, 220; Mandate, 23, 60,
100, 264n; media, 216–19; Muslim
population, 234
Buber, Martin, 142, 270n
Building and Planning Law, 1965, 256n
Bureau of Census Statistics, Israel, 241, 256n
Bush, George W., administration, 1, 44, 89,
91, 93, 96, 98, 108, 235, 239, 245

Camera (Committee for Accuracy in Middle
East Reporting), 3, 252n
Camp David negotiations, 2, 30, 97–8,
100–101, 104–8, 112, 157, 163
CampusWatch, 233
Canaanites, 16
Canada Park, 54, 100
Carter, Jimmy, 115
Christians, *see* Palestinian Christians
CIA (US Central Intelligence Agency), *World*

Factbook, 170
Clinton, Bill, 98, 100
Columbia University, 233
Communist Party, Israel, 157, 240, 242, 282n
Coordination Forum for Countering Anti-
Semitism, 232
Corrie, Rachel, 225, 279n
Custodian of Absentee Property, 28–30, 35,
73, 74, 255–6n

D'Alema, Massimo, 106
Dahlan, Mohammed, 114, 275n
Darwish, Mahmoud, 272n
David Project, 233, 280n
Davies, Wyre, 217
Davis, Uri, 40
Dayan, Moshe: archeology, 15; 'creeping
annexation', 7, 69, 134; Israeli Arabs, 32,
159; Six-Day War, 49–50; West Bank,
57–9, 117
De Soto, Alvaro, 113
Declaration of Independence, Israel, 26, 179
Deir Yassin massacre, 26, 103
Democratic Front for the Liberation of
Palestine, 241
Dichter, Avi, 132
Diskin, Yuval, 166, 272n
Doucet, Lyse, 217–18
Drobless, Mattiyahu, Plan of, 84–5

East Jerusalem, 27, 51, 184, 196, 236, 256n;
Absentee Property Law, 74, 264n;
annexation, 52–3; Camp David, 2, 98–9,
106; holy sites, 52, 163; Jewish
settlements, 52, 76, 77, 83, 87, 90, 144,
198; Mughrabi Quarter, 52, 54;
Palestinian MPs, 184–5, 276n; Sheikh
Jarrah, 91; Silwan, 90; *see also* Jerusalem
Eban, Abba, 48
Egged bus company, 94
Egypt, 59, 61, 62, 110, 146, 181; Gaza role,
114 119–21, 131, 135, 202; Sinai, 49–50,
84, 129, 131, 231; Six-Day War, 47–50
Elad settler organization, 90
Eldar, Akiva, 68, 76, 93–4, 106
Elon, Amos, 56–7
Elon, Benny, 69, 103
Elon Moreh settlement, 77, 88, 178, 264n
Eshel, Ilan, 123
Eshkol, Levi, 48–9, 57, 59–60, 75, 118
Etkes, Dror, 84
Europe, 229, 231, 234
Euston Manifesto, 235, 281n

Fahima, Tali, 161
Farhi, Gabriel, 281n

Index

Fatah, 108, 110, 128, 129, 203, 222; civil war, 112–14, 118, 119–20, 185, 187–90, 276–7n; Oslo period, 112, 188–9, 239
Feldman, Avigdor, 72
Felix, Menachem, 78
Findlay, Gillian, 224
Finkelstein, Israel, 17
Finkelstein, Norman, 14, 144, 231
Fischbach, Michael R., 29
Fourth Geneva Convention, 61–2, 64, 75, 262n
Foxman, Abraham, 3, 232
France, 19, 281n; Muslim population, 234
Friedman, Thomas, 220
Froman, Menachem, 276n

Gadish Committee, 42
Galilee, 24, 38, 42, 238; Christian communities, 32; Judaization, 34
Galili, Yisrael, 56
Gandhi, Mahatma, 207
Gaza Community Mental Health Programme, 124, 135
Gazit, Shlomo, 60, 121
Geneva Initiative, 195
Germany, 20, 232
Givat Ze'ev settlement, 91
Golan Heights, 49–50
Goldenberg, Suzanne, 224
Goldenhagen, Daniel J., 234
Goldstein, Baruch, 111
Gorali, Moshe, 67, 78
Goren, Shlomo, 52
Gorenberg, Gershom, 117, 261n
Government Press Office, Israel, 224, 226–8
Grossman, David, 191–6, 199
Guardian, 215–17, 221–2, 224
Gulf War 1991, 146
Gush Emunim, 76, 77
Gush Shalom, 196–9, 244

Ha'aretz, 86–7, 88, 93, 97, 99–100, 114–15, 120, 128, 161, 170, 176, 180, 231
Habash, George, 241
Habibi, Emile, 240, 282n
Hague Regulations, 61
Haider, Jorg, 153
Haifa, 30, 179; University, 15, 159
Hajjar, Lisa, 63–4
Halleli, Avraham, 75
Halper, Jeff, 16, 124, 199
Hamas, 147, 162, 187, 204, 213, 217, 239, 278n; 2006 election, 108, 112–13, 124, 184, 200, 238; civil war, 113–14, 119–20, 185, 186–90, 222, 276–7n; first intifada, 110; Gaza rule, 121, 124, 131–2; MPs, 113,

184–5, 202–4, 217–18, 221–2, 275n; Oslo, 111–12; resistance, 120, 127–30, 207
Handelzalts, Michael, 127
Har Homa settlement, 149
Har-Tzion, Meir, 61
Hass, Amira, 88, 129, 171, 176, 181
Hasson, Israel, 166
Hawatmeh, Nayif, 241
Hebrew language, 21
Hebron, 57, 76, 122, 144; massacre, 111
Herzliya Interdisciplinary Centre, 134; Conference, 43, 156, 246
Herzl, Theodor, 13–14, 22, 50, 101, 142
Herzog, Chaim, 50, 58
Herzog, Ze'ev, 16
High Follow-Up Committee, Future Vision, 165
Himanuta, *see* Jewish National Fund
Hirst, David, 85
Histadrut, 103, 267n
Hitler, Adolf, 21, 142, 235
Hizbullah, 128, 161–62, 207, 249
Hockstader, Lee, 224
Holmes, John, 124
Holocaust, the, 127, 142; 'Industry', 145
Honest Reporting, 13
Hook, Iain, 227
Horowitz, David, 280n
Human Rights Association, Nazareth, 159
Human Rights Watch (HRW), 192, 205–11, 277n
Huntington, Samuel, 239
Hurndall, Tom, 225, 279n
Hussein Saddam, 110, 146
Huwara: checkpoint, 170, 177–8; village, 168

Independent, 216, 221
India, 126, 207
International Court of Justice, The Hague, 74, 237
International Herald Tribune, 1–3, 252–3n
International Solidarity Movement, 225
Iran, 153, 245
Iraq, 59; colonial creation of, 19; embedded journalists, 223; oil fields, 146; US occupation, 8, 126, 213, 225, 249
Irgun militia, 102
Irish Republican Army, 203
Islam, 230; 'fascist' label, 236
Islamic Jihad, 147
Islamic Movement, 162–3
Israel Democracy Institute, 160
Israel Lands Authority, 39, 41–2, 74, 91
Israel Nature and National Parks Protection Authority, 90
Israeli Committee against House

Index

209, 274n
Nahmani, Joseph, 34
Nakba, 27; Day, 152
Narkiss, Uzi, 51
Nasser, Gamal Abdel, 47–8
National Defence College, 48
National Democratic Assembly party (NDA),
 164, 272n
National Water Authority, Israel, 122
Nationality Law 1952, 43, 257n
Nazareth, 238–9, 243, 257n, 259n
Negev, 32, 42; Bedouin, 36–7, 158, 259n
Netanyahu, Binyamin, 43, 120, 153–6, 198,
 231–2, 235, 239, 271n
Neumann, Michael, 245–7
New York Times, 1, 103, 255n
Niva, Steve, 126

Obeid, Kais, 271n
Observer, 213–14, 216
Olmert, Dana, 171
Olmert, Ehud: and Lieberman, 152–3, 155–7;
 Annapolis conference, 98; checkpoints,
 170; Gaza, 132, 184–5, 274n; Greater
 Israel, 13; Israeli Arabs, 164–5; regional
 plan, 120–21; separation, 105, 108, 182,
 195; settlements, 89, 91; two-state plan,
 45, 245–7
Operation Defensive Shield, 230, 232
Operation Hafarferet, 33
Operation Summer Rain, 224, 278–9n
Orwell, George, 207
Oslo process, 2, 113, 197, 261n; creation of
 PA, 111–12, 146–7, 187, 188, 189; division
 of West Bank, 82–3; residency, 72;
 separation, 117, 123, 169; settlers, 87, 94,
 98, 149, 223
Oz, Amos, 196

Palestine Liberation Organization (PLO),
 109–10, 146, 149
Palestinian Authority (PA), 123, 124, 181,
 230; under Arafat, 83, 111–12, 147, 169,
 188; under Hamas, 113, 184, 238, 243,
 275–6n
Palestinian Bureau of Statistics, 65
Palestinian Christians, 229–30, 236–8,
 240–41, 243, 256n, 281n
Palestinian Population Register, 181
Palestinian universities, 242
Palmon, Yehoshua, 258n
Pappe, Ilan, 23
Peace Now, 82, 88, 94, 96, 146, 148, 150, 192,
 196, 199, 270n
Pedatzur, Reuven, 119–20
Peel Commission, 101

Peled, Matityahu, 48
Peres, Shimon, 35, 45, 120, 148, 153, 156, 157,
 197, 262n
Peretz, Amir, 153, 186
Peters, Joan, 14
Philistines, 17
Phillips, Melanie, 235, 281n
Piterberg, Gabriel, 35
Plan Dalet, 25, 102
Popular Front for the Liberation of Palestine,
 241
'present absentee', 35, 258n
Primor, Avi, 105, 106
'Prisoners Document', 222–3

Qaadan family, 41, 260n
Qalqilya, 54, 171, 261n
Qassam rockets, 127–8, 182–3, 222, 239,
 271n

Rabin, Yitzhak, 27, 48, 95, 146, 192, 193,
 197, 255n, 271n, 275n
Ramla, 27, 30, 180
Ravner, Zvi, 183
Red Cross, 64
Red Pepper, 279n
Reschid Bey, fictitious character, 14
Revisionism, *see* Jabotinsky
Rice, Condoleezza, 91, 113, 186, 271n
Right of Return, 194, 250
Road Map, 89, 94, 223
Roy, Sara, 70, 85, 124–5
Rubinstein, Amnon, 67–8
Rubinstein, Danny, 130
Rubinstein, Elyakim, 30

Saban Center for Middle East Policy,
 Washington DC, 44
Safieh, Afif, 72
Said, Edward, 3, 241
Salah, Sheikh Raed, 162–3
Sand, Shlomo, 17–18
Sarid, Yossi, 125
Sasson, Talia, 273n; report of, 95–6
Saudi Arabia, 61, 131, 246; oilfields, 146
Save the Children, Sweden, 65
Schattner, Mordechai, 29
Schechner, Ron, 94
Schiff, Zeev, 187
Sderot, 127–8, 214
Seaman, Daniel, 224, 279n
Segev, Tom, 17, 24, 31, 36, 58
Shahar, Yoram, 134
Shai, Aharon, 31
Shalhat, Antoine, 240, 282n
Shalit, Gilad, 186–7, 200, 214, 216–17